Russia's War

To my Ukrainian friends, colleagues and heroes.

Russia's War

JADE MCGLYNN

polity

The right of Jade McGlynn to be identified as Author of this Work has been asserted in accordance with the UK Copyright, Designs and Patents Act 1988.

First published in 2023 by Polity Press

Polity Press
65 Bridge Street
Cambridge CB2 1UR, UK

Polity Press
111 River Street
Hoboken, NJ 07030, USA

2

ISBN-13: 978-1-5095-5675-5 (hardback)
ISBN-13: 978-1-5095-5676-2 (paperback)

A catalogue record for this book is available from the British Library.

Library of Congress Control Number: 2022949945

Typeset in 11 on 14pt Warnock Pro
by Cheshire Typesetting Ltd, Cuddington, Cheshire
Printed and bound in Great Britain by CPI Group (UK) Ltd, Croydon

The publisher has used its best endeavours to ensure that the URLs for external websites referred to in this book are correct and active at the time of going to press. However, the publisher has no responsibility for the websites and can make no guarantee that a site will remain live or that the content is or will remain appropriate.

Every effort has been made to trace all copyright holders, but if any have been overlooked the publisher will be pleased to include any necessary credits in any subsequent reprint or edition.

For further information on Polity, visit our website:
politybooks.com

Contents

Acknowledgements

On the 24th of every month, I take a picture of my baby daughter. But there is no photo to mark the day she turned two months – 24 February – because that was the day Russia invaded Ukraine. This was the day that meant Ukrainian parents, in their thousands, will never again be able to take a photograph of their babies. Because they have been kidnapped, deported or killed. This is a book about Russians – the people who committed, approved or ignored the kidnappings, deportations and killings – but Ukrainian resilience is the real protagonist. For this reason, as paltry as it is, I would like first to acknowledge the millions of personal tragedies happening to ordinary Ukrainians, who should be worrying about bad hair days, what to have for dinner or how to afford this or that item – not how to bury their son in the front garden, or where to scavenge for food, or what to do now their house is destroyed.

I am grateful I do not personally know such tragedy but also that I have Ukrainian friends and colleagues who have helped me to see through some of this privilege and to understand Ukraine, and how to help: Yulia Bidenko, Sasha Danylyuk, Aliona Hlivco, Olesya Stepanchuk, Dmytro Tretiakov, and many others who prefer to remain anonymous but who know who they are.

As is inevitable for a book written in five months, there are numerous people I must thank who made this possible. First of all, Altynay Jusunova, for her excellent research skills and assistance with the Telegram study, and Yanliang Pan, for his assistance across a bizarrely wide spectrum of activities and for making it possible for me to focus on this book. Beyond these two superstars, I would like to make special mention of the following people, all of whom supported me with time, advice, edits, discussions and inspiration: Lucy Birge, Thomas Brenberg, Ruth Deyermond, Clare Evans, Mark Galeotti, Polly Jones, Michael Kimmage, Ivan Krastev, Felix Krawatzek, Natasha Kuhrt, Marlene Laruelle, Adam Lenton, Aleksei Lokhmatov, Edward Lucas, Hennadiy Maksak, Daria Mattingly, Mira Milosevich, Andrew Monaghan, Jeremy Morris, Patrick Porter, His Excellency Vadym Prystaiko, Lena Racheva, Alan Riley, Issy Sawkins, Bob Seely MP, Ira Shcherbakova, Andrei Tsygankov, Pany Xenophontos, my students on the Monterey Trialogue, Monterey Summer Symposium and the Studienstiftung, Uilleam Blacker, Tim Frye, Ian Garner, Paul Goode, Anna Vassilieva, and my Russian colleagues who would prefer to remain anonymous.

I am grateful to my editor, Louise Knight, and to Inès Boxman for their support in making this an accessible book on a very tight deadline. The two anonymous readers also provided me with invaluable advice that greatly improved several chapters and the overall structure of the book. I would also like to thank all of my interviewees for agreeing to share their time and views with me during a period when that was either emotionally strenuous or politically inadvisable, to say the least.

Although this book is aimed at a non-specialist audience, it is inevitably informed by the two decades I have spent studying the history, politics, culture and languages of the post-socialist region in Europe. While I am originally a Russianist, I first started studying Ukrainian history, politics and language in 2014, when I was still living in Moscow. What was originally a knee-jerk response to Russian aggression (and public support for it), grew into a profound interest in Ukraine's cultural nuances and riches. Russia's invasions of Ukraine have long been a prominent feature of my research, from MA to post-doctoral studies, and I would like to thank my Ukrainian teachers – Olha Homonchuk and, later, Anastasia Ktitorova – for ensuring I could access the Ukrainian perspective, as well as the Russian.

Finally, I would like to thank my family. This list must start with my dad and nan for offering childcare, all sorts of toy- and food-related assistance and for not questioning why I was always writing at 2am in the morning. For similar reasons, I would like to declare my undying gratitude to my husband, who has put up with me writing two books within the space of twelve months. Despite the incredible inconvenience this has caused, he has always been there to help me, read my drafts, and support my work. He has done this even as he juggles his own very important work and ceaselessly fights, by my side, a doomed battle to maintain a sense of authority over our rambunctious son and infant daughter. And so to the other two main protagonists in my life: my darling son Sasha possesses a rare kindness, sense of fun, and inquisitive character that have helped me maintain a work–life balance and rekindled my love of Thomas the Tank Engine. My beautiful daughter, Lara, has accompanied me to most of the interviews in this book, on work trips to California, Madrid, Warsaw, and to meet the Ukrainian Ambassador. She has never failed to bring light to even the darkest of days. Even though there may be many such days ahead, these three will always remind me of the goodness and wonder in life.

Prologue

Credence and incredulity

There is a grave in Mariupol, overflowing with human bodies, murdered in cold blood by execution squads. None of the people had been properly identified, most never would be now. 'We can already see that there's quite a large number of corpses here. Locals say that uniformed soldiers came in cars and dumped the bodies into these pre-dug trenches.'[1] The mayor, Konstantin Ivashchenko, frowns as he explains, in clipped language, that some of the corpses were not properly covered. When Mayor Ivashchenko, who is a local man, stops talking, his eyes are void. The television camera crew turn off their equipment and leave the ruins of a city stalked by cholera and crime.

The following day, this clip spreads across Russian mainstream and social media. It makes a strong impression on viewers, who watch it in horror. They feel the same revulsion as Western audiences do when watching footage from Mariupol. Some are moved to act, or to turn away, or to despair, or to take the fight to the monsters responsible. Almost all share a hatred of those who murdered these poor souls and glazed the traumatised eyes of the Ukrainian mayor. They share a profound sense of outrage at the foreign-backed criminals killing innocents in Ukraine: Zelensky and his Western-backed Nazis.

As a reader, you are probably thinking: Nonsense, the Russians killed them. I agree and there is plenty of evidence to support our assertions. And yet, we haven't been to the crime scene, carried out a full investigation, or developed the expertise to assess when these people were killed and when their bodies were transported to the mass grave. Our knowledge that the Russians are culpable, rather than the Ukrainians, is based on informed assumptions and the wise decision not to give any credence to the claims of Russian news or collaborationist mayors like Ivashchenko.[2] But Russians do give credence to these sources, or at least few give any credence to Western and Ukrainian views. For many of us watching the daily onslaught in Ukraine in horror, the Russian viewpoint is incomprehensible – as baffling as it is appalling. But if we look more closely at the powerful forces shaping those perceptions, the reasons why Russians back the war become much clearer, if no less disconcerting.

On 24 February 2022, Russia launched a genocidal war against a peaceful neighbour. The violence the Russian Army has unleashed is calamitous for Ukraine, the world and Russia itself. There can be no justification for what Russia is doing now, or for what it has been doing in Ukraine since 2014. And yet many, many Russians do justify, even approve, the war. It is their war, Russia's war, not Putin's alone. I respect the brave Russians who have actively opposed the invasion and worked tirelessly to support Ukrainians in often unacknowledged ways. They possess unfathomable courage. But this book is not about them, nor is it about the true believers, the soldiers committing atrocities – neither are representative groups. Instead, it is about the Russians who acquiesce to the war, the ordinary people, the majority. I have zero hope of solving the Russia 'enigma' with a neat label but I do want to probe the complexities of the context through which these same Russians understand their war.

Russian approval of the war is honed by the paradoxical nature of Russian society, the mixture of militarised ritual and apathy that the Kremlin has sponsored and delivered through narratives that resonate in different ways with different groups. Since 2014, the Kremlin and its supporters have devised an entire strategic language around Ukraine, a story with familiar characters and events that play on people's emotions, biases, hopes and fears – to encourage certain types of support, discourage others, and eliminate active opposition. These narratives are often co-creations, selected for their resonance, rather than artifice imposed from above. Just as with Kremlin-sponsored disinformation campaigns abroad, the Russian state-affiliated media, with its varied and competing actors vying for popularity and impact, is adept at identifying what resonates and using it to their benefit.

The war propagandists know how to attract a crowd and how to impress the Kremlin, they are story makers not messengers. In the coming pages, I argue that Russian media content is not the result of the Kremlin imposing a narrative but of various actors, including ordinary Russians, co-creating a more amenable version of the world around them. To do so, I draw on ten years of close analysis of Russian state media, data analysis of almost 75,000 posts on the Russian social media platform Telegram, interviews with officials, elites and ordinary citizens from Russia and Ukraine, and my own experience of living and working in Russia for long periods, researching Russian media, history and politics. There will be no grand claims about the Russian soul. My purpose in writing this book is to explain why Russians support the war and what that support actually means in a context (almost) devoid of political agency.

In my efforts to explain this support to the reader, I will use comparisons and analogies with other countries, especially in the West.[3] These are not meant to relativise but to show where other peoples have faced the same choices and reacted in similar ways. That said, each unhappy country is unhappy in its own way. Russian society is haunted by its unresolved bloody history, the wounds of which the Kremlin reopens constantly, instrumentalising the trauma of twentieth-century terror, war and famine for political gain. Resistance is futile, given that the heirs of the men responsible for all of the terrors, most of the famines, and some of the wars still run the country and have instilled a cult of the perpetrator, reinforced by historical myth. Combined with continued authoritarianism lurching into dictatorship, Putin's patrimonial power vertical has created the ideal conditions for a particularly diseased conception of Russian identity to flourish. Treating Putin as the symptom not the cause, I examine the myths, memories and myopia fuelling the country to disaster, keeping its people clinging to a juggernaut of resentment, insecurity and fear.

1

The bad Tsar

'You will upset a lot of people.' Vadym Prystaiko, former Foreign Minister of Ukraine and now the ambassador to the United Kingdom, supported my premise but had endured enough discussions of Russia's war to forewarn me that my book title wouldn't be popular. 'Many Western policymakers want to paint this just as Putin's war, it suits them better.'[1] The notion that Putin invaded Ukraine despite the Russian people is often espoused by Westerners with a large circle of Russian acquaintances who all hail from an entirely unrepresentative sample of liberal Muscovites. The notion that just one bad Tsar is spoiling the barrel reinforces a reassuring sense that once Putin's generation has died out, the Russian people will trot merrily onto the path of progress, steamrollered forward by a liberal youth who admire and envy the West. I understand the appeal of this narrative as I would like to believe it too but it has the disadvantage of being untrue. Russia's war on Ukraine is popular with large numbers of Russians and acceptable to an even larger number.

Naturally, statements like 'Russia thinks' are inherently flawed: Russia is a diverse country, with diverse people holding diverse views. But most of these people do not oppose the war on Ukraine and they like Putin, or at least they like what he tells and sells them. To understand the roots of such approval, you need to place yourself in the context in and through which many Russians understand and experience the world. Their perspective is coloured by the trauma of the Soviet collapse, the country's institutions' and leaders' refusal to recognise the crimes of the past, and several governments' inability to embed the country within the 'international rules-based order'. Together, these challenges have contributed to an identity crisis and resentment that Putin has been able to channel into a resonant political force. Based on atavism, aggrievement and aggression, this force acts upon the Russian people in diverse ways that serve the Kremlin's needs. It leaves no space for hope, only revenge; no space for improvement, only redemption; and no space for the future, only a reproducible past in which people can take shelter from the present.

People without a past, or who are struggling with identity, often turn to genealogy, buying ancestral DNA kits to understand who they are, where they come from, and to reconnect with the culture of their ancestors. In their past, and in blood relatives whom they never knew, many find a more stable version of themselves. This turn to the past interacts paradoxically with the urge for reinvention or renewal: rather than embrace the human ability to grow, change and adapt, it is about finding an essence, the source from which we spring, proving we are not fully constructed or imagined. Nations who feel a need to prove their lineage can follow a similar path, tracking down their dead, metaphorically unearthing their forebears to understand 'who are we?' by answering 'who were they?' In honouring the dead, using traditions and rituals to connect to them and bring them back to life, nations affirm their own existence and future.

In Russia's all-consuming identity crisis, politicians and ordinary people also raise the dead in their search for meaning. But the dead bring no closure, only more deaths. The historian and cultural theorist Aleksandr Etkind has argued that post-Soviet culture is 'the land of the unburied', a country where the events of the mid-twentieth century are still very much alive, and still contentious within the political present.[2] Russia's leaders are unable to make sense of the blood-drenched pages of their past, unable to assemble them into a positive story in a way that acknowledges the depth of tragedy. Instead, they ignore or externalise the tragedy, burying it in shallow graves alongside those murdered by the Russian state and its predecessors.

On top of these graves, Russian officials and secret services put memorial stones to mask the cause of death, passing off the victims of Stalinist purges as Russians killed by fascists in the Second World War, crudely appropriating the bodies of those they murdered to serve as falsified evidence of their own heroism and victimhood. Such is the process underway in Sandormokh, Karelia, where the local FSB (secret police) insists that the mass graves filled with Stalin's victims, executed during the Great Terror, are actually mass graves of Soviet POWs slaughtered by Nazis. As well as pursuing local historians, such as Yuri Dmitriev, for providing evidence that disproves their claims, Russian officials are using these victims, many of them Ukrainian writers and artists from the so-called 'executed renaissance', as evidence in a campaign to recognise the Second World War as a genocide of the Soviet people.[3]

The use of corpses to assert rights over the living isn't peculiar to Russia. When the Yugoslav dictator Josip Broz Tito died, Serbs started to dig up relatives murdered in WWII. In many cases they hadn't been able to mourn their loved ones or even acknowledge the ethnocidal nature of their killings. They had to repress their trauma in the name of 'brotherhood and unity', the maxim of the Yugoslav state. But the exhumations were a reliving rather than resolution of trauma, a grotesque carnival. All of a sudden it turned out those relatives weren't dead at all, they had come back to life, possessing their children and grandchildren with all the unresolved tensions of 1941 to 1945, ready to refight past battles. In eerie echoes of Russia's war on Ukraine, Serbia attacked Croatia and Bosnia, recalling their (admittedly more significant and recent) Nazi collaborator pasts to justify slaughtering erstwhile neighbours and annexing 'historic Serb' lands.

At the same time as Yugoslav television camera crews were fixing the screen glare on their film of disturbed graves, 800 miles away the Berlin Wall was falling. In 1989, Europe's leaders celebrated this new era as a march towards liberalism; but they should have looked south, to see the return and revenge of history. Yugoslavia, so often orientalised as Europe's subconscious or a backwards-looking harbinger of past hatreds, serves rather as a glimpse into Europe's atavistic future. The region possesses histories that the West and Russia alike have preferred to ignore or to violently suppress. In this, Francis Fukuyama was more right than wrong, given that his *End of History* thesis did not suggest that the countries of the world would sail off into the sunlit uplands of liberal democracy but rather predicted that countries would find new things to fight over.[4] In the absence of ideology, the source of conflict has become identity imbued with genealogical essentialism and historicism – a fight over the past for civilisations unable to imagine, let alone provide, a better future.

Nowhere have these tendencies been better exemplified than in Russia's war on Ukraine – both the full-scale invasion and the ongoing conflict waged since 2014. It is obviously an existential war for Ukraine and Ukrainians – Russia's leaders have openly declared their intention to destroy Ukraine as a sovereign entity and identity. The Russian government, having conflated itself with the nation, also sees the war as existential, even if the Russian people do not, on the whole, share this view. As described in the following pages, Russians occupy a range of positions on the war, with many viewing it as a far-away military operation of which they knew little – at least until the Kremlin's announcement of 'partial' mobilisation in September 2022.

How to understand this paradox whereby a war is existential but ignorable? Squaring this circle is crucial to understanding how Russians have come to acquiesce in the crimes committed in their names. The apathy and the extremism stem from the same root of unresolved historical traumas in which the crimes go unpunished and the criminals stay in power. On its own, this state of affairs prevents the healthy development of society, as we see around the world, but the effect in Russia is exacerbated by the Kremlin's use of historical and other narratives, which reinforces the inherent power and fear of memories for some sections of society as well as nodding to the resonance of these same memories among other sections of the Russian population. These two sections are not static or divisible. The same person can and often does belong to both, just as many of the NKVD officers who delivered the first waves of Stalin's terror would be executed or sent to the Gulag in later rounds.

This indivisibility complicates a tendency in Western thinking to see people living in autocracies as heroes or villains, a binary that overlooks the corrosive nature of fear and how it encourages people to justify their actions. What is more, most Russians have no support structure through which to manage and overcome that fear. The closure of Memorial, a civil society organisation dedicated to human rights and the study of Soviet state terror, just a couple of months shy of Russia's full-scale invasion of Ukraine, feels retrospectively loaded with symbolism. It completed the state-sanctioned politics of selective amnesia. But fear, amnesia, and negative emotions are not the only drivers. Putin doesn't shape Russians' views on foreign policy or Ukraine so much as he articulates them. The Kremlin has used smoke and mirrors to encourage Russians to support the 'special military operation' – but the Russian people are co-authors of this deception.

In other words, the Kremlin's sales tactics are heavy-handed, but many Russians are in the market for buying. As I show in Chapter 2, there is enough sociological research to confirm that a significant number of Russians approve of what they believe is happening in Ukraine. Russians aren't the first nation to support a ghastly and unjust war,[5] and nor will they be the last, so this book wants to look further, asking not if Russians support the war but *why*, what does support mean, and to what extent are these phenomena peculiar to Russians? Ultimately this war does not stem from some genetic Russian exceptionalism – although that would have made for a much easier book to write. It is a choice. From the outside it may appear a binary choice but that is not how it is perceived and experienced in Russia.

Our quarrel is with the Russian people

In discussions of the war on Ukraine, and why it is popular, there are two simplistic streams – and a third group of insights. The first categorises Russians as evil, we need to ban them, destroy their country and cancel anything they have ever produced. The second group tries to depict the war as Putin's alone, an approach summarised by US President Joe Biden's bizarre line that 'our quarrel is not with the Russian people'.[6] (Given how many lethal weapons the USA is sending to Ukraine, it would be terrifying to see them have a real quarrel.) The notion that this war is imposed upon the Russian people follows the rhetorical tradition in the West of characterising the Soviet regime as an evil empire but its people as long-suffering liberals chafing at the bit of autocracy. Policymakers may view this framing as politically expedient as if – or when – Putin, or Putinism, does fall, it allows Russians to externalise his crimes as something done not *by* but *to* them. In theory, this would more easily facilitate a move toward liberalism.

But this approach didn't work in 1991, nor would pretending Russians were in no way complicit be just and, as the title of this book suggests, it most certainly wouldn't be correct. More importantly, it would reinforce a lack of responsibility and introspection that has contributed to many Russians' inability to accept the truth of the war.

This is Russia's war. The Russian people are largely complicit in the war's launch and the way it has been waged, just as the US and UK populations have been complicit in their nations' wars. This book wants to probe that complicity because it is an important part of why and how the war is fought: Putin banked on the population's approval and he cashed it. Most people had a choice. Russia is an authoritarian country but until recently it would not have been correct to categorise it as a dictatorship; it is rather an autocracy that offers its citizens lots of carrots to avoid the stick, as the journalist Joshua Yaffa explains so eloquently in his book *Between Two Fires*,[7] which spells out the many compromises liberal Russians made to live a meaningful and comfortable existence. It might be useful here to picture what choice you would make in the same position: would you speak out about a discriminatory company policy if it also meant losing the promotion that would help you afford your son's healthcare? Would you insist on calling the war in Iraq a war crime even if it carried the threat of jail time? Do you care that much? It is only by posing these questions to ourselves that we can even remotely understand the context in and through which Russians understand the war.

Pick your propaganda

Each war-supporting Russian interprets the propaganda in their own way and approves of the war for their own reasons; very few people simply parrot copycat versions of Kremlin lines. In any country, the same piece of propaganda can produce varied results in audiences. It might mobilise support in some viewers, while in others it will simply spark what the anthropologist Jeremy Morris calls a 'defensive consolidation' – we're here now so what can we do, let's stick together.[8] In others still, it will demobilise opposition, either directly through fear or indirectly by encouraging people to disassociate from the war. In research on China, the academic Haifeng Huang, found that heavy-handed, over-the-top propaganda actually backfired in the sense that viewers were less likely to trust and support the narratives and state media producing them. What it did achieve was to make those watching such extreme propaganda less likely to protest, because this propaganda did not – and was not trying to – demonstrate the trustworthiness of the Chinese state. It was a demonstration of the power of the Chinese state, such that it could confidently present such unbelievable lies as news.[9]

In other words, propaganda works but not necessarily in the way you think it does. This is markedly so in Russia where what one might term 'support for the war' is better understood as an acquiescence borne of many factors: apathy, lack of sympathy, self-interest, avoidance of cognitive dissonance, and so on. This is why, if the first half of this book examines what Russians are watching, then the second half switches focus to why they want to watch that in the first place, drawing in more detail on interviews and first-hand analysis of Russian society. Both elements are needed to make sense of Russians' complicated consent to this war. Of the almost sixty interviews I conducted for this book, a discussion with a Russian friend from a normal middle-class Moscow family summed up the complexity for me. In his view, for most Russians, it is natural to 'care more about a Pushkin statue than a dead Ukrainian child. My parents would say as much even though they don't really engage with the war – such things help them to accept the war, it is like an attack on their very being.'[10] But he also added that such attitudes were not dependent on age, insisting he had heard similar comments 'from young people and from people who aren't in Russia. I don't think the location matters – it's the question of belonging to a discourse, a discursive group. Here in Germany, I saw some demonstrations of the Alternative für Deutschland and some Russians with them bearing Russian flags and singing the Soviet war anthem *Katyusha* – it was the day after the discovery of mass graves at Bucha . . . I wanted to throw a stone at them.' But there was no stone and so he walked on.[11]

This quotation visualises and groups some of the more prominent and frequent reactions of Russians to the war: those who don't engage with the war, and sometimes may not even support it, but are emotionally consolidated around the Russian side; people who support it by performing certain rituals, albeit rarely with as much agency as the German Russians noted above; and people who are opposed but lack the tools to do anything about it, they have no stone to throw. As I argue throughout this book, one way to understand the difference between the groups – which are imperfectly drawn and in constant flux – is through the spectrum of allies model, used by pressure groups to change minds and influence people.

The original spectrum of allies comprises active support, passive support, neutral, passive opposition and active opposition. Pressure groups and political parties work on the assumption that movements seldom win by overpowering the opposition; they win by shifting support out from under it. Their hypothesis is that, rather than focus on active supporters and active opponents, to change views you need to acknowledge that most people are somewhere between these two points and try to nudge them further along the spectrum of allies: from passive opponent to neutral, from neutral to passive support, from passive support to active support. Likewise, there isn't much point bothering about the active opposition – you won't convince them. It is much more productive to work on moving people up into a more supportive, or at least more neutral, category.

The Kremlin's spectrum of allies functions according to similar principles but with some adaptations: their spectrum comprises active support, passive ritual support, loyal neutrals, apathy and active opposition. Notably, in their version, the Kremlin doesn't just ignore but sets out to destroy active opposition, or at least render them hopeless and apathetic. Then they nudge the apathetic into loyal neutrality ('my country, right or wrong'), and loyal neutrals into ritual supporters. A further twist is that the Kremlin does not view active support as the ideal end result but as undesirable. Distrusting any freely made political act even if in support of the regime, the Kremlin tries to shuffle active supporters down into the ritual support category, creating clear boundaries for what is and is not an acceptable way to show allegiance.

In any authoritarian country with active censorship, ordinary people's views are inevitably difficult to ascertain with full accuracy, which also complicates any generalisations. Whatever the Kremlin wishes to present, Russia is a country of atomisation, not of collective coming together. There is no society in the sense of a collective group of people made up of social relationships founded on solidarity or mutual interest without any sort of hierarchy. Consequently, it is much easier to explain why elites support or oppose the war because they care about rationalising and intellectualising – and because there are fewer of them. They provide more clarity of views, as you are much likelier to find active war supporters among the elites, intellectual or political, than among ordinary citizens. The spectrum of allies approach is of limited value in understanding their views, so it is worth briefly outlining them here.

First, you have people like Nikolai Patrushev, Secretary of the Security Council of the Russian Federation, one of Putin's closest advisers. Patrushev is representative of *siloviki* hawks who genuinely believe Ukraine shouldn't exist and that the war was necessary, preventative and civilisational. Among this

so-called 'party of war'[12] there are outsider political manoeuvr-
ers such as Ramzan Kadyrov, leader of Chechnya, and Yevgeny
Prigozhin, head of the Wagner mercenary group, who understand the popularity of pushing a more maximalist view of the
war and how it ought to be fought. However, traditionally,
most Russian elites are brutally realist, in that they want to
maximise Russian power, which the war obviously has failed to
do, bleeding its military and human forces, and making Russia
much more dependent on China.

There are different groups of realists, including those
who want to contain the West and those who are realist
Westernisers, not in the sense of being liberal or anti-liberal
so much as in the way they prioritise sovereignty and prestige.
A typical example of the latter would be Andrei Kortunov at
the Russian International Affairs Council, who has publicly
criticised the war. Another group is the Eurasian regionalists,
who believe Russia's status as a major power must be based
on its regional identity rather than any alliance with the West.
The more extreme wings of this group, such as the nationalist
and Eurasianist publication Tsargrad, funded by the Orthodox
oligarch Konstantin Malofeev, express a demand for more
war and coalesce with figures like Kadyrov. Yet, on the more
philosophical wing of this same group, where you will find
academics and thinkers like Vadim Tsymbursky and Boris
Mezhuev, there is a preference for reducing the war aims to
creating a buffer zone of Ukrainian territory.[13]

Some elites are entrepreneurial in their approach to the war,
such as Dmitrii Medvedev who was previously seen as a hope
for a more liberal, democratic Russia during his brief stint as
President, but is now a vehement supporter of the war. Among
the foreign-policy elites, Dmitri Trenin's transformation has
been much discussed in the West. As the former Director of
the Carnegie Moscow Center, Dr Trenin might previously
have been classed as belonging to the Westerniser realist
camp. However, since the war began his position has shifted

and he now outlines why a clear win for Russia, including inflicting serious damage on the Western 'enemy', is a matter of survival.[14]

Of course, most ordinary Russians have little time or energy to pontificate about Eurasianism or the merits of classical versus offensive realism as a way of explaining the world. As such, the narratives that resonate with them originate from different sources that are not always easy to identify, although I attempt to do so in Chapters 5–7. A team of Russian sociologists that has been collecting in-depth interviews with Russians has also tried, grouping respondents supportive of the war into five categories:[15]

1. State propaganda audiences: These people trust official sources of information, feel compassion for civilians, but ultimately believe that the Ukrainian army is responsible for the war and are ready to endure the consequences of sanctions.
2. Supporters of the 'Russian World': These people don't trust propaganda, but have nationalist and imperialist sympathies. For them, the conflict between Russia and the Western world has been going on for a long time. The war is just an attempt to establish peace and order by Russia.
3. NATO threat group: These people don't trust propaganda and criticise Putin. They didn't want war but now they use NATO threat rhetoric to justify the war.
4. Personally connected with Donbas: These people are often critical of Putin and not interested in Russia's march on Kyiv but rather hope the invasion might end hostilities in Donbas.
5. Incoherent attitudes group: These people don't really think about politics or even the conflict much but feel confused and overwhelmed by conflicting narratives, meaning they acquiesce to the war since they don't really understand what is going on.

These views will continue to evolve and to merge with one another as the war continues. A person's reason(s) for supporting the war will rarely fit neatly into one group alone and even if they did, that could change over time due to a shift in relative importance. Moreover, people can be motivated by contradictory reasons, or might use a political stance to articulate a certain sense of fairness unrelated to geopolitics and instead linked to personal experience, e.g. if an ethnic Russian had a relative who ended up in Uzbekistan after the fall of USSR, and struggled to obtain a Russian passport, then they might be a strong supporter of the Russian World concept in a way that has nothing to do with Ukrainians. In other words, these groups are useful guides but must still be taken with a pinch of salt: they provide insights, not answers. As the Professor of Political Science at Columbia University Timothy Frye explained to me, 'sociological polls are bad tools for working out why people do things – people rarely know themselves – but they can tell us lots of other things'.[16]

2

Putin's polls

Putin napav. Putin has attacked.

These are the words with which many Ukrainian mothers woke their sleeping children in the early hours of 24 February 2022. Nothing could have truly prepared Ukrainians or anyone with a connection to the region for the sight of the Russian Army bombing the place they proclaim 'the mother of all Russian cities'. A new age of barbarism was ushered into Europe. Kyiv was under siege. Westminster was in chaos. Paris was trying to get its bearings. Berlin was in shock. And in Moscow there was a sneering silence. Where were the Russian people? Surely they didn't want this? Did they even know?

Ira Shcherbakova is a brave and talented young journalist who was arrested for protesting the war in the immediate aftermath of the invasion. On her release from jail, she accompanied her family on a four-hour trip from Moscow to the house of her step-grandfather, to celebrate his birthday. In her interview with me, Ira painted a picture of gilded ignorance pregnant with imminent disaster – an image and setting worthy of a Chekhov play. 'We were at this country house party and we realised that only those who were from Moscow knew that the war had started. Everyone else was coming up to us and asking "Why are you so sad? What's wrong?" Just imagine, there was me, my mum, my stepdad all sitting there glued to our phones, anxious, almost shaking. But everyone around us continued to drink, to sing, to dance and to ask us "Why are you so sad? What happened?"'[1]

This phrase, 'what happened?' (*chto sluchilos?*) has become a meme on the Russian internet (RuNet). It is a mockery of the censorship but also of the way people are continuing their normal lives, moaning about the hindrances caused by the war without referencing the war itself. For example, headlines like 'In 2022, record numbers of Russians have applied for passports' or 'Authorities are increasing the plots available at the military cemetery by 17 hectares' are then followed by the ironic question 'Oh, what happened?' It draws attention to the way that for many Russians, unlike Ira, the war is everywhere and nowhere, like background noise. Or radiation.

Evidence of support for war

'They use Putin as an excuse for why they can't change anything. What Putin? Is Putin shooting women and raping our children? Is he? No, it isn't Putin, it is Russians.' Olesya Stepanchuk is a friend from Kharkiv, by way of Rivne. Her views are representative of many Ukrainians with whom I have spoken and this chapter will chart the extent to which this statement – 'It isn't Putin, it is Russians' – is a fair assessment. After all, Putin is legally culpable for starting the war but Russian soldiers committing war crimes in Ukraine also carry both legal and moral culpability. The Head of the Russian Armed Forces, General Gerasimov did not give Russian soldiers orders to rape children; Minister of Defence Shoigu didn't command an Ahmat Brigade fighter to castrate and then execute a terrified POW with a boxknife. Every war criminal has committed their crimes of their own accord, often while comrades-in-arms cheered.

Efforts to blame Putin alone are not credible, especially when his approval ratings are apparently so high. The most reliable polling available, from the independent Levada Center, puts approval of Vladimir Putin at above 82 per cent every month between March and September 2022.[2] Putin's post-war approval rating was almost twenty points higher than his pre-war numbers, a discrepancy Aleksei Levinson, head of the sociocultural research department at the Levada Center, sees as crucial to unpicking where exactly support for the war lies:

> Sixty per cent of Russians almost always approve of Putin's actions – he has had this level of rating since the first months of his presidency [in 2000]. One time it dropped to 59 per cent but generally it never really falls below 60 per cent. Whenever Putin starts a war, like in 2008 and 2014, another 20 to 30 per cent is added to this 60 per cent. We need to ask why this 30 per cent, who normally do not support Putin, mobilise towards support. We have to break down this scary figure of 88 per cent or 82 per cent by understanding that 60 per cent approval ratings are guaranteed, that's not interesting.[3]

It may not be interesting to Mr Levinson but it is worth noting that since 2014, various academics have tried to gauge the reliability of Putin's popularity, with the most methodologically robust study using list experiments to conclude that, yes, he really is very popular.[4] This shouldn't be surprising: it is easier to be an autocrat if you are popular, since you will still need to rely on millions of bureaucrats and citizens to get anything done. The alternative is to rule through the barrel of a gun but this is expensive and empowers your security forces, who could then overthrow you.

Since the full-scale war began, Putin's popularity has increased, in Mr Levinson's view, as 'the military operation is playing a mobilisational role, just as any such campaign would in any country, because it is about marginal values, or whose side you are on? It overcomes any issues about liking this or that government policy, or about whether you are living well or badly. Existential questions overcome this sort of concern – this is not specific to Russia.'[5] Following an invasion there is a tendency for populations to rally round the flag, an effect political scientists first documented in the USA but that has since been applied to numerous countries and contexts. Putin's approval ratings in 2022 were indistinguishable from those seen in the aftermath of the 2014 illegal annexation of Crimea, when support for Russian aggression in Ukraine was incredibly high and people partied in the streets with t-shirts depicting Putin on horse-back. The similarities end there: Russia's invasion of Ukraine has not been a bloodless annexation but a disastrous and largely futile bloodbath.

While support for the war and the regime are not identical, those who support President Putin are likely to support the invasion and vice versa.[6] For example, according to Levada, in March 2022, just after the invasion, similar numbers approved of the actions of the Russian armed forces in Ukraine as approved of Putin.[7] Social desirability bias also plays a role in such cases, meaning that when state television flaunts the latest surveys from the state pollster VTsIOM showing that over 77 per cent of Russians approve of Putin's actions and that almost 80 per cent trust their president, this will then act as a cue to other citizens to adopt pro-regime positions – lest they stand out or look stupid – fuelling further circles of consensus.

Not everything is consensual in Russian politics, of course. For example, age is a point of fissure, with 70 per cent of respondents aged 18 to 24 supporting the war, compared to 92 per cent of those aged 55 and above. Among respondents aged 18 to 24, 29 per cent definitely support, and 42 per cent rather support the war. Of those aged 25 to 39, the same responses comprise 42 per cent and 31 per cent, respectively.[8] These two age groups represent the highest proportion of those who do not support the actions of the Armed Forces of the Russian Federation on the territory of Ukraine.[9]

Research into youth attitudes just before the war showed that this constituency, so often feted in the West as the coming messiahs of Russian liberalism, have become somewhat desolate. The Kremlin has mobilised significant resources to shape young people's political thought and social values. While there is little evidence these have succeeded, the Kremlin appears to have at least convinced young people not to hope for anything better. In late 2021, a survey of young Russians showed how little value they attach to protests and how isolated they think Russia is internationally.

> The state has depoliticised large swathes of the younger generation, who find it pointless to get politically involved. Across all focus groups, young Russians are united in their view that they are powerless to influence their country's development [. . .] There is no positive, forward-looking momentum and participants complain about lacking any possibility of realising a future they themselves desire. The youth of Russia were already affected by this situation before the war. And, whereas some may see the war as a moment of national revival and strength, many of those who took part in our focus groups will feel increasingly isolated.[10]

Putin's popularity is undoubtedly an important factor in creating this isolation but also in promoting the war's specific aim of 'defence of the Donetsk and Luhansk People's Republics' (henceforth D/LPR). Most Russians would not otherwise be especially bothered about these territories. In the two years prior to the invasion of Ukraine, the proportion of Russians supporting independence for the D/LPR ranged from 23 to 29 per cent. In February 2022, just before launching a war designed to submerge these Ukrainian territories within

Russia, only eighteen per cent of respondents supported the inclusion of the unrecognised republics in Russia. This figure has been relatively stable since May 2014.[11] Nor could the general attitude of Russians towards Ukraine be described as bloodthirsty in the run up to war; for example, even against the tense backdrop of Russian troop movements in 2021, 55 per cent of Russians had a positive attitude towards Ukraine and 31 per cent – a negative one.[12]

Such findings raise more questions than they answer and can be interpreted in different ways: perhaps people don't care much about the war? Or perhaps they are fully subscribed to, even co-authors of, Putin's conception of historic Russian restoration, willing to go along with whatever he does. As ever, I am inclined to think that these positions are not mutually exclusive and often co-exist, perhaps uncomfortably, within a single person. Most Russians settle into the three 'passive' groups of Kremlin allies (ritual support, loyal neutral, apathetic opposition), somewhat receptive to the resonance of pro-Kremlin arguments about the Donbas but mainly desperate to get on with life, preoccupied by debt and daily trifles, and disinclined towards introspection about who or what really caused the war in Ukraine. For example, Levada has also been asking Russians: 'Do you feel personal moral responsibility for deaths and devastation in Ukraine?' In April 2022, 28 per cent said they did. By May 2022, it was 36 per cent with 58 per cent saying they didn't, down from 65 per cent. This number still tracks with a majority supporting, or not opposing, the war but it could conceivably indicate some troubled consciences.

On the other hand, it is very hard to know how respondents interpreted the notion of 'taking responsibility'– it could mean they felt guilty for not protecting 'Russian-speakers' better. This is probably the more likely option, given all the positive emotions Russians have expressed around the war, even if it doesn't quite shake off the sense of ambivalence. It is as if Russians support the ends but not the means, of the war, or didn't expect it to go that far, or support it but tell themselves they regret that it came to this. For example, some six months into the war, the dominant feeling among Russians caused by military actions in Ukraine was 'pride for Russia' (51%), but it was followed by 'anxiety, fear, horror' (31%), and 'shock' (12%). Perhaps this support is like that of the apocryphal grandmother of the 1996 Russians elections who, when asked whom she wanted to be President, replied Gennady Zyuganov, the Communist candidate. Then, when asked who would get her vote, the old lady replied 'Boris Yeltsin', explaining she would vote for Zyuganov when he became president.

Do Russians just accept the war because it's there? And if so, what does that mean in terms of gauging support and opposition in relation to the war?

Measuring opposition to the war

The phone rings, it's a woman's voice, polite, official but with a disarming sweetness. After confirming your name and address and date of birth – all correct – she asks: 'Do you support the special military operation, or would you like to go to prison for fifteen years?'

This is what many Russians would hear when pollsters ask them about support for the war. It is difficult to countenance the idea that anyone would feel comfortable expressing their dissent to an official sounding voice who knows their name and address, fully in the knowledge that spreading disinformation about the war risks fifteen years' incarceration. Most people simply refuse to answer, leading some sociologists to argue that the number of Russians who agree to respond to opinion polls has collapsed to an entirely unrepresentative level. According to Boris Kagarlitsky, before the war the Russian survey response rate was below 30 per cent, already low, but since the war it has wavered between 10 and 25 per cent.[13] Can sociological polling with this level of responsiveness, and in an atmosphere where telling the truth carries a criminal sentence, be taken as reliable or representative?

The sociologist Greg Yudin believes not. He argues that the low response rate means it is not possible to interpret the polls as a measure of public support for the war or Putin. Dr Yudin explains that under Putin, Russia functions like a 'plebiscitary democracy', in which the president relies on popular legitimacy derived from a passive and depoliticised population.[14] Elections, referenda and opinion polling function to validate ready-made decisions rather than reveal what the public really thinks. In this sense, the correct way to understand the question is 'if Putin does x, do you approve?' rather than 'do you approve of x?'

There are other measures that people cite to undermine the idea that Russians broadly support the war, including that the government has to bus in 'fake' supporters to pro-war events, such as the March 2022 'Z rally' to celebrate the invasion. If large numbers of Russians were truly enthused by this war, surely the authorities would not need to coerce school administrators into attending? More broadly, the point is that Russia is not a country where you can always believe your eyes. The investigative journalism website Proekt released a series of reports on how Russian authorities use leading questions to elicit the answers they need and massage the polls to please Putin, who is very sensitive about them.[15]

Moreover, despite the beatings and the brutal laws, thousands did come out to protest the invasion, with more than 13,000 detained across 147 cities between 24 February and 6 March 2022. The largest demonstrations on the day of the invasion were in Moscow, where 2,000 protestors gathered near Pushkinskaya Square, and Saint Petersburg, where up to 1,000 protestors gathered. Hundreds also demonstrated in Yekaterinburg, Chelyabinsk, Nizhny Novgorod, Novosibirsk and Perm.[16] These are significant and courageous numbers given how difficult it has become to organise protests in Russia. Ever since the 2012 mass protests, the Kremlin has taken great pains and efforts to dismantle opposition networks, including with the involvement of some of the West's largest tech giants (see how Apple and YouTube shut down Aleksei Navalny's Smart Vote apps).

With the Navalny network having largely fled abroad, except of course for Navalny himself, there was no opposition base to organise the anti-war demonstrations. Consequently, the empowered young oppositionists dotted around Russia in 2017, some of whom I had the privilege to meet, had no outlet – at least at the time (in October 2022 the Navalny team announced they were relaunching their regional network). Instead, they worked on online activism and Andrey Lipov, head of Russian state media regulator Roskomnadzor, revealed in June 2022 that the regulator had removed over 117,000 'fakes' about the war and Russia's armed forces, as well as 1,177 posts in support of Ukraine with a total audience of over 202 million users. What's more, plenty expressed their opinions with their feet, with up to 500,000 Russians leaving the country by August, mainly the young and economically comfortable ones, and a further 260,000 following the announcement of partial mobilisation in September.[17]

However, while some of these counterarguments provide reasons to be sceptical and robust in our treatment and understanding of what support means in Russia, they do not provide definitive proof to assert that significant numbers of the population oppose the war. First, if we are to discount the polling on the basis of the response rates then we would need to discount most polls conducted in Europe and North America at least. The response rates to Russian polls are actually in line with, and generally higher than, the response rates in the USA, suggesting that it may not be fear or the autocratic political situation undermining Russians' confidence to answer questions.[18] Moreover, preference falsification, which looks at how respondents' answers change when the questions are disguised, does not indicate that large numbers of Russians are lying about their approval. The political scientists Philipp Chapkovski and Max Schaub found that between ten and fifteen per cent of Russian respondents may not be truthful when they tell pollsters they support the war,[19] which still leaves a majority in favour of the war.

Second, we have the issue of protests. Assessing the efforts of brave Russians to protest, risking horrific forms of rape, torture and brutality, is fraught with moral qualm. It is difficult to know to whom one can compare so it makes sense to only compare like for like. Until 5 March 2022, Russian laws on media and protest restrictions were very similar to those of 2021, when people took to the streets to rally against the unjust imprisonment of opposition figure Aleksei Navalny after he returned from Berlin where he was being treated for Novichok poisoning. In the period from 23 January to 21 April 2021, between 611,000 and 880,000 people took to the streets across 198 cities, with 13,515 detained. The number of protestors and the number of cities that staged protests were considerably higher for Navalny than for Ukraine.[20]

Perhaps more pertinently, there have been no mass protests of Russians against the war in any of the places of emigration, where tens of thousands of Russians are newly ensconced. This is not surprising given that, at home, in the eight years between the annexation of Crimea and the 2022 invasion, there were no domestic public demonstrations against aggression towards Ukraine to match even one tenth of the fervour with which most Russians greeted the annexation of Crimea. Beyond liberal sections of society (especially Boris Nemtsov, murdered in 2015), there was very little public pressure on Putin to respect Ukrainian territorial integrity or de-occupy Crimea or Donbas. Putin has traditionally been mindful of constraints and limitations, as reflected in his obsessive and secretive use of private polling. If there had been a demonstrative outpouring of support for Ukrainian territorial integrity at any point since 2014, it certainly could have made an impact. Instead, those groups actively opposed to the war, such as those who took part in the 2014 Peace Marches against Russian aggression in Ukraine, were gradually demobilised – sent abroad, killed, convinced to give up.

Third, the lack of active impassioned supporters at rallies is a feature rather than a bug in the Kremlin's population management system. The Kremlin depends on being able to demobilise or disable active supporters almost as much as active opponents. The bussing in of hired supporters for pro-war and pro-government rallies is a long-established tactic that does not reflect a lack of active support but a preference for populating important events with people dependent on the state for their livelihood, to avoid risk of spontaneity. It is like a political party spin doctor using party activists for a photo shoot, regardless of whether their candidate is genuinely popular. Putin's regime is suspicious towards social mobilisation of any kind – not only against the regime, but also in support of it, its policies and decisions.

Fourth, we have other ways of measuring support than through replies to direct questions. Some six months after the war, Russian polls showed a general public optimism, with 68 per cent affirming that the country was headed in the right direction, a figure above even the peak following Russia's annexation of Crimea in 2014. Levada's index of family sentiment, which measures respondents' sense of how their household is doing financially, also jumped twelve per cent during the first six months of war, while the index of consumer sentiment jumped eleven per cent. Another Levada statistic showed that during the first five months of 2022, the percentage of Russians experiencing positive emotions increased significantly, while those experiencing aggression or depression dropped.

Such statistics arguably reveal far more than blunt measurements of support versus opposition. That said, Aleksei

Levinson believes the issue of whether or not Russians are telling the truth in polls is overstated: 'this question is relevant everywhere be it USA, Russia or anywhere. What a person says publicly and in private, will almost always differ. There is a philistine idea that honest people say what they mean and now because of the [repressive political] situation in the country, people are being less honest. But this is a primitive and false understanding of social consciousness. And ultimately the important thing is that the government gets the support it needs, not whether or not people are sincere. We need a more complex understanding of what is happening in Russian mass consciousness, but it isn't something unique or specific to Russians'.[20] Ultimately, the government got the support it needed in the form it needed – the ritual response of approval when answering the pollsters, or at least the apathetic refusal to answer them.

Fifth and finally, there is the argument that those opposed to the war have simply left. But leaving does not equate to opposition, not least because many of those who oppose the war may not have the money to leave Russia. Moreover, even of those who do oppose the war, the invasion of Ukraine was not always the direct cause of their emigration; for example, many left not out of horror at the war but because of the domestic crackdown and expectation of mobilisation into the army. Aleksandr Dmitriev, a Kherson-born academic from Moscow, is one such person. In an interview with me, Aleksandr told the story of his exit from Russia: 'we had to run away on 4 March, when there was the threat of full mobilisation. When they closed Ekho Moskvy,[21] that was a blatant signal that everything is done for. It wasn't the fact Russian tanks entered Kherson, it was the closing of Ekho Moskvy.'[22] Like many other new emigres, he didn't leave out of horror at the invasion, although he certainly felt it, but under the threat of mobilisation.

There is nothing unusual in Aleksandr's response – in any society, democracies included, most people are only driven

to protest when an issue begins to impact them directly –
but it suggests that the 'anti-war label' is not necessarily a
'pro-Ukraine' stance. As he is himself from Kherson, I asked
Aleksandr whether he would return to Ukraine to support the
war effort:

> No, I want to go to Western Europe. Ukraine right now is a
> besieged fortress. My wife is . . . look, a lot depends on family
> situation. My oldest son has a Ukrainian name, my daughter
> has a Jewish name – so there is this ethnic issue. The situation
> inside Ukraine, the academic one, is quite complicated – they
> have to decide what side they are on. And if I had been working
> in Ukraine, like in Poland now, I would have to criticise Putin
> all the time, become an enemy of my previous self – we were
> wrong, Putin is Hitler, a Nazi, all this militant cold war rhetoric.
> As a historian I don't like this sort of thing.[23]

When discussing the Russian diaspora and the Russian liberal
opposition alike it is difficult to generalise, such is the inchoate
nature of both groups; however, from many years of ethno-
graphic research, interviews, media analysis, and just chatting
with friends during the five years of my life spent in Russia,
I do not find Aleksandr Dmitriev's response surprising. The
issue is not that he will not choose a side – he has, in his own
words, chosen the Western side. The issue is that among the
constituency of people to which he belongs – incredibly intelligent people with liberal values and firm morals who came of
age in the USSR – it is hard to find many that view Ukraine as
part of the Western spectrum.

The disconnect between (some) Russian liberals and
Ukrainians has caused bitterness. Nobody is more disappointed in, and less hopeful of, Russian capacity to rise up than
the Ukrainians. Perhaps the Ukrainian saying that 'the Russian
liberal ends where Ukraine begins' is a truism but it is one
that has had frequent cause to be pronounced. Explanations

that will convince a Western audience – that Russians cannot be expected to protest in such a frightening environment, all they can do is leave – are given short shrift by Ukrainians who have staged two revolutions over the last twenty years, in the face of brutality and snipers, and who returned to fight in their tens of thousands from working abroad. Sasha Danylyuk, adviser to General Zaluzhnyi, the Commander in Chief of the Ukrainian Armed Forces, and adviser to the head of the Foreign Intelligence Services of Ukraine, perceives many Russian liberals as sharing the Kremlin's chauvinistic and dismissive attitudes towards Ukrainians as 'little brothers. They are so arrogant and condescending, even among liberals, this is just their attitude, the Russian attitude, they do not see Ukraine as really abroad, as a real country, we are just a joke to them.'[24]

Nestled alongside the contemptuousness, many Ukrainians harbour a sense of betrayal. As one Ukrainian friend and former MP, Aliona Hlivco explained: 'we watched the same films as them (Russians), danced to the same songs, went on holiday together to Crimea. We can't believe they would do this to us.'[25] Ukrainians were dismayed by the lack of support they received from their Russian friends and family and the Russian people as a whole. While the fraternal peoples narrative can be misleading, there is a great deal of intermarriage and familial connections; an estimated 11 million Russians (around 8%) have relatives in Ukraine. By comparison around ten per cent of Brits have at least one Irish grandparent. When Russia first invaded in 2014, many Russian-speaking Ukrainians in Kharkiv or from Donetsk spoke of their pain that Russia could do that to Ukrainians. After 24 February, betrayal hardly suffices to articulate the pain. Such is their disgust, many Russian-speakers are refusing to speak their own native language – anything to facilitate distance between themselves and the aggressors to the east, who insist they are 'liberators'.

This reclamation of language is also a statement about identity and existence, which many Ukrainians feel is undermined not only by pro-Putin but also liberal Russians. The former blame the latter's refusal to interrogate their own imperialist arrogance and tendency to subjugate Ukrainian suffering to their own political needs. As evidence of this, and the Western media's support in it, some Ukrainians have compared the intense coverage of anti-mobilisation protests in Moscow with the distinct lack of Western media interest in Ukrainians press-ganged into occupation armies. Analysis of certain Russian opposition social media channels supports these suspicions. In itself, the war as it is being fought against and by *Ukrainians* does not feature prominently in the major Russian liberal Telegram channels. From my analysis of three months of content from two of the most popular Russian liberal Telegram channels, Navalny and Topor, both barely mentioned Ukraine, focusing instead on Putin, and the difficulties caused to Russia. Across the sixteen channels I analysed, the average number of references to Ukraine per channel was 1,445; however, Topor referred to Ukraine a mere 89 times and Navalny's channel a mere eighteen. Such actions remove Ukraine from its own war, reflecting the solipsistic nature of some of the liberal opposition – but not all, given that the defining feature of the Russian opposition, like society in general, is its atomisation.

Who is to blame?

At first, it looks just like an ordinary price tag, perhaps a bit more expensive than you expected but it is probably the impact of sanctions. But then you notice something a bit off; what does that say? Oh, it is an anti-war slogan, how strange

It is a mundane and strangely touching gesture, to go around a small grocery shop in Kazan, in Tatarstan, writing anti-war slogans on a price tag, along the lines of '400 roubles. The Russian Army has bombed *400* people in a drama school in Mariupol.' It really won't change much except for the impact on some of the individuals involved in these protests. Take thirty-two-year-old Sasha Skochilenko, who executed this same dastardly crime of maligning-the honour-of-the-Russian-armed-forces-by-vandalising-price-tags, only in St Petersburg. In jail since April, she is now facing ten years in a labour colony, where she will perform mundane tasks, sitting uncomfortably on a too-small stool for hours at a time, subject to the whims of largely unaccountable prison guards. If found guilty – and the gross conviction rate in Russia is over 99 per cent – then by the time she is released from prison, Sasha will have missed many important events, her thirties will have passed by. And will she have changed anything? Will it be worth the pain it brings to her family? For those with children, this choice seems even starker, as police have taken away the children of mothers suspected of anti-war vandalism.[26] Is an ultimately futile gesture worth losing your children over – worth seeing them sent to an orphanage in a dilapidated former Gulag town?

The risk and pointlessness sit on people's resolve like a sediment, deliberately laid and carefully layered over the years. This is how active opposition becomes apathetic, in the spectrum of allies model. One of the few journalists to remain in Moscow, Evan Gershovich, published a piece about how Muscovites were partying and forgetting the war. There were some eminently publishable and distasteful quotes from certain of the *beau monde* ('I actually ended up being more upset about Ikea leaving than the war itself') but it is easy to follow the reasoning. As one nominally anti-war Petersburger told me: 'What is the point? Will it change anything? No, it will just upset my mother.'[27] It is much easier to disconnect, especially when the new laws brought in by Vladimir Putin on 4 March not only muzzled the media, but also introduced stiff penalties and long prison terms for those who protested the war.[28]

These same laws have led to truly Orwellian convictions; for example, a judge sentenced Moscow Municipal Deputy Alexey Gorinov to seven years in prison for disseminating 'deliberately false information' about the Russian Army. He argued that the invasion's goal is to seize Ukraine's territory and end its independence, quoting statements made by Putin and pro-war propagandists.

As well as their inability to impact the authorities, would-be protestors also decry their inability to find a common language with those 'in the regions'. When pressed on who else, except Putin, is responsible for the war, many intellectual elites blame it on the '*sovok*' or Homo Soveticus of the regions, arguing that people there are Soviet-moulded idiots or yokels who will do what any leader tells them. Not entirely unlike the North London liberals who see everyone who voted for Brexit as an idiot or a racist, or the coastal progressives who depict 2016 Trump voters as shills or fascists, Russian intellectual elites tend to see their own country from on high. To quote the celebrated Ukrainian-born writer, Nikolai Gogol: 'In Russia, there is great ignorance of Russia. Everyone lives in foreign journals and newspapers, rather than their own land.'[29] In my conversations with Westernised anti-war, middle-class Russians, they insisted they didn't know anyone who supported the war (the same was true of pro-war Russians, reflecting high levels of polarisation in Russian society) and spoke disparagingly of those who did support the war ('they sold their souls to the devil, like in 1933')[30] and of those fighting in Ukraine: 'War drags in the dregs of humanity, often people from the poorest regions, with very little education, which means they are more prone to propaganda. Also, of course, the war brings out the worst in people but why are they doing it [killing]? Because they were told to.'[31]

Stereotypes about the poor provincial yokels are frustrating. Take Pskov Oblast, on the Russian-Estonian border, where I spent two summers working in a village orphanage.

Much of rural Pskov has no running water or inside toilets. The city centre is beautiful but underfunded. There is very evident poverty and lack of investment. And yet, Pskov has a famous political opposition paper, Pskovskaya guberniya, one of the best in the country, and a long tradition of political activism, including in relation to the war against Ukraine. As in any country, each Russian city and region has its own identity, quirks and atmosphere: Nizhny Novgorod and Perm, where networks of resistance have been established to assist Ukrainians in fleeing Russia, have long felt rather liberal. On the other hand, regions like Voronezh and Belgorod, which border Ukraine, are known as the red belt, with a nod to the left-behind feeling that has lingered since the transition away from Communism.

Looking at regionalised data of support for the war, some of these differences become clear, although the most interesting places, like Ramzan Kadyrov's Chechen fiefdom, are the ones for which the data is least trustworthy. In neighbouring Dagestan, at least 300 contractors laid down their arms in summer 2022 and tried to extricate themselves from Ukraine, despite facing threats of physical violence and criminal prosecution. Following the call for mobilisation, hundreds of Dagestanis took to the streets for days of protest until the authorities promised that only men with military experience would be called up.[32] Dagestan was the region with the highest number of fatalities at the time of the protests and this imbalance led to increased resentment. The Ukrainians have been sensitive to these sentiments, aware that they might be useful to their own cause. For example, Zelensky released a hard-hitting video, delivered in front of a Kyiv plaque to the Chechen fighter Imam Shamil, calling on Russia's ethnic minorities not to sacrifice their lives for imperialist aims.[33] He evoked the shared struggles and spirit of peoples colonised by Russia, encouraging them to sympathise with Ukraine and distance themselves from (ethnic) Russian rule .

Russia is not a monolith, from the far-easterners who feel completely disconnected from Ukrainians, to the young Tatars who shared some of their Zelensky fanfiction with me, and clearly saw the Ukrainian leader as a freedom fighter challenging the overbearing Russian Leviathan. Moreover, just as people living in the regions cannot be dismissed as pro-war village idiots, neither are anti-war types all noble poets living precariously on a Petersburg waterway. Many of the anti-war people I spoke to were officials in government and government-linked agencies. Speaking to contacts from the Ministry of Foreign Affairs, where my interlocutors insisted there was much opposition to the war, I asked why there were so few resignations across government, especially in their own department, from which only one diplomat publicly resigned (Boris Bondarev)?[34] I didn't receive an adequate answer, given it was crystal clear that to stay in the foreign service and to continue to work for the government unequivocally meant supporting Russian aggression. It was a similar story for the Central Bank, for many years painted as a haven of common sense that would moderate the Kremlin's crazier proclivities. According to Meduza, fewer than fifty people resigned from Russia's Central Bank in response to the invasion. 'Three employees told Meduza that the constant criticism they face on social media for keeping their jobs makes them feel like "Reichsbank employees".'[35] They may wish to explore the validity of that feeling.

Are you really opposed to the war if you continue to work in the Ministry of Foreign Affairs, facilitating the prosecution of that war? Are you opposed to the war if you do nothing at all to help Ukrainians in any way and pay taxes to the government to spend on weapons used against Ukrainians? These questions are not intended to be flippant. The boundary between support and opposition is not as clear as it might seem in our imaginations, nor is there always a clean moral divide on closer inspection. There are older Russians, living in wooden houses without internet access, who support the war because they genuinely think they are liberating Ukrainians from the Nazi yoke, while there are younger, well-off liberals who oppose the invasion of Kyiv purely because of its impact on their pockets and ambitions and ability to feel superior to the Armenians and Kyrgyz now hosting them. To me the latter contribute more to the source of the issue from which the war has sprung: a self-centred lack of empathy and acceptance of brute force and Russian exceptionalism. Making a conscious decision not to do anything when you recognise – or have the capacity to recognise – the evil done in your name is hardly more morally upstanding than blindly supporting something you have no reason to question.

Plenty of Russians do not question their country when it comes to performing patriotism. In discussions of patriotism, it makes sense to distinguish between two core types: one form of patriotism is benign, denoting pride in one's country, another is more hostile – about blind support and hostile aggression. Russians are unexceptional in terms of benign patriotism, but real outliers in terms of the number expressing 'blind and militant' patriotism, namely the belief you should support your country even if it is wrong and that your country should follow its own interest even if it harms others.[36] As one Russian friend, who has long left the country put it: 'It is a terrible reflex: it's my country and my duty is to defend it even if it is wrong. I must defend my country. You cannot imagine how deep and powerful this reflex is. Even those who don't think this war is a good idea – say "we are wrong but we cannot lose". Do you remember the post of [name redacted] that I sent you? It is my country and I wish it to win. Why can Americans commit war crimes and stay without any sanctions but we cannot? And this kind of stuff . . .'[37] Russians have scored higher than any other country polled on the measure of 'blind and militant' patriotism since the 1990s, showing that Putin articulated, or even responded, to Russian aggression rather than creating it.[38]

The 'blind' feature of such aggressive patriotism correlates to the group I call 'loyal neutrals', who award themselves the right not to ask painful questions by declaring their support a matter of loyalty or honour. The veteran analyst Dmitri Trenin described a similar approach in an interview with me: 'In 2014, [the annexation of] Crimea was a festival: the joining or restoration of the peninsula and its people happened without one shot being fired and without any victims at all. It was some sort of miracle. This sort of thing just doesn't happen. In 2022, rather than a festival we have pain, fear, trying experiences, the unknown ahead of us, but alongside that a stronger national unity. Russia is under attack – it must withstand.'[39] In this view, when push came to shove on 24 February, everyone had to make their choice, Russia or not Russia. Dmitri Trenin chose Russia, to the chagrin of some previous admirers. So did many others, including the Director of the influential Moscow-based think tank PIR Center and close friend of Deputy Foreign Minister Ryabkov, Vladimir Orlov, who related an unusual story in his interview with me: 'my friend is a very successful investment banker in Switzerland but in March he sent me a note, "*lyubi Rossiyu v nepogodu*" – love Russia when times are hard. Then he got his Russian passport and relocated to Moscow with his wife and two children, but not because he was paid by some oligarch. They just felt it. It was a moment of choice.'[40]

Unlike for this Swiss banker, for many Russians it was an unenviable, heart-wrenching choice. Yet even that hard bargain was a luxury denied to displaced Ukrainians. It is important to recognise the constraints on Russians but it is also important to recognise and afford them moral autonomy and agency. After all, if millions of Russians had taken to the streets, then it would have had a sizeable effect and changed the dynamic. But they didn't, even after the Ukrainians asked them to. This is why there is no satisfactory or simple way to answer the famous question 'Do the Russians want war?' The title of a famous Soviet-era song and poem, written by Yevgeny

Yevtushenko during Khrushchev's Thaw, 'Do the Russians Want War?' evokes the beauty of the Russian countryside, witness to the horrors of the Second World War, to explain why Russians want peace – not conflict. Such is its cultural resonance, Volodymyr Zelensky referenced the poem in his eve-of-war address to Russians, beseeching them to rekindle these pacifistic sentiments and rise up against the Kremlin's imminent invasion.

In his interview with me, Vladimir Orlov cited this song as an explanation of why war was generically awful even if he, reluctantly, supported this particular awful war:

> Zelensky referred to the Russian song – do Russians want war – [. . .] – no, they do not, that is clear. As the poem says, ask the 27 million who died. But it is also true that when the Soviet choir went to sing that song in the country of your [the author's] ancestors in the United Kingdom, they were banned because people believed it was Soviet propaganda and not that we wanted to share our feelings. We did not want war, we don't want war. Putin's face, on the 24th [February], if I may, revealed someone who does something reluctantly, not a sadist enjoying aggression – this is my reading.[41]

It is not a reading I share. To me, it was the face of a bitter man consumed by rage and delusions of such grandeur that he had projected his own resentful view of the world onto the history of an entire region. His aggression was facilitated by the power vertical system he and his associates had built atop Yeltsin's presidentialism and by the fact that, among those close to power, nobody had the courage to tell the Emperor that not only did his soldiers have no clothes, they had no proper invasion or logistics plans either.

Fittingly, Russia's state censorship agency, Roskomnadzor, blocked videos and recordings of 'Do the Russians Want War?' shortly after the invasion as part of a crackdown on 'fake news' and the criminalisation of almost any criticism of Russia's 'special military operation' in Ukraine.[42] This strict censorship is a muzzle on the thousands of brave Russians who have spoken out, but for many others it is also perhaps a relief, an excuse not to have to interrogate how the Russian Army wages its shameful war in Ukraine. An excuse to talk about life and living instead. An excuse for equivocations. An excuse to hear only the silent Russian fields but never the silent Ukrainian graves.

Patriotism or leave me alone

Silence can take many forms. The Russian sociologist Boris Kagarlitsky has argued that 'Russian people are neither for the war nor against it. They do not react to the war.'[43] But not reacting to a war inflicted in your name is at best tacit acquiescence and at worst supercilious endorsement. It is not a neutral act, even if you wish it could be. Just as Ukrainians have had their right to sleep in peace and live without fear entirely taken away, so too do many outside the country feel that Russians have had their right to be passive, to wallow in what the cultural historian Andrei Zorin has called the 'leave me alone' mindset, revoked.[44] A typical expression of this mindset, in those unable to flee the country, is what was called 'internal emigration' in the USSR. Internal emigres carved out grey spaces for themselves, separate to the politicised and ritualised public life of Soviet Union. Putin has encouraged internal – and external – emigration in (the much less politicised) post-Soviet society as a way to manage demand for change.

These processes, and reflex reactions to political fear, have led to the aforementioned defensive consolidation, a sort of denial, in which Russians know on one level of the horrors – and they know enough that they don't want to know anymore. People say things like 'we made our choice, we will accept the consequences. If people want to leave, let them. The main thing is to hunker down until the spring. We'll wait and see. Time will tell.'[45] A sort of 'keep calm and carry on' for Russia, only stripped of all defiance. For such people, answering 'yes' to 'do you support the war' can often be read as a fatalistic remark of loyalty, rather than passivity; hence, why I call them loyal neutrals. It is as much a statement of 'leave me alone' or of wanting not to be hassled than it is of supporting the war. By contrast, to say 'no' is to take a political stance, to leave the comfort of your grey space, to shine a light on yourself at a time when they are hunting for anyone who stands out.

Beyond the academic quibbling about this or that methodology, or the various interpretations of what support means, and how one might measure opposition, it is clear that since 2014 and since 2022, a significant number of Russians have been unprepared to leave the comfort of the grey space. Many have simply acquiesced to the war, especially provided it doesn't affect them that much. The interesting question then is why this is the case. The journalist, Ira Shcherbakova, sees the war as 'a question of identity. The question is what is Russian identity, where is it? Some years ago [in his 2012 State of the Union address] Putin complained about lack of 'Ru (translation *skrepy*)'. Now, this word 'bondings' doesn't exist, it is an example of bad Russian – and Putin does speak bad Russian from time to time – but the word became a meme because it is about people trying to build a national identity somewhere where this identity does not exist. It is about a sense of belonging, belonging to something. When someone says they are proud to be Russian, it isn't clear what this feeling is based on, and this [inchoate form] has allowed it to be appropriated and taken over by propagandists of the lowest level. The concept of Russian patriotism was so vulnerable to propaganda because it was empty. On the one hand there are the propagandists and on the other hand there are people and they want this sense of belonging, they want to be part of the group because it is a perfectly human desire. But the group being offered by the propagandists is the only one available to many Russians. Unfortunately, a large number of Russians don't have many options. They want to belong to something and this is what is on offer'.[46]

The connection between a desire for belonging and state propaganda partly explains why so many of the symbols and language of the Putin era are empty signifiers; others can fill these empty vessels with meaning, conflating them with more emotive symbols. This is what has happened with the meaningless Z symbol, used to denote Russia's war on Ukraine and often dressed up in the colours of the St George's Ribbon. Itself an object of mercurial significance, the St George's Ribbon has been worn since 2005 to commemorate the Great Patriotic War; however, since 2014 it has also become a symbol of support for Kremlin aggression against Ukraine, as if British people had worn the poppy in 2003 as a sign of support for the invasion of Iraq.[47]

Brits in 2003 did not wear the poppy in this way, but most of them did support the war in Iraq. So perhaps Westerners shouldn't be surprised that Russians support the war now and a better question to pose is how long are the Russians willing to fight this war? After all, it is one thing to order a three-day special operation and another thing to launch tens of thousands of men into a quagmire of attrition. Yet, according to a July 2022 poll taken by the Levada Center, there seemed to be a readiness among the people to see the war go on for half a year, one year, more than a year. A sizeable portion of the Russian population did not expect the war to end quickly, and were ready to adjust. Over time, like all wars, it is likely to become less popular but, as Aleksei Levinson explained to me in June 2022: 'if Russia begins to have some great victories, take Kharkiv, or other military achievements that you can sell to the population as a success, then I can't exclude that there will be another outpouring of support. Of course [without such success] support for the war will be routinised and become weaker.'[48] So far, the latter pattern has been borne out: by autumn 2022, fewer Russians were following the war on Ukraine. People began to switch off their televisions to avoid the constant war coverage even before Ukraine's successful summer and autumn counter-offensives or the liberation of Kherson.

But, rather than heralding a change in the tide of public opinion, switching off, and the apathetic attitude towards politics this represents, is one of the stronger correlations of support for the war. As Aleksei Levinson explained:

> This support does not mean anything more than a state of mind. It is not an action, not everyone who says they support it is going to sign up. Of those 70 to 80 per cent, the 60 per cent I spoke about – statistically the main part of those are people of the older generation, living as a rule in small towns and villages, people who minimally participate in social life, and take no part in political life. It is not only that they themselves won't be soldiers but most of them wouldn't even have children at risk of being soldiers. It is people not included in civilian life. Our surveys are the only active engagement they have. They are passive, listen to what is said on TV and then communicate within their own bubble. They have no capacity for action. Putin isn't supported by Russian people who will come out onto the streets with flags and placards to support him. It is people who just sit at home and, if you go to their home and ask them what they think, they say yes (I support).[49]

This is the regime's strength and weakness. As seen in September 2022, the Kremlin and its regional elites struggle to actively mobilise people to fight against Ukraine. But by huddling and shunting the population across ritual support, defensive consolidation and apathy, the government can prosecute its war with a sense of control and the broad acquiescence of the Russian people.

3

How do you say 'war' in Russian?

None of the pro-war Russians I spoke to saw the war in anything approaching the same terms as people in the West. Very
few of the anti-war Russians did either. So, in asserting that
Russians support the war, it is worth interrogating not just
what support entails but what they understand that war to be.
Any such effort must draw from the television and online news
channels, including social media, as well as official accounts
from politicians that shape not only how things are described
but what it is even legal to say.

First, as has been well-documented, in Russia it is illegal
to refer to the war in Ukraine as a war, instead you must call
it a special military operation. It might sound unwieldy but
there is a long tradition of such terminology. Both recent wars
in Chechnya were classed as military operations, as was the
Soviet war in Afghanistan – although admittedly after ten
years this distinction was hard to sustain. The great benefit of a
military operation is that it can be started and ended, whereas
a war tends to be won or lost. Deploying the term 'special
military operation' is also about managing the population's
emotions and trying to not make the war appear too serious.
It is demobilising language, that helps to occlude the reality of

war. Of course, Russia isn't the only country to use euphemistic language. The Troubles is a twee term for what was a civil war in a constituent nation of the UK.

As befits a country with a casual and arbitrary relationship with the law, it is still very common for Russians to use the word 'war' in the context of Ukraine. Fedor Lukyanov, editor of the influential *Russia in Global Affairs* and an analyst close to the Kremlin, often uses the term 'war' in his television appearances. In February, Mr Lukyanov wrote on his Telegram channel in support of respected journalist Elena Chernenko, who circulated and authored a letter condemning the invasion, although he himself has not made a direct public statement of opposition. All of my interviewees except for Dmitri Trenin called the conflict a war. Yet, there have been prosecutions for doing so, a result of the Kremlin's deliberate policy of devising crimes so widely and frequently committed that almost anyone could be found guilty. This reminds people that their freedom depends not on following the law but on currying favour and staying within certain boundaries.

These boundaries are anyway somewhat blurred by the sense in Russian coverage that there are two wars, or maybe a special military operation within a war, as is evident on Telegram. With social media bans on Facebook and Instagram, Telegram's Russian audience doubled following the invasion. By June 2022, the number of Russian users that opened Telegram at least once a day had reached 40 million.[1] In my analysis of almost 75,000 Telegram posts during the first three months of the war, the term 'operation' was used more than 'war' to describe what was happening in Ukraine, although there was considerable disparity between the channels. Military channels and television referred to it almost exclusively as an 'operation', whereas nationalist, opposition and less conventionally pro-Putin channels (e.g. Baza) called it a war. Pro-Kremlin propagandists also frequently referred to 'war' but they had in mind the Russia–US proxy war, or the war against fake news and disinformation. Most of the time, the context made it clear the real 'war' was with the West.

It is difficult to overestimate the starkness of the difference between the general Western view of the war and the general Russian view of the war. According to the television channels, the 'special military operation' was not an unprovoked war of aggression or conquest but the culmination of Western-backed Ukrainian Nazis slaughtering Russian-speakers in eastern Ukraine as part of a general anti-Russian project. For example, the state news Vesti used the word 'war' to frighten viewers, with claims that others might start either a 'third world war' or even 'nuclear war' in response to Russia's special operation, also referred to often as 'Russia's operation' to free Ukraine. The state news agency RIA Novosti referred to war almost exclusively in the sense of the West's 'information war' and 'economic war' on Russia, placing the West's actions above Russia's 'operation' in Ukraine in terms of scale, aggression and malice.

On Telegram, there was also plenty of indignation at the West. That said, my analysis of sixteen of the most popular Telegram channels showed that the most viewed content pertained either to Russia or to Ukraine. Sample popular narratives included the latter's supposedly cruel treatment of the Donbas and Russia's patient heroism in finally putting an end to the subjugation of ethnic Russians by Ukrainian Nazis. These narratives were compelling distractions from the reality that in the first three months of the war more civilians died than in the eight years prior – and that the vast majority of those killed hailed from the same Russian-speaking areas that Putin claimed to be defending.[2] State supportive media – online and offline – did not place the blame for these deaths on Russia, except in so far as it held back from its heroic mission for too long, although even that culpability is implied rather than articulated. The Kremlin and its supporters admitted very little responsibility for the war or for any of the conditions that led to the war. Despite almost no pro-Kremlin Russian policy analysts predicting the invasion, many of them became fluent (almost) overnight at explaining why NATO, the USA, UK, EU, Ukraine or Zelensky made this war inevitable.

Chaotic competition

Within pro-Kremlin media, there is a competition raging for audiences and state approval. The approach is one of neoliberal capitalism, where hosts and bloggers jostle for audience figures and advertising revenue so that they might catch the eye of the Kremlin or its associated editors and be rewarded with their own show. It is this competition between media actors that explains what can sometimes look like chaotic narratives: as they vie for influence and emotional impact, the television hosts try out different storylines to see what works: is it an overdue rescue mission to liberate Ukraine or punitive retribution for their refusal to be Russian? A technical and limited operation or an all-encompassing epic battle between civilisation states? A battle to rid Ukraine of its sovereignty or a crusade to reassert the right to sovereignty? An imperial war of anti-colonialism in which Russia is only defending Donbas? Or an imperial war of anti-colonialism in which Russia is only defending itself?[3] These claims are simultaneously specific and lofty; they are all things to all men, deliberately, dizzyingly, variegated. But, while the mishmash disorientates the audience, the core message, of a good Russia reasserting its moral right to great power domination of others, seeps in unimpeded.

The sheer range of narratives is suggestive of how most Russians articulate and understand the war in their own way, rather than just following a strict pre-written government line. That is where the Russian government excels in its storytelling: it provides the characters and plot lines but you can arrange them how you like, focus on one story over another, recasting characters. As such, while everyone has their own view of the war, some of them have aspects in common. There are core ideas and assumptions underpinning support for and understanding of the war and without which the Russian position makes very little sense. These assumptions include the following: the decaying West is hell-bent on destroying Russia; Russia is fighting nationalist Ukrainians to save Ukraine from *banderovtsy* and Western machinations; Russian moral rectitude will succeed against Western hypocrisy and degradation; Russia has undertaken a defensive, pre-emptive military operation; eastern and southern Ukraine are essentially Russia; the 'special military operation' is one step towards creating a fairer international order.

Threaded throughout all these stances is a sense of insecurity, a constant need to extrapolate the war out to a greater meaning, to justify it, often with reference to past suffering and a more expansive worldview. I discussed the comprehensive philosophical background to pro-war narratives with Natalia Sevagina, a curator from the Tretyakov Gallery, who speaks about Russian art with a sincere and impressive eye for beauty and detail and who is also a strong proponent of the war. In her view, the war 'is not political but about worldview, philosophy. Sooner or later any thinking person has to ask why do I live, what is my purpose on the Earth, what is the why of my life. *This* is the why. Russia doesn't wage wars of conquest or aggression. Just don't touch us, don't touch our church, our people. And if you do, then we will fight you.'[4] Such narratives, often intellectualisations of 'the West should just keep their nose out of this' are common refrains from media and cultural figures alike.

Many foreign-policy elites and government officials have chosen to rationalise Russia's invasion as a preventative strike against a Ukraine that was growing stronger militarily and politically thanks to systematic support from the West. There have been bold and unsubstantiated claims that Ukraine was going to invade Crimea or develop a nuclear bomb. Given the shock in Russia when Ukraine did strike the Kerch Bridge in October 2022, it doesn't seem likely that anyone seriously believed in those plans. Moreover, it painted a picture of Ukrainians that did not correlate to fact – a common theme in Russian depictions of Ukrainians. Bluntly, most diplomats and Ukrainian officials are not unduly bothered about Crimea. As Vadym Prystaiko, former Foreign Minister of Ukraine and now Ambassador to the UK expressed with some exasperation in his interview with me: 'Nobody needs Crimea, yes it's okay to have a couple of beaches but that's not Crimea, Crimean beaches aren't that good, there is only a bit that hasn't been bought up by oligarchs – the rest of it is nothing, there is nothing, no water, just steppe. And anyway we have the Black Sea.'[5]

While Ambassador Prystaiko was not voicing the official Ukrainian position or suggesting that the territory does not legally belong to Ukraine, his on-the-record statement echoes off-the-record conversations with numerous other Ukrainian officials, diplomats and advisers, all espousing a marked lack of interest in retaking Crimea beyond laughing at the Russians. Prior to the war, there was also some reluctance to reclaim the territory of the D/LPR occupied since May 2014, even if the symbolic importance of the claim remained very high. This is what made Russian accusations, in late 2021 and early 2022, that the Ukrainian armed forces were preparing to attack Crimea or Russia or Donbas so very absurd.

This absurdity did not prevent Russian officials, even anti-war ones, claiming that Ukrainians were bloodthirsty warmongers or that anti-Russian Ukrainian advisers had lured Zelensky away from peaceful dialogue. In an interview with me, one Russian MFA official claimed that 'direct dialogue with him [Zelensky] started in a promising way in 2019 but was blocked due to ultra-rightists and very anti-Russian elements'.[6] This same official pointed to Zelensky's 'loose remark at the Munich security conference about revising Ukraine's non-nuclear status', calling it 'the last straw' that broke the Kremlin's military restraint.[7] In these versions of events, the Ukrainian president is a mere puppet of nefarious, more powerful, forces: the Americans, the British, the Balts, the Poles, NATO, the EU, the OSCE, Germany, liberals, fascists, Soros, the LGBT community, or just whoever takes their fancy. So who is Russia fighting then? The West or Ukraine? Yes, them, both of them. And lots of other people besides: satanists; drug addicts; liberal fascist cancel culture; pagans; Russians' own unerring sense of nobility; LGBTQ+ parades; migratory birds carrying genetic bioweapons; NATO; militant Baltic gays. Such a variegated list of enemies has given rise to a similarly incoherent set of aims. Reading Russian media, you understand that the Russian Army will give Ukrainians life by killing them. It will decommunise Ukraine by rebuilding Lenin statues. It will free Ukraine from the Anglo-Saxon yoke and help Americans not to have to finance Ukraine. By unleashing so many confusing and confused narratives at once, you bamboozle people. The viewer feels overwhelmed and stops relying on facts for contours, reaching instead for familiar concepts, things they definitely know, like national identity, historical parallels, general emotions, their own memories, perceptions of which are often reinforced by popular culture and the media.

It is against these superficially confusing but profoundly resonant narratives that many Russians will make sense of the war and accept its depiction as a defensive response to shapeshifting threats. The 'special military operation's' two core objectives were originally demilitarisation and denazification. I have heard many interpretations, of which Modest Kolerov's (founding editor of the IA Regnum news agency) made the most sense in terms of its logic, although that doesn't mean it is the way it is perceived by the Kremlin (and nor did Dr Kolerov suggest that): 'Demilitarisation is the only way to end this. War is terrifying, awful, the purest evil. The idea of the special military operation is to stop the bombardment of

Donbas, to demilitarise Ukraine so that it stops being a threat to Russia.'[8] Asked if this necessitated neutrality, Dr Kolerov said yes, but also the total removal of Ukraine's army so it could never be a threat to Russia again.

Denazification of Ukraine is the most obscene objective and proof in itself that negotiated settlement with Putin is inconceivable: how can a democratic state with a Jewish president need denazifying? It reflects the bamboozling internal reality the Kremlin has constructed and tries to impose on others. In such instances, the constant political and media analogising with the Second World War adds a sense of gravitas to absurd demands. But the Second World War also casts its long shadow in other ways; in Fedor Lukyanov's view: '22 June syndrome[9] has left its mark on strategic thinking in Russia – this trying to never end up in the same position. We can't let it happen that they attack us, if war is inevitable then we have to attack first. Putin's worldview endowed the Ukrainian question with existential importance for him – it couldn't be left for later, for his heir. He saw it as his mission to solve it.'[10]

In hindsight, and several months into a war that was supposed to last three days, perhaps Putin and his supporters would have done better to reflect on the unprovoked war of aggression they launched on their neighbour before 22 June 1941, namely the 1939–1940 Winter War with Finland, in which the USSR struggled and lost many more lives than expected. As objectives, both demilitarisation and denazification are completely intangible and incomprehensible. This is why they both failed to resonate with audiences and were soon replaced with an ostensible existential battle for truth and justice and just a general feeling of what is right. These narratives built on years of casting Ukrainians as Nazis, Westerners as Russophobes, and Russia as under attack.

Laying the ground work

One of the first things Vladimir Putin blew up after invading Ukraine was the Kyiv TV tower. Metaphorically, the same was true at home: Putin's first moves on being elected president in 2000 were to shut down and take over independent television, banning political satire shows like *Kukly*[11] for depicting him as a mean dwarf.[12] In so doing, he assured that virtually all television stations and almost all major newspapers were owned by the state or government-friendly businessmen. Although he did not change the market basis in which the outlets functioned, and which had made media sources highly dependent on advertising, Putin and his governments did curtail media freedoms drastically compared with the relative (albeit oligarch-controlled) liberties of the 1990s.

Over the years, Putin tightened the screws more and more, aided and abetted by spin doctors, propagandists, editors, oligarchs and all the people who didn't speak up for independent media. Like many things in Russia before 24 February, much of the repression was superficially deniable, as with the case of the pressure applied to Russia's last remaining independent television channel TV Rain in 2014. After they hosted a debate on whether the Red Army should have surrendered Leningrad to save lives, touching a raw nerve of the Kremlin's WWII narrative, the government forced advertisers to abandon the channel, leaving it unviable except as a YouTube channel.

Much of the state-friendly media isn't owned directly by the government but by Kremlin-friendly oligarchs, who appoint Kremlin-friendly editors. Likewise, in popular culture the state controls content creation through intermediaries, normally through the use of so-called GONGOs, or government-organised NGOs, like the Russian Military Historical Society, which is responsible for releasing a spate of heavily mythologised and presentist WWII films. None of this is to say that the government has been nervous about openly intervening, as when the Kremlin demanded the sacking of Galina Timchenko, the main editor of the popular news portal, Lenta, alongside more than half her staff, for even-handed coverage of the 2013/14 EuroMaidan protests in Ukraine. Following this, the Kremlin installed a more pliable editor and the newspaper's coverage of events in Ukraine changed dramatically.

The creeping authoritarianism of Putin's third and fourth presidential terms must be placed in the context of the mass protests against electoral falsification in the 2011 and 2012 Duma and Presidential elections. After these, Vladimir Putin unleashed much tighter restrictions on protests and freedom of speech, including repressive blogging laws, restrictions on media ownership and legislation banning 'extremist' views. The Duma then used these, superficially reasonable-sounding laws, as Trojan Horses to introduce harsher measures against the media, creating and habitually expanding a list of 'foreign agents' – essentially anyone receiving money or support from abroad – and broadening the list of activities that should not be covered by media or journalists wishing to avoid such a designation.

Like Ernest Hemingway's description of bankruptcy, the Russian government descended into dictatorship gradually at first and then suddenly. On 5 March 2022, Putin introduced a new law with up to fifteen years in prison for people who distribute 'fake news' about the Russian military, including calling Russia's war on Ukraine a war. This meant that many journalists were forced to leave the country. The government justified such draconian measures with reference to the information war the West was ostensibly waging against Russia. The government blocked many outside media sources, leaving Russians unable to directly access the BBC, Radio Free Europe, Radio Liberty, and other US and European news sources. Facebook and Twitter were blocked and Meta was proscribed as an extremist organisation for refusing to take down Ukrainian messages that called for violent resistance to Russia's invasion. In 2014, when Russia first invaded Ukraine, the audience for sources like the BBC rose dramatically as people tried to work out what was happening. In 2022, people turned to Telegram. It is sometimes assumed that if people living under conditions of censorship go online, they will search out the truth, or different interpretations of the present at least. Yet, the most popular political and news channels on Telegram are pro-war and pro-Kremlin. This is reflective not of a blood-thirsty population so much as of the years of informational autocracy that preceded the 'sudden' moral bankruptcy of 2022. 'Informational autocracy' is a useful term for understanding the nature of the Russian regime until at least the pandemic if not 2022 and denotes the way in which those in power generally used their dominance over information channels to manipulate rather than coerce audiences.[13] During this time, Russian authorities curated a media environment that had a proven ability to devise persuasive and engaging content. So appealing were the emotive narratives on offer, that viewers were not forced to watch the propaganda, they chose to – and continue to choose to – even in the free space of the internet.

To lure viewers and subscribers, Russian media actors present lies in a way that feels emotionally right. It is an appealing lie, a lie that for whatever reason you want or are inclined to believe, or at least don't want to question, as it plays on painful memories or offers respite from them. Perhaps the most important manipulation concerns the roots of the fighting in Ukraine, summed up in the plaintive question: *Where have you been for the last eight years? (Gde zhe vy byli eti vosem' let?)* The inquisitor wants to know why their interlocutor cares that Russia is bombing Ukrainians but didn't care before when Ukrainians were bombing the Donbas. This is a useful way of deflecting the feelings of guilt or horror at the deaths caused by Russian bombs. Such rhetorical questions often contain a reference to the Alley of Angels, a Donetsk memorial to the children killed during the war in Donbas since 2014. These children are largely forgotten except when their deaths are thrown in people's faces as a propaganda argument. All sides should remember them for their innocence and what their lives could have been if Russia had not started a pointless bloody war. But that is not the Russia you find on Kremlin TV, instead there you find an absurdly patient Russia that is reclaiming lost territories from genocidal Ukrainians who view ethnic Russians through a Nazi lens of racial hierarchy.

Revolution or coup?

These Nazis, although figments of a feverish imagination, did not appear overnight. They have been crafted and developed as characters for eight years, if not longer, based on real people and exaggerated into something meaningful. In Russians' view, Nazis have been in power since 2014, the year when 2022 really began and when supposedly far-right radicals took power following the EuroMaidan protests across Ukraine.

The EuroMaidan protests (also known as the Revolution of Dignity) were sparked by then President Viktor Yanukovych's decision not to sign a trade association agreement with the EU. This decision followed an offer by Vladimir Putin of major discounts on energy prices and fifteen billion dollars in aid to Ukraine, with Yanukovych seemingly lured by these promises and frightened at the prospect of alienating Russia. Admittedly, the EU had been inflexible about accommodating Russia in the trade deal, even though it would clearly impact Ukraine's economic ties with Russia.

To many Ukrainians, tariffs were beside the point. Yanukovych's decision symbolised an unwelcome choice about Ukraine's future on a Russian, as opposed to Western, path. Amateurishly, Yanukovych rejected the deal at the very time of year when activists would gather on local squares, or Maidans, to remember the struggle of the 2004 Orange Revolution. As such, the type of people who were disgruntled already had plans to meet and gather, making it much easier to bring them and others to the streets, recreating the protests across the country. Hundreds of thousands joined in the EuroMaidan, protesting all over the country, from Chernivtsi to Donetsk.

Over the winter of 2013/2014, the protestors remained steadfast despite, or perhaps because of, the Ukrainian riot police's violent response. At least 130 people lost their lives during the Revolution of Dignity, most of them shot by interior ministry and special forces snipers in a series of events that quickly overtook the political manoeuvrings of those jostling for power. Eventually, just thirty-six hours after more than sixty protestors were shot on the Kyiv Maidan and twenty-four hours after an EU-brokered agreement for early elections, President Yanukovych realised he had lost the confidence of the police, much of his party, and his security services and decided to flee Kyiv for Rostov, Russia. In the chaotic power vacuum that followed, opposition parties represented at the Maidan and in the Rada formed an interim government. Russia protested the legitimacy of this action, characterising the demonstrators and the interim government as far-right extremists in the vein of the WWII Ukrainian nationalist leader, Stepan Bandera.[14]

Asserting the need to protect Russian speakers in Crimea from impending genocide by these *banderovtsy*, Russia carried out a swift and immaculately executed annexation of the peninsula, later 'legitimised' by an illegal referendum on 16 March 2014. The 'return' of Crimea was greeted with mass support at home and spontaneous parties took place in central Moscow. While everyone was still sobering up, Russia amassed troops on its border with Ukraine and sent both regular and irregular troops to encourage separatism and violence in east Ukraine. In Russian parlance this was dubbed 'the Russian Spring', but the uprising found less support than expected and faced a

Ukrainian army that was better prepared and ready to put up resistance. What began as skirmishes between loyalists and separatists had descended into armed conflict by April 2014. This war cost the lives of 14,000 people and evolved into the even more brutal 2022 war, which Russia launched against Ukraine ostensibly to defend the Donbas and denazify the rest of the country.

Russian commentators and politicians have often cited moments from 2014 to justify the 2022 invasion; for example, Putin frequently referred to the fire in Odesa's Trade Union building on 2 May 2014, when running battles between pro-Ukraine and pro-Russian Odessans spilled out into armed street fights, with the latter pushed back to a tent fort near the Trade Union building. With each side throwing Molotov cocktails, a fire broke out and tore through the building, killing 47 pro-Russian activists. Tatyana Gerasimova, head of the 2 May Group, an organisation of thirteen local experts investigating the tragedy on a voluntary basis, described it thus: 'There was a lot of heroism and cruelty on both sides.' This was Odessans against Odessans, an awkward factor for both sides and yet Russia has repainted it as a fascist effort to burn pro-Russians to death, just as *banderovtsy* set fire to villagers in Khatyn, Belarus in 1943. In his eve-of-war speech, Putin directly referenced the opportunity to bring those responsible for Odesa to justice.[15]

The polarisation surrounding 2014 makes the historical roots of the war particularly worth studying as one's interpretation of EuroMaidan will at the very least colour one's understanding of the root causes of Russia's full-scale invasion and the questions you pose about the contributing factors. Was EuroMaidan a Revolution of Dignity or a putsch by the mob? How central was the far right to the success of the protests? Was the ensuing war in the east purely a Russian concoction or a civil war? What were the Minsk agreements: vessels for Russian control of Ukraine or the only option for peace? Your answers to the above will often have considerable bearing on your position on today's war, or at least its causes and potential resolution.

The standard Russian answers to the questions above are starkly different from most Ukrainians' answers. For example, I discussed with Dmitri Trenin why so many Russians support the war. Dr Trenin saw this support as being shaped by three main factors:

1. The eight-year war in Donbass (2014–2022),[16] during which the Russian language regions of Donetsk and Lugansk Oblasts were constantly subjected to artillery strikes from Ukraine, and by the inability of Moscow to put an end to these strikes through diplomatic means (Minsk 2, the Normandy format, 'Putin's ultimatum' in December 2021);

2. A general refusal by the majority of the Russian population – excluding its relatively small liberal part – to accept the policies and practices of the Ukrainian government. The issue here is Kyiv's official adoption of Banderite (ultra-nationalist) ideology as the ideological foundation of the Ukrainian nation, attacks on Russian language (the cessation of higher education, and then schooling, in Russian, the removal of any official status from the Russian language, the downgrading of it to the position of a foreign and undesirable language), the open hostility towards all things Russian and towards Russia as a state and so on;[17]

3. The West's extremely severe blanket reaction to the Russian armed forces operation in the Ukraine heralded a shift from a hostile standoff between Russia and the West to active confrontation in the form of an unlimited hybrid war. The West has been actively and effectively interfering in the internal politics of Ukraine since 1991, but since 2004 (the Orange Revolution), this interference has become large-scale. The 'Revolution of Dignity' in 2014 was seen by many in Russia as a state coup organised by the USA with the aim

of finally cutting Ukraine off from Russia. Since February 2022, the USA and Western countries' involvement in the Ukrainian situation has reached the level of proxy war between a united West and Russia. In such conditions, the larger part of Russian society has united around its leaders and its army, while a smaller part was required to shift from being in opposition to the Russian political regime to being in opposition to the state, basically to their own country. In conditions of war many oppositionists preferred to go abroad; some came out on the side of Ukraine and the West. And so the war in the Ukraine is seen by many in Russia as a war with the West, which has flagrantly interfered in its own interests in a domestic row between Russia and Ukraine and those parts of the historical Russian state that are still in play.[18]

Dmitri Trenin's reference to a 'domestic row' and his final three words – 'still in play' – emphasise that ultimately these debates are not just about history but also about duelling questions of legitimacy. On the one hand, there is a conspiratorial and brutal realism, in which smaller countries are but pawns of major powers, devoid of agency except to choose between puppet-masters. On the other hand, an idealistic but highly selectively applied notion that Ukraine is a test case for the principle that every nation can decide its own fate and seek security and economic guarantors. Different interpretations of EuroMaidan are central to the Russian explanation of the road leading to war but also central to why it is so very hard to find a compromise or peaceful resolution: underpinning the war is a complex, unbreakable and mutually exclusive set of histories and values that have populated increasingly different realities and identities for over eight years.

Media depictions of the 'special military operation'

Russian state media describe the war in Ukraine using very similar terms and parameters to those employed by Western media. There are the same narratives about the war in Ukraine, the same claims of genocide and war crimes, the same images of dead civilians. They even use the same tropes – that of a president in a bunker, the enemy's unspeakably high losses, Mariupol as Stalingrad.[19] But, in the Russian version, they are the heroes and Ukrainians are the perpetrators.[20] Russian television paints its air forces' horrific assault on Ukrainian towns, cities and people as a clinical operation to target villains and save civilians. They punctuate this agitprop with clips of Russian soldiers celebrating the successes of a pre-emptive mission to free Donbas from genocidal Ukrainian butchers. Clips and quotations from Putin's interviews are repeated across Russian media for days on end. Vesti nedeli, a flagship weekly news roundup show, fronted by Dmitrii Kiselev, is no exception. It intersperses Putin's wild accusations with seemingly inchoate stories about Pentagon bioweapon networks in Ukraine, Nazis torturing children, economic collapse in the West, efforts to cancel Russia, and transgenderism.

To complement my own research into this topic, I spoke to Paul Goode, Chair of Russian Studies at Carleton University, where he has been researching Russian television coverage of the war. Professor Goode's findings reveal how the television has painted Russia as engaged in an existential struggle in which it fights for justice ahead of any rational motivations and faces sanctions as a result of its commitment to what is right.[21] For the first month of the war, television settled into this cadence of existential enemies, sanctions and liberation. The enemies were largely Ukrainians and Ukrainian nationalists, with much less focus on the USA, despite initial shock at sanctions.

There was some divide between regional and federal television; on the former, the 'sanctions talk' declined steadily from mid-March and became background noise by early April. So too did the 'war talk' become background noise for most regional Russian media by April, as audiences begin to switch off from the relentless horror. There were substantially fewer mentions of the 'special operation', refugees, liberation, and D/LPR on regional media, as opposed to federal channels,[22] and mentions of Donbas were dramatically reduced. This will not necessarily surprise those in Donbas, as one contact from the DPR replied: 'We hate them [the Russians] as much as we hate the dill-eaters', using an offensive term for Ukrainians.[23] By contrast, federal television still spends considerable time focused on enemies and the legitimacy of the war, telling Russians who they are fighting and that their 'not-war' is a just war, a liberation not only of Donbas, or even Ukraine, but of the entire world. With the exception of sanctions, the topics that dominated at the start of the war, especially Donbas, bio-labs and refugees, quickly faded out of view.

Superficially, Russian media coverage can seem choppy or eclectic but this is a flawed understanding. The changing narrative themes are better understood as the toppings on a never-changing pizza base. Over the last eight years, sometimes the media has offered a larger pizza, or smaller pizza, pizza with pepperoni or with mushrooms but always, the base has remained the same, comprised of core ingredients from which Russian media, and audiences, make sense of the war. So, while the uninitiated may find the Kremlin's falsehoods completely farcical, they are less so when seen as embedded within longstanding media framings of the war, which developed out of 2014 and are broadly as follows:

The Little Patriotic War[24]

In this propaganda world, Nazis have ruled Ukraine for years, crucifying Russian children, burning people alive, and pursuing a genocide in Donbas. Social media data provided by

Zignal Labs showed a sharp increase in references to Nazism in Russian language tweets that matched a spike in references from Russian news media. 'You see it on Russian chat groups and in comments Russians are making in newspaper articles', said the lead researcher. 'I think many Russians actually believe this is a war against Nazism.'[25] According to their data, Russian state media and tweet references alike peaked on 24 February 2022 and before that in March 2014, something that is corroborated by my own research into Russian WWII analogies.[26] Mentions of Nazis aren't nearly as prominent on Russian television (as opposed to online) but then the term 'Nazi' has never been at the core of the argument that Ukraine is a fascist state. Instead, the comparisons have often been far more detailed, making them difficult to recognise using traditional quantitative search functions. In 2014, for example, the term 'Nazi' was several times less common than references to Stepan Bandera or to events during WWII, which would evade detection by any computer-led model.[27]

The notion of Ukrainians as Nazis is really a support act to a description of the war in Ukraine as a Little Patriotic War, or rerun of the Great Patriotic War (Soviet war against Nazi Germany 1941–1945). I have been tracking the comparison of the conflict in Ukraine to the Second World War since 2014 and wrote a 40,000-word research thesis from 2015 to 2017 that was dedicated to this topic. It was also a central part of my PhD thesis. Looking at my data, the intensity of this analogy has waxed and waned since 2014, with a relatively flat use of the narrative between late 2015 and 2018, and a marked lull from 2019 to early 2021. However, there was a sharp increase around February 2021 and into April 2021 when Russia began massing troops on the border with Ukraine before returning most of them to base. As discussed, references to Nazis, *banderovtsy* and the Great Patriotic War again increased with Russia's February 2022 invasion.

The Little Patriotic War analogy created the context through which many Russians understand events today. In this warped version of reality, Russia's 'denazification' campaign is about restoring Russian historical mores and battling Nazis and *banderovtsy*. Russian state media paint anyone who advocates a sovereign Ukraine as an unrepentant admirer of the Ukrainian nationalist leader, Stepan Bandera. Efforts to undermine Ukrainian identity by painting it as besmirched by a peculiarly ethnic – even fascist – bent have been used since Ukraine first voted for independence in 1991, as well as during the Orange Revolution of 2004. The Kremlin only intensified its accusations following the Revolution of Dignity and annexation of Crimea, which Putin justified by claiming that Ukrainians intended to ethnically cleanse the peninsula and country of all Russians: 'Everyone can already tell exactly what they will do next, these Ukrainian heirs to the Bandera ideology, to a man who collaborated with Hitler during WWII [. . .] they will try to create an ethnically pure Ukrainian state.'[28]

This narrative is not just about discrediting Ukrainians but also about reinforcing an image of Russians as kind-hearted liberators from tyranny. In support of this, 2022 Russian televisual coverage of the war has been saturated with unconvincing footage of impoverished villagers welcoming considerate soldiers bedecked in St George's Ribbons (a symbol of the Second World War). In one example, coming under fire just as the cameras happen to turn on, Russian soldiers decamp to a nearby field before retaliating, ostensibly so as not to give the Ukrainian army an excuse to shell populated areas. The viewer learns that this same field was the site of major battles between the Wehrmacht and Red Army in the Second World War and hears how now, Russian soldiers, descendants of the heroes of that war, are back to liberate Kyiv from Nazis once again.

These Second World War analogies are a constant among a vast range of claims about what is really going on in Ukraine. For every biolab accusation, there are comparisons between modern Russophobia and Nazi antisemitism, for every allegation of Western-sponsored terrorism in Crimea, there are articles on Ukrainian shrines to Adolf Hitler. Such seemingly incoherent narratives are better understood as paving slabs on well-trodden narrative paths that are rendered even more familiar by the invocation of popular historical myth. In this alternate reality, Russia is under attack from the West, as so often in its history, and must either fight back, like in the Second World War, or be destroyed like the USSR.

Paradoxically, as well as raising the stakes, the use of historical analogies simultaneously adds a sense of predictability, covers up logical inconsistencies (by providing a temporal consistency) and reinforces the hero/victim dynamic. Russian audiences are led to believe that history will repeat itself, either as triumph or as tragedy. For example, before the 2022 summer, United Russia MPs received instructions from the party leadership to stress the following analogies: Stalingrad and Poltava, basically symbols or bywords for existential and bloody conflict fought against the West.[29] For many watching, such analogies will frighten them into defensive loyalty, while for others the knowledge that Russia won then, so it will win now, calms them into ritual support.

Russia as 'misunderstood angels'

The Little Patriotic War myth intersects with, and feeds, the notion that Russians are the good guys. One of the difficulties when discussing the war with Russians is a frequently encountered belief that 'Russians are by nature good.' Or, as another put it: 'I know our boys, I know they wouldn't do what your [Western] politicians accuse them of. So why would I believe anything else they say?'[30] This must be incredibly rage-inducing for Ukrainians; as if it wasn't enough that the Russians are bombing your homes, they also insist on being ever so smug about how considerately they are ravaging your lands. Given Russia's (often fair) criticism of the West's military interventions in the Middle East, it is ironic it is mimicking its self-satisfied claims of bringing people freedom and rights by bombing them.

In my interviews, even among many of those who elsewhere tried to present themselves as dispassionate observers, there was often a strong reaction to any questions pertaining to the unmet expectation that Ukrainians would greet Russian soldiers as liberators, with bread and salt. Rather than accept that Russians might, in fact, be occupiers, speakers said that 'they misjudged how much Ukrainians had been infected with Banderite ideology', or that 'the pro-Russian part had just always been less passionate but Ukrainians [in occupied territories] weren't resisting now'. In his response, Modest Kolerov combined both of these answers and cited the Russian occupation of Kherson as an example of how kind Russians were, saying that they allowed opposition and 'they let people wear Ukraine ribbons in Kherson and say things about the authorities because they have that confidence, they know they are in the right. Even in wartime, can you imagine that? That is because Russians really are bringing freedom to Little Russia.'[31] It is worth noting that Dr Kolerov's son had previously volunteered with the occupying authorities in Kherson.

Sources close to the Ukrainian intelligence agencies admit they were initially disappointed in the low level of armed resistance in Kherson and in the surrender of the city to the Russians, although by summer 2022 they felt the tide was beginning to turn. In November, with the Russian Army's retreat, the Ukrainian Armed Forces liberated the city. In the aftermath, both Russia's crimes and the importance of Ukrainian resistance in the region became much clearer. Even before this, it was obvious that resistance had been far more impressive than wearing a few ribbons (although some residents were tortured even for that small act). There was a suspiciously large number of Russian collaborators' cars blown up in Kherson, including – fatally – that of Oleksiy Kovalyov, an MP from Zelensky's party, Sluha narodu.[32] Just as with missile strikes on Belgorod or Crimea, Russian sources are very tight-lipped about such attacks, not wishing to show domestic audiences that the war is coming home. That does not mean the ghastliness of war is hidden; for example, typical television battlefield coverage will see the camera zoom in on the corpse of a young Ukrainian soldier. This brutalising image will then be followed by efforts to humanise the Russian occupiers, who will use the cameras to tell their wives that they love them or tell their mums not to worry.

Russian soldiers stroking kittens, pining for lovely wives, and helping little blonde children. These images are not just what Russians want to see, they are also the ostensible answer to why the special military operation is taking so long: Russians are just too kind, they don't bomb civilians, if they did, it would be quicker. Of course, if Russia isn't bombing civilians it rather begs the question as to who is bombing them? The Ukrainians themselves, comes the reply. 'Ukrainian soldiers have orders to shoot innocent civilians' is a claim made frequently by politicians and officials.[33] Another variation on this is the idea that Ukraine uses civilians as human shields. In support of such claims, Russian media has cited extensively if selectively from a controversial Amnesty press release available on the NGO's website, which is blocked in Russia. From speaking with my own contacts in Kharkiv and Chernihiv, they had some complaints about the Ukrainian army's lack of care around residential areas but they did not ultimately hold them responsible. They understood that any carelessness was not deliberate and that it was not the soldiers' fault they had to fight in populated urban areas or to fight at all. Unfortunately, and unintentionally, the Amnesty report has reinforced pro-war Russians' 'misunderstood angel' complex, which they have used to distract from their disastrous and cruel military performance.

David versus Goliath

Who killed Darya Dugina? The daughter of the Eurasianist ideologue Aleksandr Dugin, pro-war television commentator Darya Dugina died in an explosion as she drove home late one evening in August 2022. There are many competing theories about her death. Did the Ukrainians plant the explosives for her father? Was it the Russian Republican Army, as claimed? Was it the FSB – as a message to the nationalist wing to tone down their criticism? We don't know, but the conspiratorial nature of some of these suggestions is in itself telling, as is the popularity of the notion the FSB lashed out.

Following Ukraine's successful autumn counter-offensives in Kharkiv and Kherson regions, nationalists became more open in their criticism of how the war was being fought. Nationalists are the group that could cause the most hassle to Putin and his coterie as they are an active pro-war minority, who draw their legitimacy and support through the unwieldy power of ethno-nationalism. This party of war – sometimes called the party of war correspondents, given the prominence of the latter among them – wanted full (as opposed to partial) mobilisation, believing that everyone feels as intensely as they do about national rebirth or Eurasian landmasses as opposed to lack of rubbish collection in the local vicinity. Figures such as Igor Strelkov, aka Girkin, a key military commander in Donbas, who bears the most personal responsibility for starting the 2014 war in Ukraine's east, have been especially generous with their criticism. They appeared to overstep the mark in October 2022, when the authorities began to clamp down on their more vocal criticisms following a string of military defeats, Ukrainian advances, and the chaotic queues of young men fleeing mobilisation. However, even these criticisms take place within the status quo rather than against it: Yevgeny Prigozhin and Ramzan Kadyrov were not criticising the war when they insulted the army or generals, they were criticising the lack of war success.

On television, the notion that the war may not be going to plan was largely ignored until September 2022, despite the glaring obviousness that everyone overestimated Russia's military prowess. Especially Russia. After the Russian military's success in Crimea and performance in Syria, accompanied by glitzy propaganda videos, its reputation was at an all-time high and they appeared to believe their own hype. For example, in early March, TV host Vladimir Solovev and guest Yakov Kedmi claimed the army would just need a few paratroopers to take Odesa and it would fall in 72 hours, maximum. So confident were the Russians that the Ukrainian leadership would surrender and flee, that publications had pre-prepared content, as with the RIA Novosti op-ed published by accident on 26 February. The article celebrated Russian victory in an 'operation that is a defeat for the West's anti-Russia project'. It also lauded the way that Putin had acted to save Ukraine and, with it, Russia, ushering in a new era by 'restoring [Russia's] historic unity: the tragedy of 1991, that terrible catastrophe of our history, that unnatural aberration, has been overcome'.[34]

The appearance and swift removal of the article was a brief glimpse of reality penetrating Russia's information vortex. Stepping through this looking glass, the viewer enters a world of Russian invincibility, where all evidence to the contrary is ignored or rationalised, with embarrassingly unconvincing justifications, including the notion that Russian forced retreats are simply 'goodwill gestures'.[35] Crippled by contact with reality, the Russian media's reaction to Ukrainian victories is simply to lie harder or to blame the West – in their view a much more dignified enemy.

The influx of Western weapons is a common theme on the evening news and social media channels alike, as with this colourful analysis: 'And so the Yankies have decided to deliver powerful weapons to the Ukraine. And? And this is fcuked. We aren't the ones raising the stakes but we have to react. Ukraine won't win. Not in any sense. Not today's anti-Russian Ukraine.

The question is only how much Ukrainian blood will be spilt on the road to defeat.'[36] The refusal even to countenance defeat, combined with the claim that the West is willing to fight until the last Ukrainian, reinforces the idea that really the Russians are the good guys, while also feeding an increasing tendency to depict, somehow, Russia as the little guy, the David versus the Western-backed Goliath, in an almost mind-altering twisting of reality. One such example is the myth that 200 Russians defeated ten times as many Azovstal fighters in Mariupol, a claim that spread like wildfire across Telegram.

To back up this highly spurious framing of poor little Russia fighting wildly against the odds, Russian media make many references to foreign mercenaries, who you would think had flooded Ukraine in their millions, not their hundreds. Every foreign fighter is depicted as a wild soldier of fortune, even those who are simply foreign-born members of the Ukrainian armed forces with Ukrainian citizenship and families. It almost goes without saying that the actual wild mercenaries, from the Nazis of the Rusich battalion to the freshly released murderers and rapists stuffing the ranks of Wagner, are depicted as gentlemanly officers – because they fight on the Russian side.

In the early days of the war, when the Russian army made advances, Russian war correspondents would constantly find 'evidence' of Nazi paraphernalia and English or foreign things in abandoned Ukrainian bases. Perhaps my favourite such story saw First Channel correspondents entering a war bunker recently abandoned by foreign mercenaries. What should the hapless presenters find but a copy of Shakespeare's collected works. If your credulity is strained by the idea that a sanguinary English mercenary was lugging around a full volume of Shakespeare, then you will be even less impressed to learn that this copy was a Russian-language edition.

It seems incredible that people believe such nonsense and I am inclined to argue that they don't believe it literally, especially since Soviet propaganda created rather more sophisticated consumers and parsers of news than one might find in the USA, for example. But even without believing the literal event, you can still buy the vision of reality it represents, one in which Russia is fighting a larger, more bloodthirsty and extreme enemy.

Fake news

On 1 July, Colonel-General Mikhail Mizintsev, known as the 'Butcher of Mariupol', delivered a statement about recent attacks on apartment blocks in Odesa. In a familiar tone of Soviet bureaucratese, he read aloud: 'To implement the provocation across 26–28 June, twenty foreign mass-media representatives, as well as employees of the international organisation UNICEF, were brought to Odessa [to watch] a mock attack, planned by the military administration of the Odessa region, on a social facility where a crowd of up to 30 anti-Russian activists had been prepared in advance to act as victims and casualties. Each participant in the staged scenes was paid $100 in advance and they also received a cash reward of $500 after the videos were filmed.'[37] This is just one small example. It did not make headlines in Western media and it certainly is not the most bizarre or exciting claim of false flags but these everyday types of distortion set a scene where every-thing is a bit mad, so you stop noticing the general insanity all around you.

Russian political discourse is obsessed with fake news, or *feiki*, a term they use to denote any news that doesn't corre-spond to the official ministries' versions. Pro-Kremlin Russian think tanks, such as the unevocatively titled Social Research Expert Institute, release reports like 'How They're Killing the Free Press: Fact Checkers as an Instrument of Western Counter-Propaganda & Censorship', to undermine Western efforts to pierce Russians' information bubble.[38] The television programme *Anti-feik* is a treasure trove of accusations and revelations about Western fake news, plots, conspiracies and 'Buchas'. To Ukrainians, the word Bucha will bring to mind Russian soldiers' occupation and massacre of civilians in a small town of that name to the north of Kyiv. In Russian, the word Bucha is a neologism and it means a staged atrocity. From my interviews and Telegram analysis, it is clear that this term is a popular, if colloquial, shorthand for fake news. For example, Vladimir Orlov, head of the pro-Kremlin PIR Center think tank, used it in the following context: 'foreigners shouldn't get involved with the pains and history of Slavic peoples. The French will not play or will play their own game, not intervening, but the Brits will be playing the game of causing more trouble, making more Buchas, creating more fakes. And I am sorry to say that, having many British friends [. . .] It is a new Great Game, we have to play and Russia will win. That's it.'[39] His accusation was not that Britain was responsible for the crime scene at Bucha but that Britain was responsible for staging a fake crime scene at Bucha.

Given its entry into the Russian lexicon, it is important to revisit the coverage of Bucha, which is illustrative of the way in which Russia discredits evidence of its crimes in the audience's mind before then folding its version of events back into one of the broader and more consistent master narratives it uses to explain Ukraine, the conflict and Russia's role in the world. As soon as – but not before, even though they must have known it was coming – images of civilian corpses from Bucha began to spread on social media in the West, the Russian state and social media launched an intense campaign of deceit to sow confusion around what really happened. While journalists, intelligence specialists, and disinformation experts confirmed that the victims were killed by the Russian forces that had occupied the town for a month before being driven out by the Ukrainian army, Russia had its own version, in which the whole thing was, predictably, a conspiracy against Moscow.

Russian media largely ignore stories of crimes against their own people, or people who can't fight back, but spin any revelations of Russian crimes that make headlines in the West into outrageous stories. Bucha was no exception to this rule. At first, Russian TV stayed silent, waiting to see how much attention the story caught at home and abroad. By the morning of 3 April – two days after the news broke – it was clear that the massacres had outraged the world and unsettled even supporters of the Kremlin. More firestarters than firefighters, Russian media and propagandists launched an information offensive; Russian state TV personality Vladimir Solovev, for example, posted about it 39 times in 24 hours on his popular Telegram account.[40]

News agencies, newspapers, and other media channels barraged their audiences with spiralling and ever more dissembling stories to discredit the Ukrainian version of events. There were claims that a small group of Ukrainian forces had killed the civilians as punishment for helping the Russians, or that the civilians had been killed accidentally by Ukrainian shelling, or that the bodies had only appeared two days after Russia left, or that the whole affair had been staged, just like the ostensibly faked chemical gas attacks in Syria. This dizzying range of narratives all appeared within twelve hours of each other on one Telegram channel, like a microcosm of mendacity.

Over the next day or so, the narrative began to stabilise around two axes: the Bucha affair was a staged massacre to cause the breakdown of peace talks and the dead civilians were the result of Ukrainian armed forces killing the local residents who had naturally supported the kind and helpful Russian troops, who were emphatically not the same Russian troops seen on camera shooting them at random, locking them in basements, and looting all their food. These two versions allowed the narrative to circle back towards the phantom spectre of Ukrainian fascism and a Western conspiracy to use Ukraine to destroy Russia.

The initial contradictions were not the result of panic, however, but deliberate moves in a time-worn ritual whereby Russian media and politicians slowly dismantle the truth and then replace it with a forgery. The process starts with the idea of 'wanting to ask questions' about the event being discussed (recalling RT's tagline: 'Question More?'), sowing doubt before offering alternative explanations expressed as mere suggestions or hypotheses, since the truth is ostensibly unknowable. One of the most egregious examples of this approach occurred when Russian and Russian-backed fighters in east Ukraine shot down passenger jet MH17, killing 298 passengers. The media's immediate response was to interrogate random slivers of the actual story and slash away at them. To do so, they introduced fake characters such as 'Carlos', an imaginary Spanish Air Traffic Controller working in Kyiv, who could 'prove' Ukraine had downed the plane. This fabulism lay nestled between preposterous theories that the plane had been pre-loaded with corpses or that the Ukrainians shot it down in an attempt to assassinate Putin. Over time, a more stable Russian narrative – the Ukrainians did it and the West used it as a chance to malign Russia – emerged, fuelling the argument that historical and external forces are always aligned against an innocent Russia, which is forced to pick through fragments of reality in order to discover the 'truth' of the 'provocations' committed against it. Those provocations in turn justify whatever action Russia takes and reinforces the broader mindset used to explain and excuse Russia's aggression around the world.

The consequences of normalising such a distorted view of events are devastating. They are designed to, and can only give rise to, further hysteria among the Russian elites and public. Russia uses its own crimes as further evidence that it is the victim and as a justification for committing ever more atrocities. This cycle, and its two stages of dispersing truth and reaffirming core narratives, is central to the Kremlin's spectrum of allies approach. While some doubt may linger, preventing full, and undesired mobilisation of support, many Russian viewers will be convinced of the injustice of the West pinning others' crimes on their country, leading them to become ritual, if not especially enthusiastic, supporters, or at least loyal neutrals. The less credulous will at least feel unable to discern the truth and sink into apathy. This is an essential feature of Kremlin propaganda and population management: it uses techniques that simultaneously demobilise active opposition among those who are overwhelmed by trying to argue back against different interpretations and solidifies ritual support and loyalty among those who believe that Russia is the victim of external attacks, especially since the confusion is eventually deftly folded back into a more coherent alternative worldview. This is what gives the impression that Russians live in an alternate reality and explains the connection between the idea that nobody and nothing can be believed and the firm foundations of a broader Putinist worldview.

4

Washing brains

The Kremlin's control over the airwaves permeated every aspect of Russian federal television schedules for months after the invasion. There were no longer soaps or series during waking hours, just relentless propaganda. The popular and execrable 'news' discussion show '60 Minutes' lasted two to three hours. It was as if you replaced Eastenders and Coronation Street with 200 minutes of hate. According to calculations by journalist Arina Borodina, the pro-Kremlin firebrand Vladimir Solovev appeared on air for nearly 218 hours in the three months following the invasion. On both 27 February and 13 March – respectively, the dates when Russia's initial invasion and efforts to take Mariupol were clearly failing – Solovev was on screen for over five hours.[1] Out of the ninety days from 24 February to 24 May, his trademark show 'Evening with Vladimir Solovev' was on air for seventy-two days. This man may be one of the few Kremlin-linked elites to have actually earned his garish villa in Italy through hard work.

So successful and persuasive is Mr Solovev that Russia's main television channel gave prime-time slots to his shows, scrapping the soaps they normally showed on Mondays to Thursdays. On Mondays, from 21 March though to 23 May,

Solovev appeared twice every evening, on average for two-and-a-half hours each time with a break in the middle for the viewer to relax by watching Besogon TV, a stridently nationalist programme hosted by Nikita Mikhalkov, Russia's only Oscar-winning director and close friend of Vladimir Putin.[2] The consistent flow of television propaganda ensures that audiences are kept in a state of high emotional engagement as opposed to intellectual or critical engagement.

Zombification

The intensity and frequency of Russian state propaganda, especially to the uninitiated Westerner, makes it easy to blame the television for Russians' detachment from, and derision of, facts: people have simply been brainwashed. After all, whether or not someone takes their information from state media sources is one of the key determinants of support for the war.[3] Certainly, understanding support for the war is not possible without understanding how the media works on audiences, as this chapter will set out. Pro-Kremlin media tries to persuade audiences of a certain viewpoint with the aim of furthering an agenda. It seeks to create an emotional state in people that diminishes their critical thinking, and to develop cognitive filters and heuristics that reject any alternative version of reality – like implants that construct an internal reality. 'News' shows follow the rules of drama and aim to create an addictive effect within their audience.[4]

Propaganda is more effective on low-knowledge issues, such as foreign policy and events abroad, which partly explains why Russian state media focus the vast majority of their content on foreign affairs. This is a feature that preceded the full-scale invasion but that has only become more prominent during the turbo-regime of propaganda unleashed since 24 February. The opposition journalist, Ilya Shepelin, counted no fewer than ten hours of war propaganda every day. The Kremlin media deploy repetition well, constantly referring people back to earlier theories (unless and until they are no longer convenient) to suggest there is a body of evidence for anyone who wants to see. It works according to Goebbels' principle that a lie said 100 times becomes the truth; for example, on 17 May, Russia's First Channel showed the swastika twenty times, coinciding with whenever they were talking about taking the Mariupol defenders prisoner.[5] Russian media's use of *kompilirovanie* is a popular tactic that fuses images and clips into a montage that has nothing to do with the voiceover but reinforces associations in the viewer's mind.

Despite the intense nature of the subject matters under discussion, these propaganda shows are packaged in a glitzy format and comprise a form of 'infotainment', also called 'agitainment', in a reference to its entertaining format and propagandistic content.[6] The discursive and multimedia format makes the content feel less dictatorial, more exploratory, and distracts from the uniformity of the narratives. As one interviewee explained: 'I like Solovev, his programmes are interesting because they have lots of different people on there: Kurginyan, Kedmi, Shakhnazarov, Satanovskii, a kaleidoscope of opinions', referring to all the (pro-war) guests.[7] The main purpose of such a pronounced use of guests is to provide a diversity of voices to camouflage the lack of a diversity of views. Instead of providing both a *for* and *against*, there is a wide range of different voices presenting the same position but using different arguments, creating an illusion of the polyphony of democratic discussion, without the disagreement.[8] This would appear to be a deliberate tactic given the producers' deceptive use of language around guests, who are said to be offering alternative views to the media source, even when this is clearly inaccurate. For example, the title sequence of Vladimir Solovev's Sunday night show describes itself as offering 'ferocious debates' even though everyone almost always agrees with one other.

These tactics can take their toll. Over the last eight years of watching Russian state media, there have been moments where I have paused to ask myself, what if they are right? The West does have its flaws, just think of the Iraq War, of the 2008 crash – what if Russia is right in saying that we (the West, NATO) are helping the Islamic State or have staged an attack? I have thought these thoughts in the comfort of Oxfordshire and in spite of the fact that I have access to all the sources and the education and freedom of movement to check the reality. Now, imagine someone without that access, who is not critically engaged with the media, but simply watches the news for information and has no reason to doubt it. In those cases, Russian propaganda could be very effective, latching onto your naivety and warping the world. This is why I wasn't surprised when Hennadiy Maksak, head of the Ministry of Foreign Affairs-linked Prisma think tank in Kyiv told me the story of his schoolfriend.

Like many Ukrainians before the Revolution of Dignity, Hennadiy's friend, let's call him Anton, was working in Moscow illegally, primarily on building sites. He had been there around six months when the Maidan protests began in November 2013. Anton watched the news in horror, as far-right activists attacked the Berkut riot police and he heard how innocent civilians were at the mercy of wild-eyed Nazis marauding around Kyiv, attacking anyone and everyone. Anton 'darted off to Ukraine, to Kyiv, with a firm mind to liberate Ukraine from Nazis. He, a Ukrainian brought up in the USSR, arrived, was there for two days, and realised that what he heard had no connection with reality. He had to adapt, all his friends were confused, asking "Nazis? What Nazis are you talking about?" And in the end he realised and he joined the Maidan. But think about it, six months, that is all it took. So this is how you end up with daughters calling their mums in Russia and saying "You Russians are bombing us" and the mum answers "My darling, don't tell tales, our guys don't bomb civilians."[9] That is one way you end up there, it's certainly part of the story, but to my mind it isn't the whole story, it isn't enough.'

Listening to parents believe the state over their children's terrified cries is a terrible and complicated thing. Far too complicated to be blamed on propaganda or 'brainwashing', a term that implies you are washing people's brains with things they wouldn't otherwise believe. By contrast, Kremlin propaganda is washing people's brains with things they do want to believe, helping them to stay within certain comfortable cognitive frameworks where they are the good guys and they've always been the good guys. I discussed this issue, one of resonance and the all-too-human need to tell certain stories about ourselves and the groups we belong to, with Hennadiy. He viewed Russians' reactions to the war as reaching back much further than the media coverage, describing the propaganda as a way of reactivating a dormant infection:

> it already largely existed in Russian minds, but has been reactivated. Perhaps it could have never been reactivated, it could have just laid there. But it was and all that rhetoric about murder, war crimes, aggressions against a peaceful state, they all just accept this as what needs to be done. All of them, the soldiers, their mums, and their wives who say 'suffocate them [Ukrainians], beat them up, kill their children', all these awful things we have heard on the intercepts of wives and mothers supporting their sons at war. They see it as normal. So all these implants within the brain, they are difficult to overcome.[10]

The zombification narrative is an alternative form of propaganda, one that refuses to acknowledge there could be any basis on which people could come to an opposing narrative. This interpretation dismisses alternative views as brainwashed rather than engage with the complexity of how people, like us, come to support or acquiesce to terrible crimes against innocent people. Instead, we want a nice culprit, an algorithm or

maybe a face, like that of Vladislav Surkov, the former adviser
known as Putin's Grey Cardinal. Of course, there are Russian
organisations that work on influencing popular opinion, from
the FSB's second service to the E Centre of the Ministry of
Internal Affairs, both of which study and apply the political
science of consolidating society and interpreting what is happening, inculcating values and, in theory, creating an image of
the future. But, again, they are providing content that certain
people want, or at least view as credible: academic studies show
that people who like Putin are more likely to trust Russian state
media, be open to its messaging, and vice versa.[11] This is not
the same as tricking people into believing whatever they want
overnight, that is a misunderstanding of how information and
human beings work. Much easier, and more effective, is to
isolate events, stories, motifs that resonate organically with
people and deploy them in such a way as to steer people in a
certain direction.

   One of the Kremlin's preferred directions is political apathy,
an important part of the effect of propaganda and especially
in modern warfare, which is 'hypermediated, hyperreal, with
most people seeing what they want to see, refracted through the
crooked prism of social media and the online more generally'.[12]
People living in an autocracy tend to be politically disengaged.
The lack of transparency in government and governance leads
them to question their ability to understand politics, meaning they easily adopt the frameworks of interpretation of the
conflict provided by the state media. In turn, regime narratives
reinforce pre-existing apathy by performatively demonstrating the manipulative nature of politics abroad and, for more
sophisticated viewers, by performatively demonstrating the
manipulative nature of politics at home as well. It makes no
sense to protest if you think that any politics is just a form
of cheating and so, capitalising on distrust, the Kremlin and
its media assistants can shunt those actively opposed to the
Kremlin's agenda into the apathetic grouping, not encouraging

them to believe in the Kremlin view so much as to question the idea of objective reporting in general and especially in the West.

However, when people believe nothing can be trusted, they will still look for, and need, some support and criteria through which they can understand the world and evaluate events. Often they will turn to something they feel they instinctually understand, such as national identity, or a self-inscribed narrative of their own life as better or worse after X event. They might feel such knowledge is beyond the reach of propaganda but that would be a mistake. Rather, this is where the Kremlin's propaganda excels itself, on this hidden level, since so much of it concerns identity, history, and that pivotal moment in so many Russians' lives: the collapse of the Soviet Union. So, even as people disengage from the propaganda, it still is able to reinforce the viewpoints that the Kremlin needs and espouses.

Pronouncing nonsense

Divergent interpretations rarely occur because one side has the facts wrong. They mostly occur because both sides have interpreted the facts differently due to conflicting perceptions, interpretations and values. 'It's never about truth, it's about identity.'[13] The type of propaganda now seen in Russia is the result of when perceptions, interpretations and values supersede facts entirely. Such propaganda is needed when ontological security, described by the sociologist Anthony Giddens as the need to experience oneself as a whole, is shaken.[14] The fundamental nature of mankind's need for security, as famously highlighted by Maslow,[15] leads to an increasing demand for propaganda in times of crisis. Propaganda is essential to surviving a crisis in a highly authoritarian state, where people have no agency over their own lives as a result of their political environment. In such instances, the purpose of propaganda is to protect the audience from reality by creating a fake construct of order, stability and security and also, in Russia's case, a space where supposedly immutable values, culture and history are depicted as even more important, even more real, than reality. In this light, propaganda can be considered the ultimate protection – and, equally importantly, defence mechanism – against reality.

The supply of propaganda by the state is driven not only by the political goals of the authorities, but also by the audience's demand for safety and to resolve increasing contradictions that lead to continuous stress. People try to escape from any sources that may potentially lead them to question and challenge propaganda and its messages, or that would make their view of the world unsafe. For example, how can Russian soldiers be fighting a defensive war when it hasn't been attacked? To resolve this contradiction, and attendant stress from cognitive dissonance, the Russian government and its facilitators have turned abstract issues not usually seen as security matters – language, culture, historical interpretation – into threats, even existential ones, and then depicted the government as protecting people from these threats.[16] Such abstractions encourage a philosophical style detached from reality that can ignore contradictory evidence by zooming out to the bigger picture and then zooming back into the minutiae, disorienting the audience.

This is just one discursive strategy for ignoring or rejecting the contradiction, another is the *Ne vse tak odnoznachno* ('not everything is black and white') approach, which insists on nuance for the sake of nuance even where it may not exist. According to Hennadiy Maksak, these strategies are used not only by Russian media but also by ordinary Russians:

> Because they are not ready to move away from their viewpoint or into a new framework, even if they suspect that they are being told lies, they have this defensive mechanism. They are not ready to take responsibility. They understand on some level

[that the TV is lying] but it is so frightening – Bucha, Mariupol – it is better not to see it. It is easier not to believe it and to not take responsibility, not to have to say sorry, the media combined with these pre-existing defensive mechanisms has created in Russia a society that is in its shell and not ready to leave it.[17]

Everyone wants an easy life and it is much easier for Russians to accept the official position. If you believe you are a good person, going about life, and that your neighbours are good people, going about life, then it is very hard to understand why distant relatives and former schoolfriends are sending you photos of bombed-out houses and heads on sticks and demanding to know what you will do about it. It goes against everything you are hearing in society, from friends, from leaders. It is uncomfortable, bringing up a threat of cognitive dissonance, which renders you unable to act, to behave as normal because you have two competing maps of the world. You have to choose one, which one do you choose?

The easier one.

Popular content

Propaganda only works if audiences, at least on some level, want to believe in the 'big lie' it underpins. Rather than focus exclusively on what the television tells people, we need to examine why audiences tuned in and then kept watching. Following Russia's invasion of Ukraine, the political scientist Sam Greene argued:

> now more than ever, it's tempting to think about Putin's power as imposed from above, the result of an all-powerful security state imposing its will on an entirely unwilling population. Now more than ever, it's important to push back against that idea

[without] blaming Russians for their own political plight, or denying the considerable coercive power that the Kremlin has amassed. But to focus too much on those factors is a mistake [it is better to examine] the ways in which horizontal ties of sociali[s]ation among ordinary Russians – rather than vertical ties of coercion from state to citizen – have been the source of Putin's power for the past two decades.[18]

After all, television towers are not what they once were. People do have access to different sources; even with the recent censorship of social media, the overwhelming majority of Russians have internet coverage and could access VPNs – with one quarter of Russians already using VPNs, and one half of young Russians.[19]

Russian propaganda relies largely on advertising revenues to flourish in what is a relatively neoliberal environment, so most channels are dependent on producing content that is popular. Nor do Russians buy all the messages the Kremlin transmits to them. During the Coronavirus pandemic, the Kremlin launched a large-scale campaign to persuade the sceptical Russian population to take the vaccine but it was an uphill struggle with underwhelming results and one of the lowest vaccination rates in Europe.[20] That so many Russians were able to maintain their critical faculties when it came to Coronavirus supports the argument that many Russians have wanted to hear the Kremlin's 'story' of Ukraine since 2014, because they liked what it told them – about Ukraine, the West, the world, or themselves and their own group identity.

Of course, this story has built up over time and is far from uniform but between 2013 and 2018 television was the main source of information for almost 90 per cent of Russians; in 2021, even after the suspicions relating to Coronavirus, over 50 per cent of Russians voiced trust in the television channels' portrayal of events, considerably more than for any other source.[21] The types of extreme hate speech televised almost nightly in Russia, and then disseminated to shocked Western social media users, come from genuinely popular and influential shows in the Russian mediaspace, although they are not beloved by everyone. Most of the pro-war Russians I interviewed told me they supported the war but had no television or barely watched it: 'I don't watch TV. I haven't since Covid when Skabeeva was screaming and shouting about the vaccines' said one. Another replied 'I don't have a TV, I prefer Dostoevsky' (!). A third interviewee opined that 'I don't like the way Skabeeva and Popov express themselves and deliver information. It's like she is throwing stones or hammering her opponents with nails. Out of all those political shows, the most respectable one is Vremya Pokazhet with Artyom Sheinin. He is the best in terms of how he presents information and in terms of the quality of that information.' Skabeeva was particularly unpopular: a fourth said 'I can't watch Skabeeva and her bazaar', while a fifth interviewee said that she didn't 'like how Solovev and Skabeeva and all the rest conduct their programmes. They are just propagandistic one-sided programmes. They've turned information into a show, where everyone shouts at the same time and chats the utmost rubbish.' These people were all under 45, supposedly set free by the relatively unregulated – if manipulated – RuNet.

Much of the information online is also shaped by the Kremlin, in one way or another. In part, this is because the news sites they visit are owned by the government (like Rossiiskaya gazeta) or businessmen with close working relationships with the Kremlin, as is the case for the owners of Lenta, Komsomolskaya pravda, and VK. It is also the result of algorithms that deliberately expel any non-approved sites from the search listings on Russia's most popular browser, Yandex. It is not accurate to define the Russian internet as free or unfree, rather it belongs to a controlled and saturated hybrid media system where narratives are repeated and amplified by digital intermediaries (news aggregators and search engines, trolls and bots on social media). That said, the tendency is towards unfreedom, with websites deemed to be publishing especially egregious information sites banned. As mentioned, the list of such websites expanded considerably after 5 March 2022 to include Instagram, BBC and Facebook.[22]

Among pro-Kremlin online news sites, the stories tend to be to quite similar even if the framing is adapted to the readership. This is hardly surprising given that the Presidential Administration hosts weekly meetings with the editors of state-controlled media, including broadcasters and publishers, to coordinate topics and talking points. This has long been established practice but the process in 2022 appears to have become much more micromanaged in comparison to state journalists I spoke to for my PhD in 2018. According to the journalist Masha Gessen, a state-controlled consultancy issues a detailed list of topics five days a week. Each list generally contains six to ten topics per day 'which appear designed to supplement the Ministry of Defence's war updates that constitute mandatory coverage'.[23] Consequently, the effect of propaganda is often a result of cumulative exposure: television, print media, online, the people you meet – since if Russians meet Ukrainians in Russia they will likely be collaborators or too afraid to speak openly. Even if an ordinary Russian did come across contradictory information, they would discount it as exceptional and not verifiable, as opposed to the other pro-Kremlin sources. Especially since these sources also correlate to the much more pervasive and persuasive worldview embedded within the wider culture.

Popular culture, from soaps to pulp fiction, is an area that has long been under-researched, dismissed as trash or propaganda unworthy of analysis, despite its importance to creating a shared identity, sense of meaning and purpose for society. As Ambassador Prystaiko recalled during our interview:

> I started to realise they [Russian writers] were introducing Ukrainian characters. While Russians are described almost like

angels, Ukrainians are like orcs on the ground, above whom the elites are flying. And they (orcs) always had these accents, like Ukrainians. So I started to understand that they are actually creating something more dangerous than media propaganda because, in Russia's case, the media propaganda may change tomorrow. Papers will start saying something and then in a week they will think Ukrainians are good again. But books and films are different. I understood that from the mid-2000s,[24] the younger generation were being educated to, not to hate, but to have contempt for Ukrainian-ness, to have contempt for everything Ukrainian – our ways, traditions, church, all these things. Over the years Russians came to understand that this contemptuousness is expected social behaviour, it is the norm: you have to hate Ukraine a bit – just a bit.[25]

Russian popular films and television shows have almost consistently depicted Ukraine in a negative way since 2014. There has been a glut of funding for war films of a very particular plotline, in which Ukrainians often feature in a certain way. Take, by way of example, Kim Druzhinin's *Tanks*, released in 2018. It strove to marry re-imagined Soviet war myths and Putinist cultural politics with Hollywood action. Funded and partly devised by the Ministry of Culture, it followed Koshkin, one of the T34 tank's inventors, as he drove a prototype from Kharkiv to Moscow in 1940 while Nazi spies sought to intercept him and steal the tank. Rather than ask why exactly Nazis were free to roam the Soviet countryside in 1940, the film painted Ukrainians as unreliable would-be Nazi collaborators ready to sell the tank to the Germans. In a more benign yet condescending stereotype, another film of this genre, *Panfilov's 28* told the legend of a mythical brigade who defended Moscow in 1941 by throwing themselves under German tanks. The film abounded in racial generalisations: Russians as big brother, central Asians as kindly, stupid and obedient, and the token Ukrainian as simple and cheeky, with the odd word of Ukrainian thrown

in to stress the latter's role as a dialect. Similar content could
be found across post-2014 television series, such as the con-
demnatory overtones and Crimean setting of the series Major
Sokolov's Hetaeras, which depicted the brutal crimes of the
terroristic anti-Soviet organisation, ROVS, a thinly concealed
commentary on the active *banderovtsy* who fought the Soviets
from the 1930s through to the 1950s. All these examples, and
many more, adhered to the golden rule that only nationalists,
Nazi collaborators and class-clown yokels speak Ukrainian in
Russian film or television.

Engaging narratives: Telegram

It is important to understand the context within which Russians
have the war explained to them but it is also important to
understand the content with which they engage, including
online. Telegram has over forty million users in Russia and –
unlike Twitter, Instagram or Facebook – is accessible without
a VPN. This is where much of the discussion around the war
has been taking place. The terms of this debate would not
appear to be drastically different to what was found on television, given that the most popular channels are pro-war but I
wanted to examine the details of this online discourse. To do
so, I downloaded all the Telegram data for sixteen highly popular but variegated channels between 24 February and 20 May
2022 – some 74,853 posts – and coded their content by viral-
ity (as determined by the amount of viewer engagement) and
theme. I selected the channels with an eye both to popularity
and diversity of viewpoint as the pro-Putin media all expresses
approval of the war but is far from a monolith in terms of *how*
it expresses approval. To this end, I included the channels
of news figures Vladimir Solovev (1,176,117 subscribers) and
Margarita Simonyan (312,488); media outlets, RIA Novosti
(2,016,262), Vesti (126,593), and the tabloid Komsomolskaya

pravda (179,712); the popular well-connected political gossip channel Baza (689,565); opposition channels, Topor (1,177,401) and Aleksei Navalny (328,229); military channels like Operation Z (864,307), Sladkov (855,348) and The World with Yurii Podolyak (2,164,655); nationalist channels Tsargrad (79,970) and Zakhar Prilepin (211,076); and the channels of the politicians Maria Zakharova (392,247 followers), Ramzan Kadyrov (2,511,577), and Dmitrii Medvedev (333,849). These channels had combined viewing figures of 20,575,926,858 (so over 20 billion views) of their posts during the period in question.

I coded their material in terms of themes, devising twelve core categories for the pro-war channels: traitors of Russia; patriots of Russia; the failure of Western sanctions, including the Western cost of living crisis; the notion of the decadent and immoral West; Ukrainians as Nazis; depictions of Russian military prowess; Ukrainians as weak or cowards; calls to rally around the flag; Ukraine as a puppet of the West and the role of Western weapons and fighters in Ukraine; the cruelty of Ukrainians; cancel culture and Russophobia; and miscellaneous. There was a thirteenth category for content that did not relate to the war in Ukraine, although this was negligible in terms of the most viral content. There were also four additional opposition themes to which only three channels (Navalny, Topor and Baza) contributed: criticism of the invasion and war; criticism of Putin; discussion of Russian economic and trade problems; pro-Western sentiment. I describe the main findings below, tracking how the core narratives evolved depending on the channel and in relation to the timeline of events to which they were responding.

On 24 February, when Russia launched its invasion of Ukraine, setting out to conquer Ukraine and replace its government, Putin announced his decision to launch a 'special military operation' in a pre-dawn speech. There followed a full-scale invasion of Ukraine from Belarus to the north, Crimea to the south, and Russian territory to the east. In response,

Volodymyr Zelensky declared martial law and general mobilisation. As this invasion came on the back of weeks of the
Kremlin's mocking denials about any such plans, there was
no coherent line among the pro-Kremlin channels at first. In
the chaos, many of the propagandist channels fell back on the
'Ukrainians are Nazis' and denazification lines that had been
used in the President's pre-dawn speech and had a long history
of use since 2014. In the first two to three days of war, there
was not much variety in the way of anti-Ukraine Telegram
content – just comparisons with Nazis and a cautious, generic
support of the President's invasion. Commentators who just
days earlier had scoffed at predictions that Russia would
invade, often affected an 'I'm sorry it had to come to this'
tone in the immediate aftermath. Then, as it became obvious
the invasion was not going according to plan, they substituted
their condescension for spite.

By 27 February, it was already clear that the Russian plan
was not progressing as anticipated, thanks to the bravery of the
Ukrainian military, Zelensky's refusal of a US offer to evacu-
ate, and Russia's own military failings. Meanwhile, Russia's
assault on Kyiv, the eastern city of Kharkiv, and Chernihiv
in the north stalled as the Ukrainian armed forces targeted
supply vehicles with British Javelin missiles, exacerbating the
Russian army's logistical handicaps. The USA and European
Union responded to Russia's invasion with much harsher
sanctions than expected, banning major Russian banks from
SWIFT and freezing Russian central bank deposits. They also
banned Russian aircraft from EU airspace. After the initial
few days of shock, a more coherent line and set of arguments
began to emerge on the pro-war Telegram channels, as did an
enduring divide in the coverage between the 'military channels' and the media and political channels. Amid early anti-war
protests and a sense of unease at the failure of the Russians
to quickly take Kyiv and Kharkiv, pro-war media and political channels focused on traitors and anyone who disagreed

with the Kremlin's war, encouraging potential doubters to view this as a 'my country right or wrong' situation and join the loyal neutrals while also discouraging active opposition by promising punishment for traitors. The military channels on the whole ignored this context and pushed ahead with war propaganda and glitzy videos that suggested everything was going swimmingly (this approach would break down some five to six months into the war).

Russian forces finally had some good news with which to fuel their propaganda when they entered Ukraine's southern city of Kherson on 2 March. By the same time, a million Ukrainian refugees had left the country, fleeing Russian bombs and soldiers. At this point, the West barely featured in the pro-war Telegram channels' most viral content. The situation only really changed from 11 March, as sanctions continued to ratchet up. Certain narratives remained fairly consistent throughout, such as the moral decadence of the West, already entrenched in Russian political coverage of Europe. Other consistent narratives across the first three months depicted Ukrainians as Nazis and Russophobia as rampant in Europe. These were narratives that had been fully developed before the invasion. Meanwhile, attempts to encourage audiences to 'rally round the flag' were few and far between both in the most viral tweets and in the overall content, further supporting my argument that the Kremlin and its supportive media were not trying to mobilise people for war so much as ensure public acquiescence to it in the form of ritual support, loyal neutrality or apathy.

The prominence of 'patriots' as a theme reflects the sources' attempts to model 'ritual support', depicting ordinary everyday activities as a template for behaviour, rather than throwing oneself under a tank. Channels also made use of 'celebrity patriots' as role models to emulate. Although there were abstracted calls about the honour of sacrificing one's life for the motherland, these never featured among the most viral content, suggesting people did not engage with such material as much as they did with celebrities – an unsurprising finding that should have made public backlash to partial mobilisation easy-to-predict. The only channel to make much use of calls to 'rally around the flag' (as opposed to calls for defensive consolidation) was that of Zakhar Prilepin, who belongs to the systemic opposition but is not an entirely tame political force (in keeping with most nationalists lured to fight in Donbas in 2014). The other 'nationalist' channel, Tsargrad was obsessed with traitors, paying almost five times the attention to traitors as any other channel, although 'patriots' was their most popular theme.

On 16 March, Russia bombed a theatre in the southern port city of Mariupol, killing at least 300 civilians sheltering there. Despite increasing evidence of Russia's brutal assault, the focus on pro-war Telegram remained centred on Russian patriotism as they tried to shore up support for an operation that was clearly not going to be a second annexation of Crimea. In this case, as at other moments, the prominence of viral messages about patriotism followed an uptick in messages about traitors, in keeping with an expected pattern of demobilising opposition and then controlling support: discourage and encourage. The only time when the themes of patriots and traitors did not appear in close conjunction was in the run up to 9 May, when Russia celebrates the Soviet victory over Nazism. At this time, there was plenty of focus on patriots but no mention of Russian traitors, which could have detracted from the Kremlin's ongoing efforts to nationalise the Soviet victory as a Russian one. The theme of Russian military might was prominent throughout the entire three-month period and especially around 11 and 18 March when the Russians needed to avoid the sense that this was a failed special military operation in Ukraine.

Around the middle of March, it became clear which types of channel preferred which types of narratives. For example,

although they are both anti-Putin, the Navalny Telegram channel avoided any comment on the Western cost of living crisis,
which was very prominent on Topor. The military channels
(Sladkov, The World with Yurii Podolyak and Operation Z)
also failed to engage with any of the content around Western
sanctions or decadence. Most of their references to the West
pertained to weapons deliveries and volunteer fighters. These
channels, managed by war correspondents embedded in or
around the front, were much more anti-Ukrainian than anti-
Western, reflecting the fact that they were facing and fighting
Ukrainian soldiers and not gay parades. It is therefore unsurprising that of all the channels, Sladkov, First Channel's war
correspondent, made the most references to Ukrainians as
Nazis or *banderovtsy*.

By the 23 March, almost one month into the war, NATO
estimated the number of Russian dead, wounded, captured
and missing at approximately 40,000. Russia was forced to
refocus its efforts on the eastern and southern regions as
Ukraine launched counter-offensives in the north and south,
taking back more than 1,000 settlements. With the West
staunch in its support of Ukraine, and the US and UK sending
advanced missile systems, there were some tentative negotiations, and Zelensky told Russian journalists on a video call on
27 March that he was willing to consider geopolitical neutrality
for Ukraine, and to compromise on the status of the eastern
Donbas region. On 29 March, Russian and Ukrainian negotiators met in Istanbul and Ukraine put forward a detailed
proposal of neutrality. However, the Russian negotiators had
no real authority and did not even report directly to Putin,
who refused to meet with Zelensky to discuss any of the more
sensitive issues, such as territorial agreements, needed for a
peace deal to work.[26]

Despite this obvious lack of interest in finding a diplomatic
settlement, the term 'negotiations' featured prominently in
viral posts, meaning either that Russian Telegram users were

keen to have a negotiated settlement (a conclusion not supported by polling of the wider population at that time) or that
this was the preferred way for Russian channels, and users, to
cast Russia as the good guys; for example, there were seven
times as many references to negotiations as to refugees. The
prospect, and mention, of negotiations faded away from 1 April
when, as Russian troops withdrew from Bucha just outside
Kyiv, hundreds of civilian corpses were found on the streets.
In the concocted online world of Russian Telegram, pro-war
channels unleashed a firestorm of falsehoods, dismissing the
Ukrainian version of events before eventually declaring Bucha
as staged. They also raised the theme of Ukrainian cruelty as
a distraction from Bucha (and again from later atrocities in
Mariupol and elsewhere). The military channels shared graphic
footage to support the 'Ukrainian' themes (of cowardice, weakness and cruelty), including alleged torture of Russian POWs,
dead children and dismembered body parts.

Offline and in reality, the horror of the Russian occupation
galvanised further international support for Ukrainians, who
continued to flee the fighting, with the number of internally
displaced Ukrainians hitting seven million by early April. The
pictures from Bucha of carefully manicured nails tied behind
the backs of executed corpses seared into Ukrainians' minds
and gave extra impetus and meaning to solidarity from allies.
War is the failure of politics but it is also a time in which symbolic politics can acquire profound significance. On 8 April,
Ukraine's EU membership application process formally com-
menced. Russian coverage was enviously dismissive of this
development as reflected by the narrative shift to rubbish
everything and anything EU-related, including by focusing
on how the EU sanctions on Russia were now reverberating,
causing a cost-of-living crisis. Popular posts from mainstream
Russian media, laughing at Germans who couldn't wash, or
Brits who couldn't afford to heat their homes, reached millions
of viewers.[27] Russian propagandists and politicians sought

to undermine the desirability of Europe just as Ukraine was welcomed. It was their way to distract from the reality that while Ukraine has allies and at least the outline of a future, Russia does not. From this point onwards, the Western cost of living crisis remained a popular theme in politicians', media and personal propagandists' channels, flaring up whenever new sanctions were imposed on Russia and often accompanied by selective, or misrepresented, incidents of Western Russophobia.

In mid-April, the Russian Army's launch of 'phase two' of the war led to a renewed propaganda drive. Stories of Russian military invincibility and flashy war porn videos abounded, accompanied by exaggerated claims of Ukrainian collapse. Across all channels analysed over the entire three-month period, the theme of Russian military might was the most popular in terms of viewer engagement overall, and on RIA Novosti, the World with Yurii Podolyak, Ramzan Kadyrov, Komsomolskaya pravda, Operation Z, Solovev and Sladkov's channels specifically. First Channel's Sladkov hardly wrote about anything else and 90.3 per cent of his most viral posts comprised flashy war shots, largely unrepresentative of facts on the ground. However, the military might theme did not feature at all in Vesti's coverage or on MFA spokeswoman Maria Zakharova's channel. Former President Dmitrii Medvedev used it only once and then really just as a veiled threat-cum-reminder that Russia is the world's foremost nuclear power – in case anyone had forgotten in the five-minute interval since Russia last threatened nuclear annihilation.

Around the same time, on 14 April, Ukraine sank the Russian Black Sea fleet flagship Moskva, after hitting it with two Neptune missiles. Russia denied the sinking before suggesting there was an accident onboard. To distract from the incompetence of the military operation and to dissuade anyone from active opposition, the theme of traitors (i.e. those who criticise the war or the state) gained in prominence

across media and propagandists' channels. Keen to take back
the initiative, on 18 April, Russian forces launched a new,
large-scale offensive in east Ukraine to take full control of the
Luhansk and Donetsk Oblasts and, on 21 April, Putin declared
premature victory in the battle for Mariupol, even as some
2,500 Ukrainian fighters remained barricaded in the Azovstal
steel plant – alongside hundreds of civilians – subject to
constant bombardment. The theme of Ukrainian cowardice
and weakness also grew in prominence at this point, although
it never gained anything like the thematic prominence of
Russian military might. Every single channel engaged with
it, even if the military channels, particularly The World with
Yurii Podolyak, used it the most.

On 28 April, Russia, for the first time in a long while, lost
the initiative on the 'WWII analogies' front when US Congress
revived lend-lease facilities to speed up weapons shipments
to Ukraine. This was one of the few times when the military
channels, plus Kadyrov, focused on Western intervention in
any meaningful way. Politicians and media outlet channels
remained focused on Western actions and reactions for most
of the period, from Medvedev's gloating about the cost-of-
living crisis to Vesti's obsession with European immorality.
Maria Zakharova also shared comments on both topics and
really on anything that gave her an excuse to criticise the West.
Yet, even among those channels, the notion of cancel culture
and/or Russophobia was not a prominent theme among viral
posts (although a keyword search shows it is a topic these
channels discuss, people just don't appear to want to read
about it all that much). This raises the intriguing prospect that
this narrative may have far more resonance with middle-class
or even liberal voters, since the Moscow government decided
to erect billboards around the city centre decrying the cancelling of Russian culture in the West. In support of this theory,
it would be a useful way to shunt those actively opposed to the
war into the apathetic group: what is the point in protesting or

even leaving when the West hates you, or at least doesn't share your cultural values either?

On 4 May, a Ukrainian counter-offensive north and east of Kharkiv pushed Russian troops further back from the city, in the first significant Ukrainian success since winning the battle for Kyiv. Coming just a few days before Victory Day, this further fuelled baseless speculation (in the West) that Putin would call for general mobilisation. He failed to do so, unable or unwilling at that point to risk engaging the broader population in the war. Any examination of the narratives used by the most popular Telegram channels in the run up to Victory Day would have hinted at this refusal to mobilise given that the most emotive narratives – Ukrainians as Nazis, Western mercenaries and arms supplies – largely disappeared from view. A few days later, on 12 and 15 May respectively, the damage caused by Putin's invasion of Ukraine to Russia's security was further underscored by the announcement that Finland would seek NATO membership, followed by Sweden. The Kremlin did not react in any significant way, undermining its arguments and threats about NATO expansion, and nor did the pro-war Telegram channels.

On 20 May, Russia finally took the Azovstal factory after months of Azov resistance in Mariupol and the period of analysis closed on a large burst of references to Ukrainians as *banderovtsy* and Nazis, the very same narratives with which I first began my discourse analysis of 2014 media coverage all those years ago. But, as well as examining what topics are (still) in use, it is also worth considering what subjects are conspicuous by their absence. Missing elements that featured in 2014 but not in 2022 included comparisons between fighting in east Ukraine with Second World War-era atrocities, when media and politicians accused the Ukrainian forces of Nazi-esque crimes against the inhabitants of Donbas. Actually, quite a few atrocities are missing, all of them Russian. There is, unsurprisingly, no discussion of Russian crimes, the words are all there – Bucha, Kremenchug, Kramatorsk, Mariupol, Izyum – but they mean something else, they have been demented and twisted into something unrecognisable.

The Russian media's perversion of the facts is sometimes so horrible that it is hard to focus on much else, you feel almost compelled to stop everything and perform an autopsy on the truth. But in doing so, you allow Russian lies, rather than the crimes themselves, to become the focal point of criticism. This is a tried and tested technique for shifting the focus from moral aberration to an abstracted conversation about who is lying, who is exaggerating, what is truth and how we define reality. Perhaps some of the Russian opposition's tendencies towards introspection stem from not only how easy it is to fall into this trap but also their need to engage in a conversation with the Kremlin's form of reality, a need driven by the fact that most Russians (their putative voters) inhabit a world shaped by this (un)reality. It is difficult to conceive of how opposition forces could ever come to power without embracing at least partially the Putinist mindset, even if they reject Putin the person. That may also explain why in many ways the techniques of the opposition and pro-Kremlin channels can appear complementary; for example, they both share a sarcastic and bitter humour and a relentless negativity in their depictions of the world.

But, regardless of who openly discusses them, the atrocities linger. They are everywhere and nowhere, like a dead family member, in photo frames and in the fabric of the house. Across Telegram, users know that they are only one click away from seeing the pools of blood, from visualising the mutilated corpses and knowing deep down once and for all, if only they really wanted to – but they don't. Or rather, they don't want to see it in its proper context. Much gruesome pro-Russian content was not hidden from view but boastfully splashed across the type of popular mainstream channels I analysed. Take, for example, the 'denazification' videos that appeared on the Telegram channel of the pro-Russian blogger, (alias)

Romanov Lait, in which frightened and exhausted residents of the Kherson and Zaporizhzhia regions repent of disloyalty to the Russians. On a daily basis, half-naked men and women with shaved heads and trembling voices acknowledge the error of their ways. When I asked some of my contacts who were ambivalent towards the war about these daily uploads, they responded tersely: What about Azov? The Ukrainians do worse! He is just some silly boy, it hardly matters! Beneath it all, there is an annoyance but also maybe some pain: Why are you bothering me with this when we both know it is awful and that I can't do anything about it?

One constant, across all pro-war Telegram channels, all state supportive media, and all my conversations with those who did not oppose the war, was a firm aversion to any proper discussion of where this violence comes from and, relatedly, of Russia's internal sociopolitical situation. It is virtually impossible to learn anything of much value about Russia directly from Russian news. Any effort to discuss internal Russian problems meets with a fierce defensiveness despite their readiness to pontificate on everyone else's problems. Any internal challenges are due to the enemy within and without. Like the leaders of all secure and very popular countries, Russian politicians are always eager to stress support from unexpected quarters, be it Eritrea or a failing UFF fighter. One viral campaign during my analysis was a video series in which foreigners sent in videos or photos of themselves professing their love for Russia and Russian soldiers. It calls to mind the preacher who, recently converted, zealously proclaims his faith to random passersby, desperate to find intellectual repose from his own nagging doubts by persuading others. Both are desperate to reframe their pointless harassment of innocent bystanders into a struggle for truth and salvation. Such a noble struggle requires a worthy opponent: Satan – or at least the West.

5

We are at war with the West

Sergei Kirienko was a young reformist alongside Anatoly Chubais and Boris Nemtsov, pushing a liberal economic agenda in the newly post-Soviet Russia. If Chubais managed to find a nook in Putin's Russia as a presidential aide, he lost it when he fled Russia shortly after the invasion. Nemtsov, a vocal supporter of Ukraine, didn't have any such chance, having been gunned down by Chechen assassins just metres from the Kremlin in 2015. But what of Kirienko? After Kirienko had served as the youngest ever Prime Minister of Russia under Yeltsin, working closely with the IMF, Putin appointed him head of Rosatom, Russia's Federal Atomic Energy Company. Over time, Kirienko came to mimic the cultural conservatism of the new elites by moaning about the need to protect Russia's youth from debauched hip hop and other such dilemmas. This helped him re-ascend to the top, becoming First Deputy Chief of Staff to President Putin in 2016 and then administrator for the occupied territories of Ukraine that Putin declared part of Russia in October 2022.

It is hard to discern the Friedman-worshipping Americophile in Kirienko's current stance: 'Russia is not at war with Ukraine today – rather the united West is waging war against us on the territory of Ukraine and, unfortunately, using Ukrainians. They are mounting stiff opposition using every possible capability of the Western world.' But Kirienko argued that the smart Westerners preparing the war against Russia 'made a serious mistake' when they counted on Russians being the same as them. 'They didn't take into account the mentality that for Russia there are things a lot more important than the opportunity to acquire this or that item in the shop. A much more important question to those living in Russia is "is this fair or not fair", the issue of "we don't abandon our own", and the "right to choose what to read and what to listen to". And their mistake was that, in trying to target the material side, they received the opposite effect and confronted our moral values.'[1]

It is difficult to verify the existence of this heroic freedom-worshipping Russia that cares little for the material things, and always stands by its own, within the thousands of videos of Russian troops invading Ukraine, stealing everyone's washing machines, and then abandoning local pro-Russian collaborators, newly relocated Russian civilians, and even their own comrades-in-arms as they flee the Ukrainian liberators. Be that as it may, a lot of what Kirienko says about the collectivism and profundity of Russian identity resonates with many Russians. The war is so easily, readily and deliberately entangled with discussions of Russian identity, history, meaning and security because of Ukraine's pivotal importance to Russia's understanding of itself. But this also makes it dangerous and destabilising, meaning Russians are eager to find an acceptable answer to the question of why Ukrainians dislike them so much. This inevitably necessitates lies, as understanding the real reason would require Russians to unlearn their version of history, Russianness, and what their country has been up to in Ukraine for the last eight years. Most people are (wisely) reluctant to confront these questions.

Instead, the government and the people choose to present the collective West, led by the USA, as an eternal enemy who has led Ukraine astray. Below is a list of how Russians explained why so many countries have condemned Russia's actions against Ukraine. The poll took place in March 2022 and respondents could choose more than one answer:

- They are brought to heel by the US and NATO – 36 per cent.
- They have been misinformed by Western media – 29 per cent.
- The world has always been against Russia – 27 per cent.
- They believe Russia has violated international law and Ukraine's rights – 16 per cent.
- They fear Russia will act against them the way it did against Ukraine – 15 per cent.
- They are outraged by Russia's actions and sympathetic to Ukraine – 12 per cent.[2]

It is noteworthy that the older generation was more than twice as likely as younger respondents to choose the response that the US and NATO had brought other countries to heel. Younger people were six to seven times more likely than the elderly to say that Russia had violated international law and Ukraine's rights and that other states were outraged by Russia's actions and sympathetic to Ukraine. Unfortunately for Ukrainians, there are twice as many elderly as young people in Russia.

Many of these statements reflect the conspiratorial notion that the West controls the world and it is only now that Russia is finally standing up to them. This anti-Westernism colours political possibilities and realities in Russia. The more pro-Western and liberal opposition have struggled to overcome the taint of the 1990s, even as those responsible for the horror of shock therapy have remade themselves as Russian patriots. To deflect from their own role, Russian ruling elites have rubbished the idea of liberalism and the concept of democracy more broadly. Most Russians need little encouragement on this score. Even Aleksei Navalny, easily the most popular opposition politician of the last decade, comes from the so-called Natsdem (literally National Democrats) tradition, which is still economically quite liberal – although Navalny has made moves towards the left in recent years – but also has nationalist roots. Consequently, many Navalny supporters are not especially pro-Western and, in my experience interviewing activists within his presidential campaign in the regions, many are angry with the West for how closely intertwined they have been with the Russian elites and their money. They question why countries that are so rhetorically committed to liberal values accept such obscene amounts of money from, and give so many visas to, the same Putinist elites who repress the rights of ordinary people in Russia. It is a very apt question and also contextualises why a mere four per cent of Navalny's Telegram content could be described as pro-Western and why, in some of his other social media feeds, such as Twitter, he has openly criticised the West's approach to Russia since the war began.

Young Navalny supporters are not the only people jaded by Western hypocrisy. Despite bold statements from Brussels and Washington that 'the world is united against Russia', it isn't. China has been highly critical of the West's role in Ukraine, rather than Russia's, while India has predictably stuck to its non-aligned traditions. Many African and Middle Eastern countries see the West as the colonial power in this equation and blame the grain shortages on Western sanctions, not Russian aggression. The common denominator here is not Russian popularity but Western unpopularity. Very few of these countries actively like Russia for itself or for its actions, they just enjoy seeing someone meting it back out to the arrogant West. Therein lies arguably the majority of Russia's global appeal and soft power. Rather than undertaking detailed analysis of Africa-focused troll farms, perhaps European leaders might consider why so many people living in Africa are not fond of their former colonial overlords.

On 7 July, Putin delivered a speech to State Duma leaders and the systemic party faction heads, in which he displayed a neat summary of the core anti-Western rhetoric that appeals at home and abroad:

> We hear some people say that we started the war in Donbass, in Ukraine. No, the war was unleashed by the collective West, which organised and supported the unconstitutional armed coup in Ukraine in 2014, and then encouraged and justified genocide against the people of Donbass. The collective West is the direct instigator and the culprit of what is happening today.
>
> [. . .] But here is what I would like to make clear. They should have realised that they would lose from the very beginning of our special military operation, because this operation also means the beginning of a radical breakdown of the US-style world order. This is the beginning of the transition from liberal-globalist American egocentrism to a truly multipolar world based not on self-serving rules made up by someone for their own needs, behind which there is nothing but striving for hegemony, and not on hypocritical double standards, but on international law and the genuine sovereignty of nations and civilisations, on their will to live their historical destiny, with their own values and traditions.[3]

The message is a consistent one with Russia's major doctrines and broader political rhetoric over the last decade at least: the West is on its way out, it knows it is fading and so is becoming more aggressive in its death throes, but this will only hasten its demise, which it richly deserves because it is sinful, hypocritical and aggressive towards others. This is a waiting game and Russia is confident of its ability to outwait the West by relying on the reserves of resilience it has built up through the experience of the Soviet Union and of the Soviet Union's collapse.

Cold war, hot sanctions

The Roman Empire took around 250 years to collapse. The Soviet Union about two-and-a-half years. The end of Communism and transition to capitalism left a remarkably enduring imprint on Russian citizens, similar to the Great Depression, but much less studied or examined. It is difficult to quantify the sense of shock and of resentment but the economist William Pyle has tried. Relying on the Life in Transition Surveys, he demonstrates that Russians were exceptionally impressionable to life experiences during the years immediately before and after the Soviet collapse. According to the impressionable years theory, one's life experiences in young adulthood leave a more lasting and formative impression on a person. Pyle applies this theory to Russia as a country, relying on oral histories and testimonies and cross-referencing them with foreign policy and values surveys. Controlling for other variables, Pyle connects variation in individual labour market histories to a set of widely studied beliefs and values, concluding that 'Russians who reported experiencing labo[u]r market hardships more acutely during the 'impressionable years' of 1989–1994, a six-year period encompassing the three years before and the three years after the dissolution of the Soviet Union, were more apt when surveyed in 2006 to oppose the core beliefs and values that animated their country's transition from Communism. Instead, they expressed greater affinity for what might be termed, for shorthand purposes, 'Soviet values: scepticism of free markets and democratic politics, less tolerance for economic inequality, and greater support for government-led redistribution.'[4] The same correlation between labour market hardships after the mid-1990s does not occur.

Of those Russians who experienced the 1990s as adults, 70 per cent view the period negatively, associating it with hunger and lawlessness.[5] Even the most hardened Thatcherite could understand why. The Russian government unleashed 'shock therapy' designed to rapidly unleash market forces, electrocuting the old Soviet system. The best industrial enterprises were hurriedly auctioned off to the oligarchs for a pittance. Workers weren't paid or were paid in products, from gherkins to flour, a mark of the barter economy that existed. People finally had access to Western products and international travel but they couldn't afford anything. Excess deaths went up five times, bread prices skyrocketed 600 per cent and the murder rate averaged 84 a day. Afflicted by hyperinflation, many people lost their personal savings and their societal status, with doctors driving taxis after shifts just to afford food.[6] In 2021, Putin claimed that he too had moonlit as a taxi driver. Almost definitely false, this claim is symbolic of how the Russian president has appropriated people's private humiliations, recalling anarchy then to justify anti-Western authoritarianism now.

Putin's 2005 remark that the collapse of the USSR was a catastrophe struck a chord with the many people in Russia who lost out from 1991, people who had wanted things to be better but lost spirit when they quickly turned out like always, as Chernomyrdin dourly quipped. It is perhaps unsurprising that while polls demonstrated majority support for the dismantlement of the USSR before 1991, following the difficult transition from Communism, by 1995 people were already expressing a marked nostalgia for the Soviet era.[7] Putin has drawn strength from this disappointment, successfully positioning himself as the antidote to the 'wild 1990s'. A good deal of Putin's popularity derives from the fact that under his rule, there had been marked improvements in Russia's international status, ability to pay its debts, and GDP. There is a genuine popular gratitude for these advances, which does not appear to lessen with time, perhaps because the popular view of the 1990s also appears to get worse over time. This chimes with Pyle's impressionable years theory, which other experts such as Gulnaz Sharafatudinova[8] have noted in terms of the damage caused to collective identity during the transition.

In the 1990s, Russians were learning how democracy and elections function and drawing conclusions from that. They witnessed the cruellest form of shock therapy, democracy without institutions or rule of law, criminality, exploitation, shelling of the White House, a rigged election (in 1996), and the rich and powerful treading over the poor and the weak. Given their experience of capitalism and democracy involved having to battle, with almost zero support, the very worst excesses of both approaches in a truly perverted form, perhaps the only real surprise should be that the return to dictatorship took as long as it did. Certainly, it seems naive to be shocked that this period solidified an anti-market and illiberal worldview in those who experienced it first-hand. Putin did not create these sentiments. He taps into what is there and of course probably shares some of this worldview, having lived through the 1990s in adulthood and felt the impact of the Soviet collapse on his own career and living conditions.

Fedor Lukyanov is editor of *Russia in Global Affairs* and a foreign-policy analyst close to the Kremlin. He remembers the 1990s as a time of hope turned sour: 'There was a lot of enthusiasm, a sense that the world was coming closer, and so on. There was strong support for change under Gorbachev and Yeltsin. And naturally the fact that this support was used by those leaders in the way it was – Gorbachev didn't know what he was doing and lost it all because he stopped controlling the current and ended up being washed away by it and personally lost. But Yeltsin and the people who came to power with him, they are the most unpleasant as these people used that outpouring of enthusiasm [for change] and converted it into power and property for themselves. That was the most damaging thing for democracy. Of course, now the 1990s are a myth, full of legends and it is difficult to know what is true and what is myth but basically there is an impression that it was unfair, that what the free market and democracy brought to Russia was unfair. People were robbed, people lost things and they were exploited by a group who enriched themselves. That's why, when they [Western governments following Russia's invasion of Ukraine] started to arrest the property of our oligarchs, the Russian population was very happy.'[9]

When he was still prime minister in 1999, Putin said that 'Russia can rise up from its knees and strike hard' but this phrasing does not explain who brought Russia to her knees – the West? Russia itself? Shady international forces? As ever, the statement's ambiguity is its strength not its weakness, since it allows the pain of the 1990s to be politicised and turned against various enemies – the West first and foremost. The dominant rose-tinted Western view of the post-Soviet 1990s as a chaotic but promising interlude of democracy and freedom is just one of the ways the latter has allowed Russia's leaders to get away scot-free with pinning the blame on everyone else and never admitting their own personal involvement in the corruption and criminality of the 1990s. As Fedor Lukyanov remembers from his time working with foreign NGOs in the 1990s and policymakers since:

> in the West there is a very warped view of 90s, they try to write Russia into narrative of Eastern Europe – and it isn't like really that narrative even worked out for Eastern Europe. Poland and Hungary had their own specifics for example [. . .] Of course, it is easy to judge now, it was more chaotic at the time, the government and people were just trying to survive. But all the same the idea that Russia was on the right path and then left it is not true. I remember in the 1990s, I was working with, involved with, those bringing Western aid for our reforms. It was very funny because either out of stupidity or naivety they had no idea what country or people they were dealing with. They were really enthusiastic, especially the Americans who wanted to help transform Russia, but at the same time they believed there was absolutely no difference at all between Bolivia or Mexico or Russia. 'We will come and deliver privatisation here in Russia,

it is the same anywhere, just like Bolivia.' Never mind the fact that nobody much liked the results in Bolivia anyway and that in Russia it would end up a . . . well, they didn't understand that. And then some people started to earn money from it all, cynically. That discredited the idea of the West, and especially of the Western assistance to Russia's transformation.[10]

The West evidently made many mistakes in how it handled the collapse of the USSR and, with the benefit of hindsight, it is clear that European countries should have made a stronger case for a transition to a more social democratic model. However, it was Yeltsin and his coterie – in which Putin played his role – that inflicted unnecessarily painful economic decisions and siphoned off billions in IMF loans to their offshore accounts. Many of this era's worst actors are firmly embedded in today's political elite, like Vladimir Medinsky, the presidential aide who was originally running Russia's negotiations with Ukraine and who, in the first post-Soviet decade, ran a PR agency representing the infamous MMM pyramid scheme that bankrupted millions.[11] There is also Vladimir Putin himself, alleged to have stolen millions. Part of the reason why the narrative about the 1990s as a Time of Troubles has taken on an almost mystical aspect but so rarely involves identifying the concrete individuals responsible is because those individuals were central to Putin's career and one of them is Putin himself.

This resentful memory of the 1990s is not just a grievance against the West. It is also central to Russian media framing, and therefore popular interpretations, of the West's reaction to Russian aggression in Ukraine. It is especially relevant to the regime's framing of US and EU sanctions imposed during the summer of 2014, when the USA and EU banned state-owned banks from raising capital and Russian oil firms from cooperating with Western companies in response to the downing of passenger jet MH17. According to Russian media, these sanctions were nothing less than an attempt to destroy Russia, just as the West destroyed the USSR.[12] In the same way that Russian media coverage of these sanctions was distinct from its rhetoric on Ukraine, since 2022 Russian media has differentiated the sanctions narratives from its invasion, casting the former as a war with the West connected to but separate from events in Ukraine. The core of this narrative depicts Russian intransigence as intrepid resistance to Western attempts to wreak financial havoc on Russia and to replay the economic crises of the 1990s, following the Soviet collapse, something the West is hellbent on achieving regardless of Ukraine, which serves only as an excuse. This is an important distinction from Western depictions of the conflict, which rarely, if ever, separate sanctions from the war.

While they do not necessarily share the above interpretation, even very pro-Western and anti-war Russians deeply oppose the sanctions. It is sadly ironic that the Western sanctions imposed since 2014, and especially since 2022, really affect ordinary Western-leaning Russians the most, as they are the ones who want access to the West but are not rich enough to buy a golden visa or a private jet to bypass the restrictions. For most Russians, the sanctions have failed to change minds. Although initially surprised by the severity of sanctions imposed, especially seizure of Russian currency reserves and private property, six months into the war, some 80 per cent were categorically against making any concessions to Western countries for the lifting of sanctions and only thirteen per cent were ready to make concessions in exchange for lifting restrictions.[13] What's more, Russians have expressed confidence that they can weather the negative effects of sanctions, especially after the first few months of the war were easier than expected. By August 2022, most were no longer anywhere near as worried about sanctions as they were at the start of the war. If in March concern over sanctions was reported by 46 per cent of respondents, then by May only 38 per cent of those surveyed were worried.[14] The most concerned by restrictions were

Muscovites and inhabitants of cities with a population of over 500 thousand people (45%). The Kremlin has been cautious in their approach to sanctions, recognising the need to keep the domestic situation stable, and preparing the economy by taking drastic Central Bank measures to avoid high inflation.[15]

Even without these measures or lighter than expected impact, sanctions often incite unintended reactions, consolidating loyalty in the face of external attack, a position that benefits Putin, and creates a sense of unity. Dmitri Trenin expressed this succinctly: 'In my view, sanctions more than anything else have facilitated the coming together of Russian people.'[16] The hectoring from a hypocritical West pushed some Russians into performing ritualised support, like slapping 'off you go then' stickers on the shop windows of Western brands that left Russia after 24 February. Other Russians, who might disagree with the war but feel targeted by sanctions have became apathetic in response. The most unlikely reaction to sanctions is that they will turn people against Putin or they will weaken Putin personally. The sanctions came too late: now, there isn't really any amount of money that would make Putin abandon the war.[17] The moment to discuss money, and to show the West's refusal to be bought, came and went, and Russia kept the receipts.

So why apply sanctions if they reinforce support for the regime? Do they actually work? Whether or not sanctions work depends on what you want them to achieve. Sanctions should not be aimed at regime change but at lowering an antagonist's state capacity. Other aims can include symbolism, weakening morale, economic decline. There is evidence of the latter in Russia's case, as the number of people living below the poverty line has grown by 41 per cent in the first three months of 2022, according to official government statistics. That represents an increase from 12.4 million people at the end of 2021 to 20.9 million at the end of March.[18] The impoverishment of the Russian people is nothing to celebrate; but anyone who thinks otherwise will also need to explain how they envisage it will turn people against Putin. Many Russians already associate a 'Western way of living' with chaos, anarchy and loss of status, and such measures only reinforce negative associations with the West.

In other words, a significant part of Russian society feels that the West has taken a lot from them and now it is trying to take even more. This is an emotional response and one that often came up in conversations I had with Donetsk refugees in Voronezh in 2017 and 2018. Many of these people were not virulently pro-Russian so much as despondent about being treated as 'Soviet dregs' by the culturally Ukrainian and pro-European populations of Lviv and Rivne. The main source of their pro-Russian sentiment was a nostalgia for lost status or (self-) respect. Many of the families had connections to, or careers in, law enforcement or mining, and they missed the status they had enjoyed under the USSR or imagined they would have in Russia. From my conversations with them, it was hard to shake the impression that all they had wanted was for someone to recognise their loss, to stem the sense of humiliation – and Putin had offered them this acknowledgement. Nor does this reflect purely class divides: in her interview with me, Natalia Sevagina, whose family hailed from intellectual and military elites, recalled with emotion her father, an officer, having to lay bricks in the 1990s as he struggled to feed the family. 'Army, science, everything was broken. Now, everything that is valuable to us is returning. We are returning to our own systems, to our own education.'[19] Putin has been very adept at encouraging this sense of return, kindling the fires of personal humiliation within a broader sense of national degradation, and linking it to Western military, especially NATO, expansion and disregard of Russian interests.

National humiliation and NATO

Do you know 'Frankie Goes to Hollywood'? The song 'War, What is it Good For?'[20] They were talking about US foreign affairs. And when I was a student I thought war was good for nothing. Actually when I did military service, I was woken up at 6 am by the song – 'Uncle Sam did the best he can, you're in the army now'[21] this music from Vietnam [. . .] all my work in previous years went to hell, we didn't get a peaceful solution, we failed, so today I say it is up to the armed forces, the militias, to take care of [. . .] Russia was so patient, with its no aggression, its bla bla bla, Yeltsin's talk about Yugoslavia, Chernomyrdin, Primakov's loop turning back the plane, Putin's speech in Munich.[22]

In his electic pronouncements above, Dr Orlov's message is that nobody took Russia seriously and now it is too late. In my interviews with them, several foreign-policy specialists, including Vladimir Orlov, referenced the rudeness of the West's response to Putin's so-called ultimatum. This was a gambit at the end of 2021, in which Putin suggested NATO return to its pre-1997 borders. As Dr Orlov continued:

The moment in transition was between October and December [2021] when the president and his inner team were analysing [the West's response]. They could have gone for war, for a special operation in November or December. Then Russia could have done it better, and quicker, with fewer human losses. But Russia waited. She waited for the US reply. Russia was trying to find another way. Some called [Putin's suggestion] an ultimatum, but it was just an invitation to do business and negotiate, not on Western terms, not on Russian terms. The reply he got, I analysed carefully, including with dear US colleagues, and it was basically 'haha, you Russians are doing your bla-bla-bla again'.[23]

The ultimatum read as completely absurd to NATO and its

members. It was not taken seriously and was clearly a stark signal of the type of radical change Russia wanted to see. As Sergei Lavrov commented after the invasion: 'We were told bluntly and quite rudely [by NATO] that the expansion of the alliance and the possible participation of Ukraine in this process is not your business.'[24] Certainly there was a dismissive tone in the 2000s towards Russian security complaints but the ultimatum's demands that NATO pull out its military infrastructure from Central and Eastern European member states, as well as commit to legally binding guarantees that the post-Soviet republics, including Ukraine, would never be accepted into NATO, were unlikely to encourage serious engagement. On the NATO side even the suggestion was taken as 'utter madness', as one NATO policy officer with first-hand reports of these discussions put it.

Given the content of the ultimatum, and in the context of Maria Zakharova suggestively licking strawberries and Embassy Twitter accounts engaged in puerile trolling, it is easy to sympathise with this cynicism – many countries have stopped taking Russian diplomacy seriously. Nevertheless, the Americans did still try to engage the Russians but their worldviews were like two ships passing in the night with the added complication that the Russian Foreign Minister refused to confirm or deny whether his ship was, in fact, a submarine. Lavrov has since claimed that he had the impression that before 24 February nobody understood what was going on because Western politicians were deceiving their voters. It is tempting to view this as projection, given the many rumours circulating among Moscow-based think tankers that Lavrov only found out about the invasion of Kyiv some two hours before Russia began bombing. It would appear NATO is not the only one in the humiliation game.[25]

Russian dislike for NATO is palpable but is often aimed more at the symbolism of NATO, or at NATO as an instrument of Western power. Relations with NATO itself are a bit more complicated. Russia cooperated with NATO in the 1990s but the bombing of Yugoslavia in 1999 heralded a turning point, only further aggravated by so-called 'colour revolutions', democratic uprisings in the post-Soviet space, which the Kremlin believed were sponsored by the State Department. The sense that the West took advantage of Russian weakness has played a formative role in post-Soviet perceptions of the alliance. As one leading professor of history at a Moscow university explained: 'If politicians in the West think Russia can be beaten into submission or defeat, they have misunderstood, we can't. This issue is existential, this is not only about who wins in Ukraine but what sort of Russia emerges – and the sustainability of the Russian Federation itself.'[26] In answer to the same question about perceptions of NATO, another professor, this time from a prominent regional university, cited the axiomatic phrase: 'Russia can either be strong or it can not exist.'[27]

Even if only rhetorical, this readiness to define everything as an existential crisis has many roots, from the Soviet collapse to demographic crises. The collapse in birth rates following the chaotic 1990s is an issue that frequently emerges in Putin's speeches and that appears almost impervious to policy measures. The ridiculous accusations splashed across Russian propaganda that Western powers were seeking to isolate and extinguish the Russian genotype, including in biolabs built by the CIA across Ukraine, fuel and are fuelled by this demographic obsession.[28] It also raises a number of questions, such as why any such tool wouldn't affect Ukrainian genotypes if Ukrainians and Russians are one people. Or why launch a devastating war that will kill the very young men needed to start families. But we are unlikely to get a serious answer to either question. What is more useful is ascertaining the 'higher truth' nestled behind such claims, namely that the West is using Ukraine to target and destroy Russia.

This view of the West is indisputably paranoid but begs the question: What came first? NATO expansion or paranoia?

The answer to this question, among academics at least, often divides into two camps. The first argues that Russia's insecurity has launched into a paranoia so intense it makes its security concerns laughable and unserious. They argue that Ukraine was committed to neutrality and had fairly little interest in joining NATO when Russia began this conflict in 2014. They add that Putin didn't care about Finland and Sweden joining so clearly the issue is not NATO per se and, in any case, NATO is a defensive alliance. Even if it weren't, given Russia is a nuclear power, it should feel secure enough not to try to dictate to other countries what membership they can and can't join. This view is morally sound, if incorrect on a few points but also unrealistic: how would the USA react to Mexico joining a defence union with China? Perhaps we might ask those who continue to enforce an embargo on Cuba.

The second camp argues that Russia's aggression and paranoia were stimulated by NATO expansion eastwards – as Russianist and International Relations experts like George Kennan and John Gaddis predicted would be the case. In this view, Russia has vital strategic interests in Ukraine and, by interfering and trying to lure Ukraine to their camp, the West was looking for trouble. Ultimately, great powers like Russia are always going to behave like great powers, i.e. think in terms of spheres of influence, and others have to recognise this fact. In the context of Russia's war on Ukraine, this approach can appear overly concerned with trying to answer that perennial Russian question 'kto vinovat' (who is to blame) when Moscow really thinks in terms closer to the famous Bolshevik slogan of 'kto, kogo' (Who [will dominate], whom).

Both positions have strengths and weaknesses, although not perhaps in equal measure. I discussed this topic with Patrick Porter, a professor of international relations and nuanced thinker who would not fit neatly into either camp, despite his classical realism.

In brief, I see two impulses in Moscow's behaviour in Ukraine, both of which are coiled into one another – reactive security-seeking and imperial aggrandisement. These two points are treated as mutually hostile, but need not be. It's not so much about NATO formal expansion, as it is about a general extension of Western influence and presence into what Russia sees as its 'orbit'. A combination of EU/NATO expansion, informal presence (NATO was 'in' Ukraine, even if Ukraine was not 'in' NATO), creating what Moscow sees as a potential platform for subversion. [. . .] A fear does not have to be about a real thing, to be a real fear. States can be genuinely paranoid even of remote things. Secondly, NATO does not have to expand formally to threaten regimes or project power – indeed, the fate of Libya's Colonel Gaddafi I think was a critical alarm for Putin et al. Fixation on formal enlargement is oddly narrow and legalistic. For the most part, the West expanded NATO in its own mind as a defensive, security-seeking and stabilising measure. Indeed, a large part of NATO expansion was driven by a desire to stabilise its own members, integrate them into a benign US empire (hierarchical, constraining structure), to pacify them and lock in US hegemony in Europe. It wasn't always *about* Russia (original italics), but Russia was always in the mix.[29]

This view approximates to my own. Russian insecurity exists for reasons independent of the West but Western actions have triggered and exacerbated it, even radicalised it when combined with obvious hypocrisy and what Marlene Laruelle has termed 'normative imperialism'.[30] Potential NATO candidacy for Ukraine is seen in Russia and by Russians as a symptom of the problem, not the main problem in itself, as it's not NATO enlargement *en se* that matters so much as Moscow's perception that its 'ownership' (of Eastern Europe) was being violated.[31] In the Kremlin's view, this was a US-driven effort to push traditionally Soviet or Russia-aligned states into the

US sphere of influence, including through artificial regime change. US actions in Kosovo, Iraq, Libya and Syria were viewed through this prism (unlike say US intervention in Sierra Leone, not a traditional Russian ally) and led to diplomatic and even military pushback, as determined by the limits of Russian power at the time. This explanation that it's not about NATO so much as what NATO represents, even civilisationally, explains why Russia meekly accepted Sweden and Finland joining NATO; because even if they were neutral, the Kremlin sees them as Western countries that do not belong to Russia's sphere of influence. What's more, if NATO membership was the immediate threat, then Russia behaved entirely counterintuitively, since its occupation of Crimea and Donbas in 2014 had put an effective stop to any formal entry of Ukraine into NATO because it would have required the politically unacceptable act of Kyiv giving up its claim to these territories.

In conclusion, any discussion that centres on NATO expansion as a key driver for Russia's invasion and/or insecurity is simplistic. The question of Ukraine's civilisational status is much more complex than a basic security buffer zone issue and instead goes to the heart of Russian identity, status-seeking and historical grievance. The NATO expansion question is also over-discussed compared to other Western failures to support not only Russia but other post-communist countries in terms of sociopolitical issues and even just by not facilitating the elites' corruption. Westerners, especially Americans, should not inflate their own countries' importance in determining Russian actions but, if they insist, then there is plenty of terrain to explore without having to crowd around the topic of NATO expansion. Moreover, any proper understanding of NATO's role in aggravating tensions with Russia should not start from the alliance's engagement with Georgia or Ukraine but rather from the Yugoslav wars, and especially the bombing of Yugoslavia in 1999 – a war that, if it is remembered at all in

London or Washington, is misremembered, despite its clear relevance to the conflict unfolding in Ukraine.

Kosovo

The bombing of Yugoslavia is a crucial point of departure in Russia's geopolitical mindmap. The mainstream Russian understanding of the 78-day conflict is quite different from that of many Western countries, who see it as a humanitarian intervention that prevented, or was even a response to, genocide. Western accounts place little emphasis on the lack of UN security council approval for the air strikes or on the loss of civilian lives. But if you look at история.рф, the Kremlin-funded most popular RuNet history portal, if it does say so itself, you will read that the crisis in Kosovo was caused not by Slobodan Milošević deliberately stirring up nationalist tensions but by the USA, with the support of NATO and some EU countries, who were exploiting Russia's post-Soviet weakness and destroying its longtime ally, Serbia.

It is hard to disagree with Fedor Lukyanov's analysis that 'in the West, they underestimate the role of Yugoslavia. Of course, first, the very fact that in peacetime there is bombing of a large European capital, it caused a lot of shock. None of us really believed in the official reasons, that the bombing was about the genocide of Kosovars. Nobody thought that was really happening. Second, Western colleagues can't understand our fixation on NATO; we have made it into a monster that threatens Russia. It is an exaggeration of course [on Russia's part] but Western analysis doesn't understand the expansion of NATO; the first phase of expansion began in February 1999, when Poland, Hungary and Czechia joined, the first three countries. Just two or three weeks later, NATO began the first military operation in its history. So with expansion, NATO went from a defensive to aggressive alliance. And you can explain until you are blue in the face about the difference between this or that war but it is a fact that NATO began to expand and then it began to go to war. It had never been to war before. So this claim we hear that NATO is a defensive alliance – that was only true during the Cold War. Since the Cold War, there's been Yugoslavia, Libya, Afghanistan and Iraq (sort of). That paranoia we have is not entirely without some foundation. I remember very well at the beginning of the 2000s, I was an editor of a journal and I often met students and school kids. And in the provinces, in places like Voronezh, there was always a question: 'Can NATO bomb us like they bombed Belgrade?' And I would answer: 'No, because we are a nuclear power' – but they would reply 'Ah that is why they want to build missile defence systems on our border.' And there is some logic there.'[32]

Even at the time, as noted by Andrei Tsygankov, Western and Russian media depicted very different images of the war in Kosovo.[33] The West's support for the Kosovo Liberation Army, whom they had previously classified as terrorists, at least until they were fighting against Yugoslav forces, led even democratically minded Russian opposition MPs to vehemently criticise Western actions in the Balkans. This sentiment grew stronger after NATO's bombing campaign against rump Yugoslavia in 1999, which forced Slobodan Milošević to negotiate. The resulting Kosovar autonomy led many Serb civilians to flee the province and facilitated the ethnic cleansing of Serbs. Although Russia contributed to an international effort to send peacekeepers to Kosovo, they openly supported the Yugoslav forces there and even stormed Pristina airport, preventing NATO planes from landing. Tactically pointless, this act was rich in symbolism, conveying both Russia's disagreement with NATO policy and a renewed desire to assert its interests. In this respect, it mirrored the now much-vaunted Primakov U-turn, when in March 1999 the then Foreign Minister Yevgeny Primakov ordered his flight back to Moscow *en route* to Washington DC after learning that NATO was beginning air strikes on Yugoslavia. Many Russians perceived NATO's actions as a deliberate humiliation and a denial of Russian status in the region and beyond.[34]

Over the last decade, with Russo–Serbian relations becoming much closer under Aleksandar Vučić, Russian politicians and state-aligned media have invoked their selective retelling of the Yugoslav wars to domestic audiences not so much as events in themselves but rather as symbols of Western untrustworthiness and of why Russia must assume a strong and aggressive position in the world. In this way, in domestic political discourse, the wars have transformed into a narrative of Russia's journey back to great power status through its recreation of a strong state, a journey dated to disagreements with Western powers over Kosovo and the 1999 NATO bombing of Yugoslavia.[35]

Before 2022, there were four main ways in which Russian media and politicians told the story of the Yugoslav wars:[36] Yugoslavia as the first colour revolution; Western exploitation of Russian weakness; the need for multipolarity to prevent Western dominance; and Western disregard for international law. During the Revolution of Dignity in 2013/2014, Russian elites invoked the wars in Yugoslavia as a precursor to State Department-backed colour revolutions. By contrast, in response to Western criticism of the annexation of Crimea, Russian politicians and media would bring up Western disregard for international law when they bombed Belgrade and/or recognised Kosovo.[37] As ever, Russia's leaders shifted their perspectives on the past to meet the political demands of the present.

This framing was not, primarily, designed to antagonise the West. It was largely for domestic consumption and aimed at rendering events in the Balkans an appropriate and relevant historical frame through which to interpret the West's actions and criticisms of Russia, namely as belonging to a pattern of dubious and nefarious behavior only made possible by the collapse of the USSR. For example, at the Valdai Discussion Club summit in 2017, Putin bemoaned the West's treatment of post-Soviet Russia, arguing that the former had spurned Russian openness and trust as it 'completely ignored our national interests [. . .] for example in the bombing of Yugoslavia and Belgrade, sending troops to Iraq and so on. And it is clear why: they looked at the state of our nuclear complex, our armed forces, our economy. Then international law looked unnecessary.'[38] This interpretation renders Yugoslavia the pivotal point in the degradation of Russia's relations with the West – as the place, in Putin's words, 'where it all began'.[39]

The Yugoslav wars remained a touchstone in Russian political analysis, with references increasing in times of good relations with Belgrade, albeit not really evolving. Then, in December 2021, in the run up to Russia's invasion, the topic of the Yugoslav wars and especially Kosovo began to be discussed in new ways. While all the references to Yugoslavia as the first colour revolution, Western exploitation of Russian weakness in the 1990s and the need for multipolarity to prevent Western dominance were there, there were also two new narratives. One related to Western atrocities and attacks on civilians during the bombing of Yugoslavia and the other could be described as 'Russia becomes the West.'

In this narrative, Putin and others self-consciously mirrored the language used by NATO leaders to justify bombing Yugoslavia; for example, in his 22 February address, in which he announced Russia's recognition of the Luhansk and Donetsk People's Republics, Putin used the NATO bombing of Yugoslavia and support for Kosovo as a touchpoint and justification.[40] This was not only about providing precedent but also about sending a message: if the West can redraw borders for Kosovo, then Russia can redraw borders for the Donetsk and Luhansk People's Republics in east Ukraine. In their speeches, the Chairwoman of the Federation Council, Valentina Matvienko, and the Foreign Minister, Sergei Lavrov, also invoked the NATO bombing as justification and precedent for Russia's moves to protect the population of the Donbas from a fictitious genocide.[41] This continued after the invasion, with RIA Novosti reporting how Putin explained the objectives of the 'Special Military Operation' to the UN General Secretary by 'reminding him of Kosovo and noting that Moscow [also] had the right to provide military aid to DPR and LPR'.[42]

While there was a soupçon of trolling to these comparisons, such statements were more substantive than mere 'whataboutism'. On one level, it was a statement that the West no longer had the exclusive power to redraw borders and change regimes, and on another it was a comment on the West's ideational supremacy – the appeal of its values to other countries, which the Russian leadership believed to be hollow, was revealed as little more than self-interest and profit-making. In Russia's 2022 retellings of the Yugoslav wars, it was demonstrating (to itself most of all) not only a return to great power status, which it had assured after its intervention in Syria, but an explicit undoing of the post-Cold War security architecture, crossing the threshold into a different world order, rather than simply straining or revising the current rules. This mirroring could be seen in the justification for Russian ground forces' invasion of Donbas to 'avert the risk of genocide'. The message was: Russia is back. You defined the order before but now we do. You thought you were exceptional but you weren't – we are.

Vladimir Putin is clearly quite personally troubled by American claims to exceptionalism. The historian Sergey Radchenko has written about how this preoccupation and effort to occupy the same space reminds him of the protagonist in Dostoevsky's *Crime and Punishment*, Rodion Raskolnikov, who struggles to rationalise the abominable to prove his own exceptionalism. 'Behind all this rhetoric lies Putin's preoccupation – an obsession even – with proving to others and, above all, to himself that he has the right to Ukraine, the right not in a moral-ethical sense, nor in any legal sense, but in Raskolnikov's sense: to bend down and pick up what was his because he dared to do what no one else did – openly challenge the US-led rules-based world order.'[43] The evolution of the Yugoslav wars analogies is the evolution of Kremlin spite and anger at hypocritical American exceptionalism into the demand that Russia too be recognised as exceptional – separated from the antheap of nations and crowned as a Napoleon.

Russophobia

On 1 March 2022, the University of Milan sent an email requesting that a set of four lectures on Dostoevsky be post-poned due to a desire to avoid 'disagreements' in the context of Russia's war on Ukraine. By 2 March 2022 this request had already been rescinded but, as so often with cancel culture lore, by then the story had taken on a life of its own, simultaneously feeding a paranoia that everyone is out to get Russians and a weird (for a country with censorship) obsession with Western cancel culture. The Kremlin has often used the latter to feed into alt-right Western narratives, as seen during Putin's 2021 Valdai speech and its fake outrage at the treatment of J. K. Rowling by some trans-rights activists.

Russian television news has sought to fuel a sense that Russians are being singled out for bullying. On Telegram, the 'cancel culture' of Russians only constituted two per cent of the overall content but, when channels are examined individually, it made up almost ten per cent of the content on the television news channel, Vesti. This reflected television's broader focus on Western Russophobia and also cancel culture, a continuation of a trend seen in television media in 2014, when news shows, such as Vesti nedeli and Voskresnoe vremya, devoted much more time than print or online media to the tearing down of statues and censure of all things Russian – even if it wasn't called 'cancelling' then. The TV narrative that radicals are demolishing history has only grown in prominence in Russian discourse and it has also become a more salient issue in Europe and the USA, where one can find similarly disproportionate reactions to the idea some people might want to remove a statue to this or that murderous historical figure. In all three regions, the prominence stems, in part at least, from the amount of media attention dedicated to these 'statue wars'. As Fedor Lukyanov said of the Russian case: 'They will show someone in Ukraine tearing down a Pushkin statue ten times every hour but you won't see those places where Pushkin stands unmolested. You get the idea that it is fuelled by the purest Russophobia.'[44]

The Russian government and media's responses to the removal of Pushkin statues or alterations of curricula on Russian literature are highly theatrical and often much more distressing than the original 'crime'. Tat'yana Moskal'kova, the Kremlin's human rights ombudswoman, who probably has other work to be getting on with, found the time to declare that 'Russophobia' abroad 'can only [be] compare[d] with the Holocaust'.[45] The Russian Ministry of Foreign Affairs shares her concern, even releasing a 160-page report 'On violations of the rights of Russian citizens and compatriots in foreign countries', which it claims are 'widespread' in the 'collective West'.[46] Politicians jump on any and every opportunity to tell Russians that the West hates them, citing cancelled invitations to Russian musicians, or measures that prevent Russians from receiving tourist visas in certain EU countries. The latter is a debate that has taken up energy much better used on asking why the West hasn't sanctioned numerous Wagner supplier companies, why Russian oligarch families are still holidaying in the EU, why Putin's friends still have EU citizenships, and why Gerhard Schroeder is still a standing member of Germany's governing party. Inevitably, the Russian response to the tourist-visa-ban debate has been entirely unhinged, from Dmitrii Medvedev trying to goad the EU into introducing prohibitions, so everyone can see how much Europeans hate Russians, to Maria Zakharova obliquely threatening a deliberate strike on Zaporizhzhia nuclear power plant, teasing darkly that people need visas but radiation does not.[47] Such hysteria is most likely aimed at encouraging visa bans, since they help to stem the number of people leaving and reinforce the Kremlin's depiction of a Russophobic West.

All this drama occludes the reality that nobody has cancelled more Russian culture than the Kremlin, whether by banning leading websites popularising Russian culture (Calvert Journal) or shutting down world-famous theatres like the Gogol Centre. These failings barely register. Instead, the focus remains on external prohibitions, which fuel a penchant for self-victimisation and martyrdom. The Russian Orthodox Church very much encourages this depiction of Russians as maligned and misunderstood; in the words of Patriarch Kirill: 'our Fatherland has never done anything wrong to anyone. The world is turning against us not because we are bad but because we are different and this otherness inspires hatred, envy and indignation.'[48] While such statements may cast aspersions on his suitability as a holy man, they reiterate Kirill's skill as a religious leader, painting everything in black and white, good versus evil, Russians versus Russophobes.

Anglo-Saksy

The blackest, most evil of Russophobes, are the *Anglo-Saksy* (Anglo-Saxons), without whom Russia would never have been forced, against its own ostensibly peaceable nature, to invade Ukraine. Rather than a 4chan theory about Æthelred the Unready's dastardly but (inevitably) ill-advised posthumous conspiracy against the Russian people, the term 'Anglo-Saksy' is used to refer, insultingly, to the US and UK and sometimes also Canada, Australia and New Zealand. The most Anglo-Saxon-ish of the Anglo-Saxons are the English. Timofei Bordachev, Programme Director of the Valdai Discussion Club and Professor at the Higher School of Economics, summarised the mixture of hatred and intrigue with which many Russians view England when he argued: 'it is hard to find in international politics a state that has brought as much evil to the rest of humanity as Britain. All of its history is a never-ending succession of wars and conspiracies in pursuit of a single aim: to derive personal benefit. But this same history also gives us examples of remarkable imagination, creativity and capability of the most reckless of adventures.'[49]

Dr Bordachev's article reflects an enduring and wide-ranging Anglophobia in Russian popular and academic culture from almost nightly primetime television caricaturist attacks on British politicians to the mainstreaming of La Rouche-ist conspiracies about the British Empire. Amusing in a ludicrous sort of way, Russia's preoccupation with perfidious Albion is also unnerving, given the comparative geopolitical irrelevance of Britain and also that the UK really hasn't done much harm to Russia. One interviewee, from the Russian Ministry of Foreign Affairs, quibbled with this portrayal, referencing the Murmansk Legion, a British unit that intervened unsuccessfully in the Russian Civil War in 1918–1919.[50] When I asked for a more recent example, he mentioned the 2021 Black Sea incident when a British destroyer sailed through waters that are legally Ukrainian but which Russia claims. He said that the incident did not 'amuse' the Kremlin. However, I imagine Putin was still marginally more amused than David Cameron was after Putin's minions shot down MH17, killing ten Britons, and the Russian president couldn't be bothered to pick up the phone. Or than Theresa May was when Putin's finest sports-drink salesmen splashed Novichok around Salisbury. Or than Tony Blair was when Putin's GRU goons dripped polonium across Mayfair.

Rather than discuss the Russian state's recent attacks on
the UK, my Russian interlocutors preferred to present their
conflict with Britain as residing in the two nations' mutually
exclusive natures. I discussed this issue with Fedor Gaida, a
history professor at Moscow State University who frequently
contributes to academic and religious publications. Professor
Gaida is not, by any stretch of the imagination, an Anglophile:

> At the beginning, Biden tried to find some small compromises
> with Russia but the English were totally against it, maximally
> uncooperative. In Russia, this war isn't seen as a Russia–
> Ukraine war, it is a seen as a more global event, and as a result
> of global events. In fact, it is seen as Russia against the West,
> only not quite the West, but more narrow than that. When
> Russia says it is against the West, they don't see the West as
> a unified phenomenon. In general, the idea is that it is a war
> against the USA and Britain, and that Ukraine is not seen as
> an independent actor in this struggle but as an instrument of
> the US and Britain, and actually more of Britain. It is a dan-
> gerous instrument, like a territory that isn't independent and
> so becomes a launchpad for aggression towards Russia, as a
> territory on which the whole political system is under total
> Anglo-Saxon control.

In Professor Gaida's view, Ukraine is unable to come out from
under that control on its own and Russia must fight these
Anglo-Saxon forces to free Ukraine. He claims that this belief
is not only his opinion but that of any thinking Russian, who
understands that this is a fight against the Anglo-Saxons, and
first and foremost the Brits.'[51]
I asked Fedor Lukyanov to explain this preoccupation with
the UK, but his good manners forced him to dissemble and
say something about differing conceptions of freedom before
joking that: 'when Russia goes, so will the last country who
still thinks Britain is a major power'.[52] Russians' widely held

dislike of Britain also links to differences in the way that history is taught and what is taught. There is a whole different book to be written on this topic but, as a subject, Russian schools teach history using a very applied methodology, in keeping with the tendency, perhaps in part a legacy from the teleology of Marxism, to present history as a 'truth' and to use historical analogies with gay abandon. The notion that nations are essentialist also features in Russian curricula in a way that would be unthinkable in contemporary Western academia; for example, students at the prestigious MGIMO, which functions as a feeder university for the MFA, take courses on 'ethnopolitical history', not a subject you are likely to find at Goldsmiths or UCL. In the case of Britain, Russian historians and history teachers usually assess the country through the nineteenth century, honing in on the Great Game, the Crimean War, and Britain's efforts to undermine the Concert of Europe. I learnt more about nineteenth-century British perfidy in five years of living in Russia than I had in twenty years of living in the UK.

There is a notably conspiratorial edge to Russians' views of Britain – and of much else besides[53] – such as the Golden Billion doomsday scenario in which powerful Western elites control world events to amass great wealth and destroy ordinary people's lives.[54] Endorsed by high-ranking officials, such as head of the security council, Nikolai Patrushev, a milder version of the plot is often used to explain how the UK is dictating global events. In the words of Fedor Gaida:

> Britain is trying to expand the conflict level in Europe in order for investment and capital to come to Britain. And there are very close relations between the British and today's Ukrainian elites. Zelensky is closer to Britain (than to America). And for this very reason, in Russia we consider Britain not exactly a more serious opponent, but a more existential one. When we talk about relations with the USA, in Russia we think that, yes, we are enemies now but if the USA becomes less powerful

then we can come to some agreement. So attitudes towards Americans, especially towards ordinary Americans are fine but attitudes towards Britain are different. Britain is seen as an existential enemy. Russians can love English culture, or music, films, they can walk about in English clothes but politically the main mass of Russian people see Britain as a force that is always trying to harm Russia and as a force that needs to be destroyed. This is an enemy with whom we cannot harmonise relations. Russians think England is an aggressor, that they are defending themselves and they need to solve this problem, Let's put it simply – while Britain exists and British politics exists, this will always be a problem for Russia.[55]

As he was talking, a moment flashed into my mind from 2014. I had woken up in my Moscow flat and checked my phone, where the top trending YouTube video (in Russia) was of a nuclear bomb attack on London and in my half-awake state I believed it was real.

These conspiratorial and apocalyptical parameters of Russian elite thinking are troubling and underestimated as drivers of Russian policy – especially given that they are prominently and openly held by Putin's closest advisers. Such views are also trenchant on the nationalist and Eurasianist right, popularised by the writer Aleksandr Dugin. In his work, Dugin expounds upon the theory of Eurasianism, which depicts Atlanticist forces as ranged against Eurasianists: two supercontinents, one land-based and one sea-based, locked in struggle. In this 'philosophy', Britain gave birth to the USA and so the USA is not independent but just an extension of the British mindset.[56] Consequently, British meddling is at the root of much that afflicts Russia and the world – from enabling elites to prosper at the expense of everyone else, to the staging of Bucha. Naturally, such theories tell us far more about how Russia sees itself than how it sees Britain, or how Britain is. Yet, while I doubt most Russians know, let alone subscribe to the particulars of Eurasianism or the 'golden billion' plot, the depiction of Britain and the USA as representative of mercantile, de-racinated forces at odds with Russia's deeper, more spiritual and meaningful power, does resonate. This resonance is reinforced by the civilisational terms used in Russian media to describe the current conflict.

Clash of civilisations

The dominant Russian attitude towards the West is not one of hatred, so much as a contemptuous sense of superiority fed by an inferiority complex. Speaking to the exceptionally popular YouTube interviewer, Yurii Dud, Russia analyst Aleksandr Baunov, described this perspective succinctly: 'Russians believe that the West is richer than us not because they are better but because they are worse. They might be richer or stronger but we have truth.'[57] This harks back to a longstanding self-perception that Russians are more spiritual and sincere than the materialistic and rationalist West. Ostensibly, they prize moral justice over legal justice.

Vladimir Orlov's explanation of why Russia will win in Ukraine is a classic of this genre (we spoke before the Ukrainians liberated Kherson in November 2022):

> Because the moral right is on our side, because the Ukrainian people, although brainwashed strongly for the last thirty years, although brainwashed partly by the Germans, by the Nazis, for quite a few years, they will realise that truth and justice are more important than narrow recognition of one's nation state. It will be difficult and it will not apply to all of Ukraine but still . . . the best example now is Kherson. I will not be pushing for [us to take] the whole of Ukraine. The point is not that Russia should invade the whole country and impose its own rule. Russia is not the United States, Russia will not behave like the

Americans behaved in Iraq, where they arrived and used divide
and rule. We will not pit the Catholics against the Orthodox,
like the Americans did with the Sunni and Shia. We will not do
aerial bombardments like the Americans did in Iraq. I know
there are some issues, with shopping centres,[58] I register that,
but if Russia had wanted to win just by military force we could
have done that easily. With lots of loss of human life in Ukraine
but easily.[59]

Like real Communism, it would appear that winning the war
simply has never been tried.

Rooted in the sociopolitical realities of Russia and its
intellectual and political evolution, the argument that Russia
should not pursue a similar path of development to the West
has a long history, from Catherine the Great's naive defence
of Russia in her letter to Voltaire[60] to Putin's 2007 Munich
Speech, in which he criticised the US-led world order. Putin's
post-2007 differentiation of Russia from the West and shift
towards civilisational discourse is explained in part by his
inability to reconcile Russia's interests within the Western-led
liberal order, which made allowances for Iraq and the War
on Terror but not for the wars in Chechnya or the targeting of journalists. It was also fuelled by a sense that the USA
was interfering in Russia and its 'zone of influence' in eastern
Europe by sponsoring civil society initiatives.

Many Russians view their anti-Westernism not as latent or
innate but defensive in nature. As Dmitri Trenin explained:

> Some say that the West is trying to subjugate Russia culturally,
> to conquer or snuff out the soul of the nation and therefore the
> Russian World has to be defended in those places where it has
> historically existed, like Ukraine and Belarus. This isn't about
> the superiority of Russian culture, although it is just taken for
> given that it is a lot higher and deeper than the primitive mass
> culture of the West, a civilisation of consumption, modern

gender innovations and so on, but rather about the defence [of Russian culture] from attack by this powerful and aggressive 'cultural weed'.[61]

This need to protect Russian culture also permeates the 2021 National Security Strategy and feeds into a concept voiced by Putin and other leading politicians and intellectuals that Russia is uniquely in touch with its own culture and history – a concept I describe as cultural consciousness – and so is well-placed to save the world, especially continental Europe, from the cultural weed of Americanism.[62]

Confidence in the West's degeneracy was central to the Kremlin's calculations when invading Ukraine. The Russian leadership evidently believed the West had abandoned all sense of morality and would allow Russia to invade and occupy Ukraine, prioritising money and comfort above Ukrainian sovereignty. As Fedor Gaida explained to me:

> Russia wouldn't have gone to war if it didn't believe that the West was on the verge of collapse – cultural, economic and geopolitical. Putin didn't just decide to attack Ukraine – it is part of a very large policy – Ukraine is just one element, right now it is the most important one, but Putin's higher idea (*sverkhideya*) is to chase the English and Americans out of continental Europe. He wants Ukraine free of Anglo-Saxons and continental Europe free of Anglo-Saxons. It doesn't mean he will attack all of Europe but he considers that in Ukraine the problem will be resolved by military action and in Europe by the crisis that is coming. That is, in Russia they are certain Europe is on the verge of a very serious crisis, with energy, with food, and that this crisis will come this year.[63]

There is an established Russian tradition of predicting the demise of the West, from the Slavophiles' confidence in Western decay in the early nineteenth century to the Soviets waiting for global Communist revolution in the 1920s. Nor were they alone in such prognoses; in the evocative phrase of historian Michael Kimmage, the West is the 'empire upon which the sun is always setting'.[64] This is at least part of the reason why Putin remained confident that Russia could outlast the West even after seeing that Western resolve and support for Ukraine would be more solid than predicted. Other reasons included the confidence that Russia(ns) care more about Ukraine and they comprise a morally robust civilisation-state capable of renewal and fortitude. Natalia Sevagina, the art historian, encapsulated this idea when I asked her how she thought the war would end:

> It will end with the victory of truth, like Russian history always ends. It is always difficult but it always ends in truth, in the law of truth. In Russia truth is beauty and it will prevail. Western Europe is in crisis but Russian consciousness still has the potential to survive if it can get away from these European surroundings. They have given up on their values, they have dechristianisation even though without Christianity Europe doesn't exist. Europe has rejected its soul, its ideal. People who are against this war are those people who are not people of the spirit but people of the material world, but for Russian civilisation, the material is always secondary to the spiritual.[65]

The Russian Orthodox Church adds further legitimacy to this sense that Russia's war on Ukraine carries religious or spiritual connotations and consequences. Russian Orthodox priests have referred to the fighting as a 'holy war' and even as a defence of the entire Russian Christian world, seemingly untroubled by the fact that Muslim extremist battalions like Ahmat are doing a fair amount of the fighting. It is interesting to imagine what Jesus might think of that, just as it is interesting to think what the former Soviet foreign minister, Vyacheslav Molotov, a fierce proponent of atheism, would think of his grandson and deputy of the State Duma, Vyacheslav Nikonov, claiming that 'in the modern world, Russia is the embodiment of the forces of good. This is a metaphysical clash between the forces of good and evil. This is truly a holy war we're waging and we must win.'[66] As if this language were not striking enough, a brief perusal of the religious Orthodox channels on Russian television takes this self-righteous messianism yet further, with discussions of exorcism, and Christian rituals, to rid Ukraine of its demons and the beasts of Azov. The guests and hosts on the Spas Orthodox channel frequently discuss apocalypse, hunger and war before lunch, then move onto their core idea that Russia embraces a vaguely defined 'spiritualism' ('*dukhovnost*') that stands in opposition to an anarchic, godless West, cut loose from its moral, ethical and religious foundations.[67]

Embracing 'desatanisation' crusades, Russian politicians have sought to depict Russia's global role as almost counter-revolutionary, leading the defence of the 'true' Europe, traditional values and 'cultural sovereignty'. This last phrase peppers the 2021 National Security Strategy, especially the section entitled: 'The defence of traditional Russian spiritual and moral values, culture, and historical memory'. Here, the vocabulary, if not the prose style, is borrowed from Dostoevsky, claiming that these traditional values 'are subject to active attacks from the USA and its allies' who propagandise for a society where 'anything is permitted'. To understand Russian confidence in Western degradation, it is useful to address the idea of *passionarnost,* created by the twentieth-century Soviet historian and philosopher of Eurasianism, Lev Gumilev. It denotes a nation's, or people's, ability to forge onwards, making sacrifices to reach the climax of its powers, when great conquests are both possible and necessary. In February 2021, one year before the invasion, Putin affirmed his belief in *passionarnost* and argued that Russia as a country had yet to reach this highest point, whereas the West had passed its peak and now wallowed in inertia and decline.[68]

On 4 July 2022, RIA Novosti even published an article entitled 'America celebrates one of its last ever Independence Days'.[69] The disorderly withdrawal from Afghanistan certainly contributed to this analysis in the public sphere, as when Timofei Bordachev argued in June 2022 that Ukrainian statehood would wither and require more and more support from the West just like in Afghanistan.[70] Or when, one year prior, in 2021, during America's chaotic withdrawal from Kabul, the Russian media drew interesting parallels between Afghanistan and Ukraine and Western activity in both. For instance, on 16 August 2021, Igor Korotchenko, a 'foreign-policy expert' on the political talk show '60 Minutes', abruptly pivoted from a discussion on Afghanistan's illicit drug trade to accuse President Volodymyr Zelensky of substance abuse.[71] As discussed in the coming chapter, this sense of being on drugs, or in some way unable to assess reality – dementia, drugs, brainwashing – is a common trope in Russian media, as they try to convince audiences that their version of reality is the correct one. It is also part of the media's obsession with debauchery, as evidence of Western decadence, which often descends into such detailed descriptions that it starts to beg the question of how these moral stalwarts came to understand so much about gay sex parties or cocaine-fuelled sex workers. The salacious mind boggles.

6

The Ukrainophobes

By framing their slaughter of Ukrainians in moralistic language as a 'war with the West for a new international order', pro-war Russians can pretend that they are not fighting Ukraine but on Ukraine's behalf, liberating them from Anglo-Saxons and nationalists. They have been indulged in this depiction by others for whom this 'Russia versus the West' framing is convenient. This includes numerous Westerners, from restraint-professing Realists to more hawkish interventionists, who both discuss the war as if it were purely a proxy war, a reaction to Western overreach or, alternatively, an overdue last-ditch defence of Western values. In this way, Ukraine is decentred from a war that is explicitly about destroying its very existence and in which tens of thousands of Ukrainians have died over the last eight years.

Ukraine and Ukrainians are the missing link in so much Western analysis and virtually all Russian analysis. Many people underestimated Ukrainian society's courage, resilience and competence, but Ukrainians are the reason that this war cannot end in success for Russia. The other, no less insurmountable, reason is because Russia is trying to destroy an idea. For all the claims of fighting the West, my analysis of

Russian social media tells a different, more complicated story about who Russians think/know they are fighting and why. If Russian state television focuses its endless ire on the 'war with the West', the social media channels of Telegram present a different version, much closer to reality, in which it is clear that this is a war not only *about* Ukraine but *against* Ukraine and Ukrainians. For example, words about Ukraine are used 5.5 times more than any variants of words about the West and three times more than words relating to the USA/America. However much Russians might want to pretend they're fighting the West, we can be sure that the tens of millions of Russian Telegram users know perfectly well that they are destroying Ukrainian cities, fighting the Ukrainian army, and killing Ukrainian civilians. But admitting that means admitting Ukraine exists in its own right.

No agency for Ukraine

Addressing a general reluctance to view Russo–Ukrainian relations through a postcolonial lens, the academic and translator Uilleam Blacker has warned that, 'Russia's refusal, over the centuries, to perceive or hear Ukraine, to accept Ukraine's existence on its own terms, lies at the foundation of Putin's aggression.'[1] The refusal to accept Ukraine as it really is can be traced through the prism of Russian views of Zelensky. This is a man whom Russians expected to flee, a man being hunted by the world's second largest army as some of his own colleagues turned their coats, a man who had Russian divisions bearing down on Kyiv and Kremlin staff calling to dictate surrender terms. In the panic of that chaos, with the American president offering to extract him, the Ukrainian president replied: 'I need ammunition not a ride' and filmed himself strolling through the government quarter of Kyiv with his closest advisers. He is a hero.

Yet Russians refuse to see this Zelensky. Every one of my pro-war Russian interviewees, and all of the pro-war Telegram channels I analysed, depicted Zelensky as a nobody, a puppet, or someone who, according to Modest Kolerov, would become 'pro-Russian without much hesitation if told to'.[2] There is a common view among nationalists and Eurasianists that Zelensky is a British agent. I heard many similar claims along the lines of Fedor Gaida's: 'I believe Zelensky received British citizenship recently and has personal guarantees from the British government and the essence of these guarantees is: you can fight to the last Ukrainian, have no mercy, you can fight to the last man and when it is no longer possible to fight, then you can run here to London and we'll look after you.'[3] When I mentioned that Zelensky was genuinely popular in Britain and that British people liked him, Professor Gaida said that he believed me but that he was equally sure we Britons would shoot Zelensky in the head without a moment's hesitation should the need arise.

Russian interviewees profess an image of Ukraine (and of gun-toting Britons) that nobody who has spent considerable time in the country would recognise. One junior academic from the city of Belgorod on the Ukrainian border, explained how 'Zelensky has put in place a personal dictatorship, shutting down television channels[4] to repress the political opposition, to criminalise everything.'[5] Another Russian interviewee, whose deceased father was from Chernihiv, complained of how 'since 2021, Zelensky has ruled Ukraine with laws taken by the national security council, a small group of people who set up a personal dictatorship with no government involvement. Zelensky exploited the fact his party dominated parliament and effectively criminalised any other party.'[6] Neither comment is true but, even if they were, it is hard to accept that such criticism is offered in good faith when neither cared about the lack of democracy in occupied Ukraine, or indeed in Russia.

Another dogged criticism of the Ukrainian President is that he is a drug addict, something many Russians appear to believe both literally but also metaphorically, as if it were representative of the health of Ukraine and its leadership: weak mindless junkies. As Vadym Prystaiko noted acidly: 'Russians believed Ukrainians were worth nothing, just CIA operatives, paid by the State Department. They called us the 'Washington *obkom*', they had that obsession with those stupid cookies.[7] They believed their own propaganda and didn't believe Ukrainians could make it on their own.'[8]

Russia's refusal to afford Ukrainians agency is replicated in its administration of the occupied territories since at least August 2014. For example, in June 2022, on orders from Moscow, the DPR head Denis Pushilin fired his government and replaced the cabinet with several former Russian state officials, including Alexander Kostomarov, the ex-deputy governor of Russia's Lipetsk and Ulyanovsk regions, and Vitaly Khotsenko, Russia's former Industry and Trade Ministry department head. Kostomarov in particular has a reputation as a bulldozer who gets the job done no matter what. Ever since the full-scale invasion, tensions between the population of the DPR and LPR, their pseudo-governments, and Moscow have mounted in proportion to the conscription rate. As early as March, D/LPR officials began press-ganging men into the military, catching anyone who looked eligible and packing them off to the front. At the beginning of the war, I spoke to one family in Donbas who were hiding their fourteen-year-old son, keeping him home from school, after two of his classmates had disappeared and allegedly been sent to the front to serve as cannon fodder against their co-citizens. I have not been able to re-establish contact with them since March.

Russia has wreaked untold misery and suffering upon all Ukraine, but there is something particularly tragic about their treatment of ordinary citizens in Donbas. In 2014, Russia sent in armed thugs to exploit and militarise people who felt unwanted, derided, left behind. Whether pro-European politicians made enough effort to appeal to this constituency is certainly a question worthy of debate; the fact that Russia's armed invasion in 2014 made life infinitely worse for the people living in Donbas is not – it is indisputable. In the words of one Petersburger with extended family in the Donbas:

> I feel terribly sad for the Donbas people. They are abandoned by all, used for games. I can't stop thinking of the Alley of Angels, those are real children killed in a war that isn't their fault. They had an exhibition to the children in Petersburg – with all these pictures of their lovely little faces. I looked at each of them and I tried to imagine what toys they liked, were they good at school. I was there for ages, forty minutes, maybe longer, and in all that time, nobody stopped. I wanted to scream at all of them walking past but I didn't, I just smoked.[9]

Ukraine doesn't exist

In a speech marking the recognition of the D/LPR on 21 February 2022, Vladimir Putin asserted that Ukraine is an illegitimate country that exists on land that's historically and rightfully Russian, adding that 'Ukraine actually never had stable traditions of real statehood.'[10] Such comments built on a 2021 essay, where Putin described Ukraine in its legally recognised borders as an 'anti-Russia project' and denied Ukrainians' existence as an independent people.[11] The Russian military promptly included this essay on their list of mandatory works to study.[12]

The article, entitled 'On the historical unity of Russians and Ukrainians', provided a very Russified interpretation of Ukrainian history, in which Putin depicted Ukraine as a non-nation, a region, a subset of Russia. 'The name "Ukraine" was used more often in the meaning of the Old Russian word "okraina" (periphery), which is found in written sources from the twelfth century, referring to various border territories', he opined. 'And the word "Ukrainian", judging by archival documents, originally referred to frontier guards who protected the external borders.' But this is nothing more than a non-linguist's uninformed opinion on etymology, given there is considerable dispute among experts as to whether the name in fact comes from the word for 'oukraina', which means territory.

More insidious than such distortions, or even than the offhand way in which Putin justifies cruel repressions of Ukrainian culture, or of absences, like the Holodomor (referred to as a common tragedy of famine), was the way in which the Russian president travelled back through time to weave a narrative in which Ukraine is not an identity but a weapon. For example, writing about the nineteenth century, he claims: 'the idea of Ukrainian people as a nation separate from the Russians started to form and gain ground among the Polish elite and a part of the Malorussian intelligentsia. Since there was no historical basis – and could not have been any, conclusions were substantiated by all sorts of concoctions, which went as far as to claim that the Ukrainians are the true Slavs and the Russians, the Muscovites, are not. Such "hypotheses" became increasingly used for political purposes as a tool of rivalry between European states.'[13] Two sources with experience of ghost-writing essays for Kremlin elites confirmed that Putin was active in editing and rewriting this particular article, which reflected his view that European powers turned Ukraine's existence into an 'anti-Russia' by distorting its national history – hence his desire to set the record straight in this essay and through the war

I often think about this essay. Speaking with a prominent Ukrainian intellectual after a roundtable on memory politics in late 2021, she asked me for my thoughts on the essay and why Putin wrote it. I said two things: one, that his writing it, as with the WWII essay, was further evidence he really does believe these revanchist historicised views of the world; and two, that I was baffled as to the intended audience. The content was too obvious and dull for Russians – they have heard it all before and in much more entertaining guises; it was too esoteric for Western audiences; so perhaps it was intended for Ukrainians? But that made little sense either, since clearly such an essay would enrage sooner than appeal to Ukrainians. Still, as I walked home, I thought that Ukrainians were the most likely target audience and wondered at Putin's detachment from reality if he really thought he could appeal to any kinship of nations after all the suffering he had inflicted on Ukraine.

In hindsight, I should have dwelt further on that conclusion. Putin's essay, together with the 2021 National Security Strategy, were warning signals, not just of impending Russian aggression but also of Putin, and his advisers', isolation from reality. At the time, it was too hard to believe Russia had underestimated Ukraine and the West so much, and it was too easy to dismiss the odd claims as rhetorical devices. As Fedor Lukyanov, argues: 'It is strange we didn't expect it because if we go to Putin's essay, that he wrote, well published, on Ukraine in summer 2021, it delivers a strong historical foundation as to why Russia and Ukraine are one people. He says very clearly we consider it is one nation, any divisions are artificial, we can recognise the presence of two states but there are conditions: these two states can co-exist if one remains friendly but if one becomes hostile, like the anti-Russia stated there, then that state won't exist. As simple as that. He says the reason very directly.'[14]

Others have put it more directly still, like when Sergei Lavrov argued that 'Ukraine tried to build up its sovereignty through the rejection of its own history. Ukraine has no history of her own without the Russian nation.'[15] These views filter into a mocking denigration of Ukrainian culture and history across society, albeit in different forms. Some Telegram users, especially on the nationalist wings, refer to Ukraine as country-404

– a reference to the internet's '404 Page Not Found' error. One of Russia's largest textbook printers, Prosveshcheniye ('Enlightenment'), has ordered editors to purge positive references to Ukraine from schoolbooks on history, literature and geography.[16] Meanwhile, viewers learn from television that the Ukrainian language, history and religion are 'concocted' and Russian troops are fighting for 'their land' in Ukraine.[17] In the Russian view, these aren't two legitimate competing visions of Ukrainian-ness: one is true and the other is dangerously false.

But that isn't how nations work; they are always imagined communities, bonded together by a constantly evolving mishmash of history, ideology, religion, shared values, shared aspirations, language and beyond.[18] Their imagined-ness does not make nations any less real, or meaningful, but this constructivist view of the nation is at odds with the primordialist perspective, in which the nation is something racial or essentialist. The Kremlin's need to enforce a more primordial view of nationhood, its refusal to accept that Ukrainians have created their own bonds and national community, bred an ignorance that directly undermined its war effort. For example, even at the end of 2022 it was common to read on pro-war Telegram channels, or hear from pro-war supporters, that Ukraine could be divided into the pro-Russian East and South against the anti-Russian western part of the country. Take these words from one Moscow think tanker: 'Ukraine couldn't become whole, it was too divided. It is a country of regions, where the West and East never found dialogue. The West was stronger politically and the South-East economically and this not only weakened Ukraine but started to destroy it so that it all ended in 2014 with blood, and after 2014 today's events became almost inevitable.'[19]

Such outdated analysis played a central role in the Kremlin's plans for invasion and occupation. Russia's leaders believed that people in Zaporizhzhia and Kherson are Ukrainian if they have Ukrainian TV but once Russian TV is working, they will be Russian. Views on what to do with central Ukraine are more complicated, admittedly; I spoke to several foreign-policy advisers who were willing to concede to Ukrainians a small neutral state around Kyiv, provided it were dependent on Moscow's whim. Most Russian elites are outright hostile towards western Ukraine in a way that, oddly, means it would do best of all in this imagined scenario and be allowed its independence.[20]

The 'divided Ukraine' thesis has some basis, albeit a largely outdated one, especially since 2019 when Zelensky won the presidential elections with majority support in all but one region of Ukraine. As in any country, there are myriad divisions in Ukraine, but the east–west split, while politically lucrative for politicians eager to play to their base, is a simplification of a country with numerous languages, ethnicities and cultural legacies. Moreover, many of those Ukrainians who still harboured pro-Russian attitudes before February 2022, have now been brutally disabused of their sympathies.

Not only people but also institutions have followed this trajectory. If, previously, religion in Ukraine cemented and reflected national divisions, then since 2022 it has served to illustrate rupture with Russia. Broadly speaking, most of Ukraine is Orthodox Christian, although there are three west Ukrainian provinces dominated by the Ukrainian Greek Catholic Church, which follows Byzantine rites but is in full communion with the Catholic Church. Before the full-scale invasion, the Orthodox Church was split between the Ukrainian Orthodox Church, which was loyal to the Moscow Patriarchate and the Ukrainian Orthodox Church loyal to Kyiv, which gained autocephaly in 2020. The former was one of Russia's last bastions of influence in Ukraine – but now even they have rejected Moscow and Patriarch Kirill, destroying the last remnants of Russia claims about 'brother nations'. Described in Russian state media as a decision taken under pressure from the authorities, the actual reason for the break was the Patriarch's abandonment, even celebration, of violence against its own flock, as when Russian forces shelled Sviatohirsk Lavra, perhaps the holiest Orthodox site in eastern Ukraine, killing four monks in June 2022.

Spurred on to ever ghastlier atrocities by its need to possess Ukraine, Russia's arrogance towards its neighbour reflects the weakness of its own self-identity and the flimsiness of the bonds that cohere its people, in whom the Kremlin places very little trust or agency. Under Putin, the Russian elites have tried to enforce an essentialist vision of a never-changing historical Russia, an exceptional land with a mission to lead others in developing cultural self-consciousness. Ukraine is central to that vision and Ukraine's own identity and national renewal represents a direct challenge to Russia's conception of its nationhood. In Russia, this is not a controversial view; for example, in an interview with an official working for the Ministry of Culture, in which we discussed his role creating historical projects and initiatives, he stated outright:

> the obsession with streamlining history is so all-encompassing because they worry there is nothing there. Ever since Yeltsin there has been this struggle to articulate: why does Russia exist, why should it exist? And against the backdrop of separatism, which are issues that could flare up, this is an essential question. After the USSR collapsed, we could not cohere our people around rejecting the Soviet experience, people didn't buy that it was something done to them, not by them. And so we didn't have an idea, because we have so many different nations and languages and time zones – how do you bring that together? Those in power had no idea but we couldn't go on that way. Russia is not Canada – we need something to justify our existence. So they turned to history to ignite patriotism, to the Great Patriotic War in particular but also to some imperial paradigms, particularly around Ukraine, Novorossiya and so on.[21]

Stalked by the fear that Russia, rather than Ukraine, does not exist as a viable nation, Russian elites construct their identity on a sense of Russia as a great power, for which it needs, at a minimum, to be able to trace lineage to Kyivan Rus', and show it can control 'lesser' neighbours. In other words, Russian nationhood, as imagined by Putin, depends on suffocating and swallowing Ukrainian nationhood; hence, the prominence of symbolic politics in the newly occupied territories. In Mariupol, rather than rebuild the sewage system or repair traffic lights, the Russian occupation authorities spent the first two weeks dismantling Ukrainian language signs and concocting nightmarish visions of a land destroyed. Hennadiy Maksak recounted the following story from his colleague:

> She was in occupation in Mariupol, but she wasn't able to evacuate beforehand. She found a *marshrutka* in the end but only once it was already difficult to get out.[22] By the time she got out, she thought there was no Ukraine. Occupation troops had told her 'what Ukraine are you talking about? There is no Kyiv, there are no other Ukrainian cities. There's nowhere to go. Out of eighty people on the bus, she was the only one to travel to government territory because she has a son in Kyiv and he told her to come. Everyone else went to Crimea because they thought there was no Ukraine anymore. These are the psychological processes of the special operation in occupied territories, making people doubt everything.[23]

From the accounts of those released from Russian captivity, the occupying forces used psychological tortures to attack the foundations of people's national identity and sense of self. This has included forcing prisoners to meet guards with pioneer salutes and making POWs sing the Russian national anthem.[24] Perhaps the grisliest of such tactics has been the Russian government's kidnapping of Ukrainian orphans. In assaulting demonstrations of Ukrainian-ness, Russians only reinforce Ukrainian identity, unleashing a cycle of destruction, insecurity and hatred.

Vilifying Ukraine

'*Ne-za-leeeezh-na*'. The word means independent in Ukrainian but not the way Russian TV presenter Vladimir Solovev says it, in his thick Russian accent, dripping with condescension. When he says it, with a cruel sarcasm, the word denotes a Ukraine that is not only not independent but that has no right to be so. Like Solovev, many ordinary Russians casually treat the Ukrainian language as if it were just a Polonised dialect of Russian or an accident of the unfortunate division of Ukraine from its Russian brethren. The derision is symptomatic of the snobbery and ignorance of Ukrainian culture that rendered Russia's three-day operation to take Kyiv a failure before it even started.

In his conversation with me, when Vadym Prystaiko recalled his formative years in the Ukrainian Soviet Socialist Republic, he stressed the extent to which large numbers of Ukrainians had internalised Russians' dismissive attitude to Ukrainian identity:

> if you are educated in Ukraine you will speak Russian. Ukrainians were ghettoed in the villages, immediately categorised as rednecks because they were the only ones who spoke Ukrainian, and obviously it wasn't literary Ukrainian. To show you were well educated, you were high class, you had to speak Russian and so most things were produced in Russian, because people wanted to show they spoke Russian. When I was in school, in our internal passport, parents would write Russian for their children rather than Ukrainian.[25] Why write Ukrainian? Everyone understood it was better to be Russian than Ukrainian.[26]

The Prystaikos were one of the few families that insisted on writing Ukrainian in their passports but such families were treated with suspicion.

When the Soviet Union collapsed, activists and cultural figures worked to promote Ukrainian identity and culture, including through language laws designed to promote the use of Ukrainian in the public sphere. Russian propaganda channels at home and abroad have successfully cast these efforts as the 'banning of the Russian language' but this is a drastic exaggeration, even if you find some of Ukraine's post-2014 language laws heavy-handed.[27] The only authorities banning language learning on the territory of Ukraine are the Russian occupation authorities; upon annexing Crimea in 2014, Russian officials immediately set about excluding the Ukrainian language from the school curriculum. Moreover, nobody has done more to damage the status of the Russian language in Ukraine than the Russians themselves. In response to the 2022 invasion many Russian-speaking Ukrainians have switched to Ukrainian as their main language, a shift that many Russians have taken as a personal offence. For example, when the popular Ukrainian YouTuber Slidan, who normally communicates in Russian, posted a video in Ukrainian, his Russian audience exploded in anger, accusing him of racism and calling Ukrainian a swine language.

These responses are reflective of generalised characterisations of Ukrainians in Russian popular culture that exist on a spectrum from chauvinistic condescension to bloodthirsty racism. Again, Russia's leaders' insistence on Ukrainian shortcomings blinded them to their strengths, contributing to the 'special military operation's' failure. Despite FSB polling in 2021 revealing that even in eastern Ukraine, 71.1 per cent of people would view the arrival of Russian troops as an 'occupation' instead of 'liberation', this intelligence did not feature in the Kremlin's war calculations, perhaps because of the cronyism that rattles around the Russian power vertical or perhaps because the elites were not willing to hear it.

In conversations with me, numerous Russian officials, advisers and think tankers have intimated that Putin envisaged the special military operation as a more complex version of the January 2022 peacekeeping operation led by Russia in Kazakhstan. When riots began in Kazakhstan, the Collective Security Treaty Organisation, an alliance of post-Soviet states led by Russia, landed troops, took the main cities back under control and restored order within the week. According to one official, the plan was for Russian forces, backed up by military administrators, to make for Kyiv as quickly as possible. They would be accompanied by internal troops who would impose order on the city after Zelensky had fled, while the occupying authorities imposed a 'neutral' government. Ukraine would be demilitarised, and the 'anti-Russian, Banderite ideology would be rendered obsolete' with most of this work carried out by the Ukrainians themselves, pleased to be liberated, and then the 'Russian troops would go home after a few months, maximum four.'[28]

Of course, the actual invasion did not go according to plan. When I asked them why, my pro-war Russian interviewees were loathe to afford the Ukrainians even a begrudging respect. There was almost no recognition of Ukrainian military valour, ordinary heroism and resilience. Perhaps the most ungenerous of my interviewees was Fedor Gaida. His interpretation of the war inverted the common understanding that in trying to take Kyiv, Russian forces aimed too high from the start of the war. Instead, Fedor Gaida argued:

Russia understood its limited approach at the start hadn't worked, so from March they launched a full-scale war where the main aim was to destroy the Ukrainian army, that is, all battle-capable troops of Ukraine on the left bank of the Dniepr river, especially in Donbass. During this coming summer (2022), these troops will cease to exist. Some will be killed, some captured, some injured. But the battle-capable army of Ukraine will not exist after this summer. Approximately half of it has been destroyed already and the other half will be destroyed this summer. Although they are fighting pretty well, especially those who were mobilised in the south-east as those soldiers are in fact Russian. So right now Russians fight Russians. This is a civil war and civil war is always the most tragic.

Alas for Professor Gaida, his predictions did not wear the test of time, although the notion that, if Ukrainians do something well, it is because they are Russian is a rationalisation also found in the pro-war media.[29]

Such arguments betray the Russians' reluctance to take Ukrainians seriously. I probed this disdain with the veteran analyst Dmitri Trenin, asking whether he accepted the interpretation that the failure in Ukraine stemmed from Russians' underestimation of Ukraine. He said:

In Russian society at the very beginning there was disappointment linked to the fact that the operation was dragging on, that Kiev and Kharkov weren't taken and so on. The propaganda had for too long projected this image of a weak and half-collapsed Ukraine and had spoken too little about the real makeup of Ukraine, its society, ideology, army. From the military point of view, a small number of Russian troops (100,000 or around that)[30] didn't have any chance of taking a three-million-person city like Kiev. It would appear their aim was two-fold: to frighten the Kiev authorities into running away (that didn't work out) and to direct some forces away from Donbass and the South (this, clearly, did work out). The same was true for Kharkov. Taking a big modern city is an unbelievably difficult thing. In 2004 the American army stormed Falluja for six weeks in Iraq. There is another approach: at first to destroy and then to take (as happened in Mosul and Rakka). It's clear that this variant was not suitable for Kharkov.[31]

Dr Trenin's version of events should be treated sceptically; there is considerable evidence that the Kremlin expected the initial attacks on Kyiv and Kharkov to be successful, such as the types of troops sent (which included administrators), the pre-prepared medals for taking these cities, and leaked articles celebrating their conquest.

In my interviews, it was striking that many Russians appeared incapable of factoring in the Ukrainian people and army as a variable in their analysis. The policy elites rarely engaged with, or even acknowledged, the fierce Ukrainian resistance to Russia's invasion. For example, in my interview with Dmitri Trenin, he remained unconvinced by Ukrainian resistance to Russian aggression: 'There weren't any flowers for the liberators [Russians]. Pro-Russian forces in the Ukraine have traditionally been less passionate than pro-Western forces. On the other hand, there is no anti-Russian partisan movement on the territories controlled by the Russian army, which many – in the West especially – expected.'[32] As noted on page 65, as some official sources confirmed disappointment at the smaller than expected initial scale of armed (as opposed to civilian) resistance in Kherson, from May 2022 onwards there was an uptick in violent resistance, often in the form of car bombings and assassinations of collaborators.

Ukrainian resistance in the occupied territories and beyond was fuelled by anger at the Russian invasion and by the anarchic cruelty accompanying that invasion. Many of the Ukrainians I spoke to were understandably traumatised by the war and could not be included in this work except to direct my understanding of what was happening on-the-ground, and allow me to identify common themes and patterns in their understanding of the war, its causes and consequences. From these conversations, I was struck by how often Ukrainians referred to audio clips of Russian soldiers released by Ukrainian authorities. Such intercepts, impossible to independently verify, allegedly come from calls and messages between soldiers and their loved ones. In one intercept, a soldier's girlfriend gives him permission to rape Ukrainian women. In another, a Russian woman discussed how she would torture and kill Ukrainian children if she had her way. 'I would inject them with drugs, look in their eyes and say die, suffer.' Even though they were witnessing the evil of war with their own eyes, it seemed that many Ukrainians were still horrified at how civilians, especially women, sitting in safety, could wish such violence on them and their children. While one must be cautious as to the authenticity of these intercepts, their effect on many Ukrainians has been profound, especially when combined with the Russian media onslaught.

Regardless of authenticity, it is not so very hard for Ukrainians to believe Russians would urge horrific crimes in private when such terrible insults are aired publicly on Russian television every day; for example, when the military analyst Vasily Fatigarov compares Ukraine to a cancerous tumour that Russia needs to surgically remove.[33] Or when pundits laugh that Ukrainian children will have no fathers, no homes and a destroyed country and that even though 'They'll have McDonald's, it will be burnt.'[34] Or when a Russian MP, Oleg Matveichev, compares Ukraine to 'a prostitute who has got infected with AIDS and wants to infect everyone else, to spread the infection so that more people die so that she doesn't die alone but lots of other people die too. That is the Ukrainian state today.'[35] One media figure, Anton Krasovsky, fleetingly a darling of the West for his stance against Russia's anti-LGBT laws in the early 2010s, called on national television for Ukrainian children to be burned if they did not recognise themselves as Russian. He was briefly suspended from RT but only because of media outrage in the West. As seen above, Krasovsky's comments were in keeping with media depictions of Ukrainians. There are hundreds of thousands of such examples that show how, over the years, the Russian media conditioned audiences to expect and justify their country's atrocities in Ukraine. To do so it is reliant on the narrative that Ukrainians are Nazis.

Banderovtsy and Nazis

It is important to consider not only the intensity of the analogies between the war against Ukraine and the Great Patriotic War but also their consistency and banality. For example, in the first few months of the war, the Moscow Victory Museum opened an exhibition entitled 'Ordinary Nazism' linking current Ukrainian nationalism to Second World War-era Nazi collaborators. This was just one of thousands of exhibitions, including interactive shows, on the crimes of the *banderovtsy* since 2014.[36] Most of these exhibitions were funded or even organised by politicians and the Russian Military Historical Society and the Russian Historical Society (led by Sergei Naryshkin, the head of Russia's foreign intelligence agency). The Russian Orthodox Church has also been involved in profiting from patriotic history; by 2022, Putin's personal confessor had made around 20 billion roubles from designing militaristic historical programmes and museums.[37]

Since 2012, the Russian state has generously funded initiatives aimed at moulding youth national and patriotic consciousness. The Ministry of Education was quick to introduce into the school curriculum lessons stressing the direct relevance of the Great Patriotic War to the ongoing war in Ukraine. These patriotic lessons on historical memory start for children from the age of six. While the lessons are new, in form at least, the core message of the Great Patriotic War's relevance to understanding Russian identity and the war against Ukraine has long been underscored by popular cultural and extracurricular activities. To use a British example (not a nation known for its reluctance to discuss WWII), imagine if films, politicians, the Imperial War Museum, celebrities, books, soaps, your school, your after-school maths club, your local football club, and your gym all reinforced the idea that Irish people were Nazi collaborators. After a while, you would start to internalise it without noticing, even if only ironically at first. The only thing that might save you is the ludicrousness of the list of things that are deemed Nazi, from visa bans to the Swedish Dockworkers Union. This absurdity of Russia's accusations helpfully undermines any pretence that the politicians instrumentalising the memory of the Great Patriotic War actually care about this shared past. Instead, the Great Patriotic War is a useful way to change the conversation from a discussion of Russian perpetrators to one about Russian heroes and victims.

Politicians' (ab)uses of the Great Patriotic War are rooted in its deep resonance and emotional power among ordinary Russians. While the term 'denazification' was too vague to function as a clear objective for the 'special military operation', analogies or at least invocations of the Great Patriotic War remain very emotionally powerful as propaganda. In the words of the editor of IA Regnum, Modest Kolerov: 'The war is about defeating nationalism, defending the Great Victory, the memory of that. That memory is what ties and binds Russians together, you cannot expect us to just let that memory be tarnished. My parents lived under fascism as children. It is personal for me, it is personal for so many Russians.'[38] The Kremlin has carefully nurtured the fear that the memory of the Great Patriotic War is under attack, or being 'tarnished'. Since the mid-2000s, Russian diplomats and representatives have seized every opportunity to engage in memory battles, with the aim of showing to domestic and international audiences that Russia's liberation of Europe (as heir to the USSR) is neither properly recognised nor adequately valued.

The Great Patriotic War is a powerful cultural memory, with 89 per cent of Russians saying the Great Victory makes them feel proud. Given the epic heroism, both real and imagined, of the Soviet war effort, it is easy to see why this would appeal to ordinary Russians. It is hard to overestimate the role of the Great Patriotic War cult in demobilising critical voices, consolidating loyal neutrals and also encouraging ritual support, from taking part in the Immortal Regiment parade or wearing a St George's Ribbon. Such rituals are now associated with enmity not just towards Nazis but also towards Ukraine, and the broader West. Natalia Sevagina reflected this development in her answer to my question about whom she viewed as Russia's enemies: 'We are fighting the Western worldview. Nazism is a Western European phenomenon and now I hear people with Russian names and accents [i.e. Ukrainians] professing Nazism. When I see Nazism in my own people [i.e. Ukrainians, whom the speaker views as Russians] it is scarier than just evil it is anti-people. My grandmother spent four years in concentration camps. My grandfather was in Leningrad during the Blockade.'[39]

Many of those who claim Ukraine is swarming with Nazis cite the Azov Regiment, which the Russian media has successfully depicted as a neo-Nazi brigade. As always with propaganda, the Russians have taken a certain inconvenient truth and then used it as a Trojan Horse through which they can smuggle more lies. The inconvenient (to Ukraine and the West) truth is that in previous iterations the Azov Regiment has had Nazi affiliations and continues to use far-right imagery. However, the ragtag Azov Battalion of 2014 has little in common with the professionalised Azov Regiment absorbed into the Ukrainian National Guard in late 2014 and repeatedly reconstituted since then. Azov is now depoliticised and, although of course they still have extremists and dubious symbolism, this is not an ideology of the force, which attracts recruits due to their reputation as tough fighters, a reputation only further enhanced by their inhumanly heroic yet doomed defence of Mariupol. Perhaps the best people to ask here would be not the Russians who have invaded Ukraine based on lies and who have funded and welcomed neo-Nazis across Europe but the Jewish establishment of Ukraine, which is fully in support of the country's defenders, including those who fought with Azov.

Substantively, any Russian claims to be fighting Nazism are quickly disproven by the active involvement of far-right groups, such as Rusich, in 'denazifying Ukraine'. One famous ultra-nationalist fighting in Ukraine since 2014 is Anton Raevsky, who sports some memorable tattoos, including an intricate portrait of Adolf Hitler on his shoulder, the emblem of the Third Reich on his chest, and, on his forearm, the phrase 'Jedem das seine' ('To each what he deserves') – the motto displayed over the main gate of the Nazis' Buchenwald concentration camp.[40] Evidently, Russian politicians and media do not dislike Nazis because they are Nazis, but rather because they view Nazis as anti-Russian, using this reductive logic to also class anyone who hates Russia as a Nazi.

Russia's war on Ukraine is not only about territory but about epochs. It is a war over time as much as space, the past as much as the future, death as much as life. The Great Patriotic War lies at the heart of the Kremlin's uses of history, connecting to other events, imbuing them with further emotional power. If denazification was too technical a term, more nebulous ideas of return and redemption have wielded great effect. As Fedor Lukyanov explained to me:

> Denazification, as everyone has accepted, even on the level of the Presidential Administration was not successful, nobody knows what it means, this slogan didn't work out, especially because even if, *even if*, you think Ukraine is ridden with Nazis, what does it mean? Even in Germany, it required full occupation and rebuilding the country, does it mean that? No, surely not. So this slogan has already gone. But what remains, and clearly we all underestimated this, is the trauma from the USSR. There was a delayed reaction and now the idea that 'we aren't conquering, we are returning' – is quite well spread in society. In many people's minds, the collapse of the USSR led to the loss of things that rightfully belong to us. The aim now isn't to return everything – not Uzbekistan, not Estonia or Lithuania – just those territories with Russian populations, with a Russian kernel, territories that due to the Soviet collapse

ended up in other countries, but that don't naturally belong there. Even if at first nobody was demanding such things, that grievance was there. It is our professional failure that we did not understand this earlier. This didn't happen overnight. Like in 2014, when they returned Crimea. Crimea was Ukraine, nobody liked it but nobody was so bothered they were going to do anything about it. But as soon as it happened everyone was over the moon, super, super excited about it. Now it is different, there is a bloody war but this trauma of collapse is a very serious factor that needs to be considered further. It won't be exhausted by the war in Ukraine. Not in the sense that Russia will try to conquer other territories but that Russia will behave differently now, Russia is choosing and making its own path. It is returning to the world of thirty years ago. [41]

But that world no longer exists, if it ever did and, in trying to find this mythical, misremembered promised land, the Russian government has destroyed the security and respect it could and, at times, did enjoy.

7

Restoration, redemption, revenge

In 1982, the Monument to Commemorate the Reunification of Ukraine with Russia was finally completed. The monumental arch crowned a statue of a Ukrainian and Russian worker launching forwards into the future together, set against the majestic backdrop of the Dnieper river. Forty years on, the Kyiv City Council dismantled the statue and renamed the remaining sculpture the Arch of Freedom of the Ukrainian people. At around the same time, in the same country, only 300 miles east, Russian occupation forces re-erected a monument to Vladimir Lenin in the central square of the then-occupied city of Nova Kakhovka in Kherson region. It was the very same Lenin statue that Ukrainian activists had removed in February 2014 during the Revolution of Dignity.

Superficially, these events tell a simple story: Russia is trying to revive the USSR while Ukraine is trying to dismantle the Soviet legacy. But this isn't about the Soviet Union, it isn't about anything except proving Russian power, as represented by the irony of (re)erecting a Lenin statue in a country that Russian forces invaded off the back of a speech about 'decommunisation'. In his 21 February speech, Putin set out his ahistoric conclusions: 'Bolshevik policy created Soviet

Ukraine, which even today can justifiably be called 'Vladimir Il'ich Lenin's Ukraine. He is [Ukraine's] author and architect. And now grateful descendants have demolished monuments to Lenin in Ukraine. This is what they call decommunisation. Well, that suits us just fine but let's not stop halfway, as they say. We are ready to show you what real decommunisation means for Ukraine'.[1]

When is Lenin not Lenin?

How did we get to the point where 'real decommunisation' ends up looking like a re-erected Lenin monument? When symbolic politics came to signify not material realities but abstracted ideas and emotion. The Lenin statue in Nova Khakovka, and elsewhere, is a symbol of a worldview and of historical continuity and legacy. In such cases, these monumental Lenins have almost nothing whatsoever to do with Lenin the historical figure and everything to do with reproducing what is lost. As the cultural theorist Ilya Kalinin argues, the Soviet past is reproducible and is only ever reproduced because to update or transform it would risk splitting society.[2] By reproducing Lenin, you neutralise him as well. He loses the dazzle and authenticity of the original, instead becoming a commodified symbol of aesthetic tastes, or cultural preferences. It is like seeing a copy of an Andy Warhol print or, more favourably, of a Suprematist composition by Kasimir Malevich, in someone's house: it doesn't have the same impact as seeing the original, it isn't imbued with the same history, it is reduced to aesthetic, a stand in for and representation of the person's preferences and identity.

Of course, at the same time as reproducing the USSR, Russia is also reproducing elements of Tsarist history, as a matter of priority. This hurried renovation of the memory-scape in the occupied territories has involved erecting statues to the eighteenth-century General Suvorov in Kherson when

Ukrainian forces were barely 10km away, and claiming they would recreate Novorossiya, the area of lands in southern and eastern Ukraine conquered and annexed to Russia by Catherine the Great. This is about imposing and reproducing Russia's view of history, its own and Ukraine's, by restoring the 'historic Russia' of Putin's, and others', imaginations, as expressed in the amalgamation of Tsarist and Soviet iconography. Rather than a logically consistent idea, historic Russia is better understood as a feeling. It is the nebulous notion that the three eastern Slavic countries are one and the same and that Russians, or Great Russians (as opposed to Little Russians, Ukrainians, or White Russians, Belarusians) should be the centre and ruler of any state incorporating all three. The Yale historian Timothy Snyder has described this as the 'politics of eternity', the belief in an unchanging historical essence expressed as the organic unity of the Russian Empire and its people – especially its Slavic, Orthodox core. [3]

The legitimacy of historic Russia, of which Lenin is, suitably, both thesis and antithesis, has its roots in Kyivan Rus. A giant Prince Vladimir statue stands outside the Kremlin in honour of the prince who converted Kyivan Rus to Christianity. Meanwhile, in Kyiv there is a giant Prince Volodymyr statue to that same person. Both countries lay claim to Volodymyr's legacy and see it as essential to their claims to nationhood. According to this logic, if Volodymyr is the founder of Ukraine, then Ukraine is a nation and Russia has nothing to do with it, whereas if Volodymyr is really Vladimir and is the founder of Russia, then Ukraine is a part of Russia. This is not a new debate or claim; for example, when the Grand Prince of Moscow, Ivan III, faced the Novgorod army in 1470, he claimed he had the right to its territory because he was a direct descendant of the Kyivan, Rurik, dynasty.

The fierce political debate around the inheritance of Volodymyr has not created ideal conditions for academic historiographical debates. The excessive focus on tracing the origins also distracts from everything that happened in between to endow these historical figures with such meaning. For example, Kyiv has never been conquered by Russia; instead it joined Russia in an act of union – the Treaty of Pereyaslav – that initially allowed Ukraine to retain considerable cultural independence. Consequently, when the age of nationalism dawned in the nineteenth century, Ukrainian elites had both a living memory and experience of national independence, even as Russian rulers used every tool at their disposal to prevent the flourishing of Ukrainian national identity. Particularly destructive repressive measures included Alexander II's educational edict prohibiting publication in the Ukrainian language or even the import of works published in that language. This edict, which remained in place until the 1905 Revolution, had a major impact on the Ukrainian national project and efforts to bring literacy to the Ukrainian peasantry.

Rather than recall this long history of repression, Putin and his acolytes have instead centred Lenin's role in facilitating Ukraine's territorial and national advancement. They appear especially irked by the early Soviet nationality policy of *korenizatsiya*, which encouraged the development of national minority cultures and the downgrading of Great Russian chauvinism. This resentment is disproportionate, given Lenin's nationalities policy was short-lived and, as early as the late 1920s, Stalin opted for a policy that repressed non-Russian national identities, including by arresting and executing huge swathes of the Ukrainian cultural elites in a crackdown on 'bourgeois nationalism'. After Stalin, the preoccupation with the question of nationality persisted throughout the evolution of the Soviet Union in an atmosphere where Russia was *primus inter pares* and Russians assumed a privileged position in terms of social status and cultural capital.[4] With the fall of the USSR, this status in the so-called 'near abroad' was partially removed. The revocation of these privileges was experienced by many as a form of repression or even discrimination, reigniting Russia's imperialist tendencies.

Russian conceptions of empire

'Under the indifferent glance for him, who miraculously had risen from the dead, perished everything that asserts life, its significance and joys.' Leonid Andreev's 1904 short story, *Lazarus*, tells the story of the biblical figure's second life, once he is brought back from the dead. Unable to shake the pallor of the corpse and containing within himself the magic mystery of death, its horrible infinitude, people go mad from looking at him, and he is banished to the desert where he seeks death's return, unable to acclimatise to the world of the living. Russia's effort to revive Soviet identity after it died charts a similar course. Partial restoration of the Soviet Lazarus has brought only death, those who have seen its eyes now know only suffering.

To justify this pointless restoration, Russian leaders, intellectuals and ordinary citizens alike have woven a web of narratives in which Russia has been maligned despite its heroism. Russian elites have obsessed over rewriting their nation's history, straitjacketing the tragic nuances into a usable and unifying narrative that resonates with the imperial and messianic consciousness previous bloody empires have left embedded within Russian identity.[5] The presence of over eighty different nationalities within and indigenous to the Russian Federation reinforce the imperial, as opposed to ethno-nationalist conceptions of Russian identity, on which its claim to Kyiv and other Ukrainian territories is based.

To satisfy Russia's understanding of itself as a great power, its leaders have often had to disappoint the demands of Russian ethno-nationalists and promote Russian culture as a multi-ethnic and multi-cultural civilisation. The official conceptualisation of Russian national identity, as it emerges from state doctrines and in official speeches on Russian identity, is predicated on a particular understanding of Russia's multiconfessionalism that places it in opposition to Western multiculturalism. The Russian government depicts the country as inherently multi-ethnic and multiconfessional, rather than an 'imported' multicultural one, as is supposedly the case for Muslim communities in Western European countries.[6] This contrast of authenticity with artificiality is central to the Kremlin's positioning of itself against the West and a key point of differentiation between the supposed failure of Western multiculturalism and the alleged success of Russian multiconfessionalism.[7] In a wide-ranging interview in 2012, Putin explained how 'Polyculturalism and polyethnicity are in our consciousness, our spirit, and our historical DNA', enabling Russia to provide an alternative system to Western multiculturalism and liberalism.[8]

Russia has a strong nationalist presence and some of the most interesting criticisms of Putin have been from the nationalist side, which is probably the only force that could undermine the Kremlin. Although often forgotten, Yeltsin's early 1990s embrace of nationalism was an effective ploy to gain popularity and votes.[9] So far Putin has largely avoided nationalism, preferring to leave that bone to be gnawed at by the systemic opposition, like the now-deceased Vladimir Zhirinovsky, leader of Russia's misnomered Liberal Democrats, or the former Deputy Prime Minister, Dmitrii Rogozin, previously leader of the far-right Rodina party. The only exception was during the Ukraine Crisis and in early 2014 when, in his direct line phone-in, Putin lauded the 'ethnic Russian cultural code' as a 'powerful genetic code.[10] One employee at the Ministry of Culture explained that there was a deliberate effort to paint the 2014 conflict in Donbas in ethno-nationalist terms and language partly as a way of exporting the Kremlin's then nationalist problem by sending the most impassioned out to

Donbas. The problem still persists somewhat. Between 2000 and 2017 alone, 495 incidents of far-right political violence occurred in Russia, causing 459 deaths. This rate is five times higher than in the US and over seven times higher than in Western Europe during the same period, considering differences in population sizes.'[11]

As a rule, in their definitions of Russian identity, the government did not allow ethno-nationalist appeal to jeopardise an imperial vision of Russia's past or future. And yet, while this vision is certainly imperial, Russians are often reluctant to accept themselves as an Empire. Russia's 'colonial exceptionalism' is not entirely exceptional; China and the USA are also very defensive about their past colonising and use various narratives to escape the label. In Russia, such narratives include that Russia was a self-coloniser: 'The history of Russia is the history of a country that colonises itself.' This phrase, first coined by the historian Sergei Solov'ev in the 1840s, gained widespread currency thanks to Vasilii Kliuchevskii's *Course of Russian History*, first published in 1911 and still popular today. There is also a strain of thought that Russians were even bigger victims of Russian and Soviet imperial projects. Dmitrii, a secondary-school teacher in Nizhny Novgorod, when asked about this, complained: 'Unlike with overseas empires, there was no gap between the territories populated by Russian people and non-Russian people. This, combined with the way the Russian empire was constructed, starting from the Golden Horde, meant that the local nobility would be included in the Russian nobility, with the same terms and same rights and nobody tried to impose religious restrictions or convert new subjects to the Orthodox Church. If anything we Russians were worse off under the empire because Poland and Georgia and parts of Belarus and Ukraine didn't even have serfdom.' This has little to do with definitions of colonialism, given that the English working classes didn't bask in the fruits of British imperialism either; instead it talks more to a defensive refusal to acknowledge the crimes of one country towards another in such a way that inevitably only begets further crimes.

Yet, other relations are possible and have been in place as recently as the 1990s, when Yeltsin's Russia appeared to repudiate empire. On 19 November 1990, Boris Yeltsin gave a speech in Kyiv to announce that, after more than 300 years of rule from Moscow by the Russian tsars and the Soviet 'totalitarian regime', Ukraine was free at last. Russia, he said, did not want any special role in dictating Ukraine's future, nor did it aim to be at the centre of any future empire. This speech would be unthinkable today, when it has been replaced by a plaintive narrative of scattered Russian peoples unjustly torn asunder by the Soviet collapse.

At the actual time of the collapse of the USSR, there were different narratives in play. It was popular to describe the Soviet Union and even the Russian Empire as an inverted empire (*imperiya naoborot*), in which the peripheral territories extracted resources from the Russian centre. It appealed to the wounded pride of many Russians as well as to right-wing anti-Semitic nationalist groupings, which were increasingly popular in the 1980s. This must be understood against the prominence of what the academic Mark Beissinger has described as the 'anti-imperial sovereignty frame' in the late 1980s, which began in the Baltic States in 1988 before spreading across the Caucasus and Ukraine; various Soviet republics declared their sovereignty *vis-à-vis* the Soviet centre.[12] Yeltsin was able to fit his vision of Russia into that narrative, by arguing that the ambiguity of Russia's position had led to its mistreatment, casting Russia as the true victim of the 'Soviet Empire':

> The centre's many years of imperial policy have led to the Soviet republics' ambiguous position today, and to the lack of clarity surrounding their rights, duties and responsibilities. This is most true when it comes to Russia. We cannot make peace with the fact that we are in first place for how much we

produce but in last place (15th) for how much we spend on our social needs.[13]

Yeltsin disparaged the idea of a multi-national empire, which he equated with the exploitation of Russians by a Soviet elite. The idiosyncratic form of the Soviet Union has allowed for a colourful range of paradoxical interpretations and imaginative metaphors from scholars seeking to convey Russia's position in the USSR. Geoffrey Hosking, for example, described Russians as 'Rulers and Victims in the Soviet Union'.[14] Yuri Slezkine has employed the architectural metaphor of the communal apartment to visualise the consequences of Soviet nationalities policies, with each non-Russian nationality enjoying its own living space.[15] Only Russia, the owner of the communal apartment did not have its own defined living area: it simultaneously possessed the entire apartment but had no room of its own. In conversation with this author, he agreed it would be reasonable to apply the term empire to the USSR and this could be productive, paving way for serious discussions of the USA and others as empires too.

In his contribution to this debate, the scholar David Chioni Moore described the former societies of the USSR as 'extraordinarily postcolonial', defining this as the relationship of the subjugated to a former coloniser (Russia) who continues to play an outsize role in the former colony, preventing them from asserting full independence.[16] This functions as a near-perfect descriptor of Russia's behaviour towards Ukraine since it tried to fully assert its independence in 2014. Russia's understanding of its own empire-mindedness is linked to its understanding of sovereignty, which Putin describes as follows: 'There is no in-between, no intermediate state: either a country is sovereign, or it is a colony, no matter what the colonies are called. And a colony has no historical prospects. If a country is not able to make sovereign decisions – it's a colony.'[17] Russia's urge to restore the Cold War status quo is apparent from its recent demand to return NATO to the borders of 1997. Preaching a unilateral ban on integration for its ex-colonies, Russia proved it doesn't see them as sovereign bodies entitled to make their own decisions but as vassals either controlled by the West or by Russia. This language allows the Kremlin and elites to present themselves as the rebels and to paint their own imperial wars as actually battles against imperialism. On 18 June, a professor at MGIMO and former intelligence officer, Andrei Bezrukov, predicted the following development of Russia's war on Ukraine: 'for us this is, in essence, a liberating special operation (against the US and Britain) for independence, it is anti-colonial.'[18] While this type of language occurs elsewhere, it is usually about attempts to 'culturally colonise' Russia.

Cultural imperialism

From March to November 2022, Tatyana Tomilina was the self-appointed Rector of Kherson State University.[19] The real Rector had to flee for his life. Although Tomilina specialises in world literature, she is a bureaucrat with an academic background so dry and procedural she would be worthy of her own Gogol short story. Tomilina had long been known to harbour pro-separatist, anti-Maidan and anti-West views. When she ran for mayor in 2015, she openly made claims about Pentagon biolabs that would be recycled in 2022.[20] In the interval, she worked closely with a man named Aleksandr Gulyaev, who was an active fighter with the Russian proxies in 2014 and even represented the Kherson's People's Republic at a separatist congress, unencumbered by the fact no such republic had ever existed. According to one of her former students, Anzhelika, 'Tatyana had been unemployed since 2015 because of her social media posts (about Ukraine).'[21] Many of these posts were public pronouncements made during her ill-fated run for mayor of Kherson.[22] Unable to win office through fair electoral means, the group to which she belonged would seize power in 2022 through military means. When her partners and colleagues helped the Russians seize Kherson, she took over Kherson State University.

As another former student, the distinguished historian of ideas, Aleksandr Dmitriev, remembers:

> Tomilina is a pretty standard representative of the Russian World idea. For her, Joseph Brodsky's poem about the independence of Ukraine is a *profession de foi*, what she believes.[23] She sees it that there is Pushkin who is a great national poet, like a Goethe or a Shakespeare and there is Taras Shevchenko who is a backwards figure from a second-rate power. I knew a lot of these people in the mid-90s, some of them went to Crimea, like one old friend of mine who is dead now. He stayed subscribed to *Novyi mir*,[24] stayed in that world, that Russian World. These are people for whom Pushkin is more important than Shevchenko, for whom the sun rises in the north. They understand Ukrainian, could even have a conversation. But they remain part of empire. My generation, people of my generation had to make a choice, maybe my choice would have been different if I had stayed in Kherson or Odessa. When I was in Moscow at the beginning of March and needed to decide what to do – leave or stay – I understood then that for me Europe was dearer than Russia. It is a choice between Europe and Russia. Everyone faced this choice.[25]

It is quite clear what choice Tomilina made. In doing so, she removed freedom of choice from everyone around her. Settling into their occupation of Kherson, the Russians soon began kidnapping teachers, especially headmistresses, who wouldn't collaborate. They kept the women in a basement, threatened them with violence and then dropped them by the side of a road. Even as they did this, they proclaimed themselves carriers of a greater, more dignified culture, erecting Pushkin billboards in occupied Ukrainian cities. It was they who positioned Russian culture this way, leaving it vulnerable to being reduced to a symbol of occupation, murder and rape – tarnishing it more than even the greatest critic could have wished.

Russian politicians and state-funded cultural actors (plus many members of the liberal class) insist on the need to separate politics and culture even though the Russian government has securitised almost every aspect of culture, deliberately infusing it with the most brutal political thought. For example, people were shocked by Mikhail Piotrovsky, head of the Hermitage Museum, coming out for the war in quite virulent terms: '[Russians] are militarists and imperialists', he admits and even though war is 'blood and killing', it is ultimately a positive thing that allows Russians 'to prove themselves. And our recent exhibitions abroad are just a powerful cultural offensive. If you want, a kind of "special operation". Which a lot of people don't like. But we are coming. And no one can be allowed to interfere with our offensive.'[26]

The notion of the great and powerful Russian language and culture, much like the English language, has been used as a way to suppress national identities as inferior and spread empire. I do not agree with banning or censoring literature, perhaps especially not Russian literature, in my view the best in the world. But there is no reason Dostoevksy or Pushkin should not be approached in the same critical way that one approaches Western authors like Kipling. This is especially so when their work, such as Pushkin's poem 'To the Slanderers of Russia' has been cited admiringly by Russian propagandists on numerous occasions to argue that the poem is of direct relevance to Russia's war on Ukraine. In the poem, not Pushkin's best, Russia's canonical poet boasts about Russian military might and its right to Poland. Dmitri Trenin also sees the relevance: 'the problem from the point of view of many of those who see in the Ukraine a war with the West, comes down to the conviction that the USA/West are interfering in "family" problems among the Russians and Ukrainians with the sole aim of containing and weakening Russia. Compare this with Pushkin (in his poem "To the Slanderers of Russia"). Then, in 1830, it was about Poland and the Anglo-French alliance, today it is about Ukraine.'[27]

Whether or not Pushkin had this or that view is of no relevance to my aesthetic enjoyment of his work, just as people enjoy Salvador Dali's art without excusing General Franco's crimes or wear Chanel handbags without exonerating Nazi collaborators. However, Russian occupiers, and the Soviets before them, do not erect statues to Pushkin in Kherson, or Tashkent, as a mark of awe at the intelligent rhyme of the Onegin stanza but because of Pushkin's primacy in the Soviet and Russian canon and culture. His presence in the main square of any Ukrainian city is also the absence of Ukrainian greats. The promotion of Russian culture has a long history of also ensuring the erasure of the Ukrainian. If there is only one pedestal on the main square and it is a Ukrainian square, it is reasonable that it reflect the history of Ukrainian peoples, especially given the long history of Russification policies, which are being applied with aplomb once again. For example, in Mariupol, the summer holidays of 2022 were cancelled and dedicated to russifying children by teaching them emergency Russian language and history and 'great Russian literature'.

The horror and destruction the Russians are wreaking on Ukrainian culture makes any decision to prioritise critiquing the cancelling of Russia in poor taste. One of the most infuriating things for me has been discussions with academic contacts from Petersburg or Moscow, including professors, who, although against the war, appear much more riled by slights against Tolstoy than they do by the bombing of Kharkiv's universities. In the views of one, equally irate, Russian friend: 'It is a reflex – we are the bearers of the "Great Russian Culture". We have given the world Dostoevsky, Tolstoy, the idea of world justice and so on. What has Ukraine given the world?

Dumplings?' – this is a direct quotation from the lecture of one of my professors at the pedagogical university. The people saying such things might be unable to write an essay in their native language, might not have read a book in years but in their heads they are "the bearers of Great Russian Culture". This great culture is metaphysical, while bombing Kharkiv is just an earthly thing. Therefore, bombing Kharkiv is just a historical event, while cancelling Russian culture is a metaphysical crime.'[28]

The influence of Russian culture affects most people socialised in Russia – both Putinists and anti-Putinists – aided and abetted by an ongoing history of Russian dominance over Ukraine that helps to reinforce its chauvinist explanations. Moscow has tried so hard to destroy the best and brightest manifestations of Ukrainian art and culture, from banning publications in the Ukrainian language to shooting an entire generation of avant-garde writers (known as the 'Executed Renaissance') in the 1930s. Russian imperialism is able to blind itself to the results of its own imperialism, which it then uses to justify more imperialism, claiming that there is very little Ukrainian literature without referencing or even recognising that their representatives banned writing in Ukrainian and shot the best talents. Or insisting swathes of Ukraine are actually Russian because Russian speakers live there.

Efforts to delineate Russian and Ukrainian ethnicities are beside the point, not because they are the same people but because belonging to the Russian view is a cultural and political choice, rather than a marker of being this or that nationality. We see that in the fact there are some genuine separatists and collaborators in the east who have facilitated the destruction of their own towns and murder of their own neighbours. We see it in those (admittedly few) Ukrainians who, even as Russian bombs fall around them, still refuse to abandon their sympathies for the Russian World. We see it too in the historical crimes perpetuated by central authorities against Ukraine but often with the assistance of Ukrainians who saw their allegiance with the centre, Moscow, rather than Ukraine. It is important not to imbue nations – or political groups – with the traits of a monolith, as the tale of Lev Kopelev makes clear.

Lev Kopelev

Lev Kopelev was a famous dissident, feted by Western intellectuals, beloved by the Russian intelligentsia, and active in the Soviet human rights movement. He won acclaim when imprisoned for protesting violations of German civilians' rights after WWII. But, long before all that, in 1929, Lev was working in the countryside of Kharkiv Oblast, facilitating the brutal Soviet policy of collectivisation, distributing leaflets and papers to convince peasants to join the *kolkhozy*. As the scholar of the Holodomor, Daria Mattingly, has shown, some things don't add up in Lev's story: While 'in some villages there were revolts, put down by cavalry police and military detachments', in the villages where Lev worked he insisted there was 'not a gunshot fired or a drop of blood spilt'. How convenient. Likewise, Lev describes watching multiple trains heading north, swarming with dispossessed families and crying children, but he only once mentions his involvement in such dispossession, referring to the 'non-violent' eviction of a priest.[29]

If his involvement was so very non-violent, this rather begs the question as to why Lev had to flee the village with the chairman of the local collective farm and two district plenipotentiaries during the unrest prompted by the appearance of Stalin's 'Dizzy with Success' article that (cynically) denounced the excesses of collectivisation in March 1930. Why were some peasants throwing stones at him as he hastily fled the village? Why was he unable to return and instead transferred to help collectivisation in the villages near Kakhovka in Kherson Oblast'? What were the activities that Lev assisted with during his year on the ground in Kakhovka? Why did they lead to such unrest that an armed police detachment had to be deployed to 'pacify' the village?

Daria Mattingly knows the answer to these questions and it is a simple one: because Lev Kopelev was almost definitely lying. Like other teacher plenipotentiaries he would have had to do sickening jobs. Unlike some others, he demonstrated no regret for them. From a young age, Lev had grown used to enforcing genocidal policies on the Ukrainian countryside and in December 1932 he was sent to Popivka in Myrhorod district, a village starving since the summer of 1932. The villagers had nothing to give, they were dying, so Lev threatened them and stole their valuables. In his memoirs, Lev explained that it was easier to participate than not and that anyway he believed he was acting 'for the greater good – finding bread for his socialistic Fatherland'. He even claims he did not see anyone starving to death at the time, a fact which Dr Mattingly politely calls 'implausible' given that '2050 people died in Popivka in 1932–1933. Four orphanages had to be opened in the village.'[30] In the face of such abject human misery as starving children, Lev Kopelev, this feted dissident, continued to demand the last few grains from families, to demand more grain than was produced. While others are on record as having tried to help starving children or at least found a way to escape from performing the job, following a short break after his 'work' in Popivka, Lev Kopelev returned to the 'grain front' in March 1933 – the month of a sharp increase in the number of deaths from starvation. Again, in this terrible time, when other perpetrators quit or tried to help the starving peasants, Lev chose to continue.

In his memoirs, Lev Kopelev expresses no regret, only unconvincing efforts at rationalisation, even justification, by arguing he was a true believer, convinced by some abstract ideology to see himself as saving the nation. But he could see starving, crying children with his own eyes, their bellies round from hunger, he watched them die. Many others helped them and he did not. This man is somehow known as a great human-ist, a wonderful dissident who represents the highest ideals of humanity after he protested violations against German civil-ians during WWII and was duly arrested. But the mass killing of Ukrainian peasants provoked no empathy in him, despite his claims of commitment to humanist ideals at the time. He saw it, he caused it, and he justified it in part because he did not see Ukrainian peasants as real people. Unlike the Germans, they were not cultured. What does this say about society, when participating in a manmade famine that killed millions of Ukrainians does not prevent your access to the hallowed halls of humanism? Celebrating Kopelev without factoring in his involvement in a manmade famine is an especially stark indicator of the extent to which Ukrainian suffering, when inconvenient, is ignorable, sacrificed at the altar of Russian storytelling about themselves.

Again, the correct lens here is not racism so much as social racism, the imperial elitism towards a lesser culture, that makes their suffering ignorable. Similar attitudes are at play in illiberal stances on Ukraine, even if they are trussed up in historicised anecdotes for the sake of argument. Putin sup-ports his assertion that Ukrainians are not a separate people by insisting both Russians and Ukrainians descend from Kyivan Rus and are bound together by a historical language and Orthodox faith. In his 2021 essay, Putin even cites the prophet Oleg, calling Kyiv 'the mother of all Russian cities'.[31] But why destroy what you deem to be the cradle of your own civilisa-tion? The Russian Army has had relatively little hesitation in destroying Ukrainian cultural treasures. The aforementioned long-standing imperial arrogance among Russian elites has manifested itself as a sense of ownership over other cultures and as having the right to rebuild or reconstruct these cultures in its own image. When presented with the opportunity to take free stuff from Ukrainians, the Russians fell to it with gusto, sending hundreds of tonnes of personal belongings, from

PlayStations to vibrators, back to Russia. Russian forces also swiped a great deal of historical heritage from Ukrainian museums, including historical coin collections and art in Mariupol, as well as Scythian gold and historical weapons from Melitopol. This ownership is based on an aggrieved and messianic sense of history that has bequeathed Russia the moral right to defend what it sees as historical truth and heritage, making it its own. Such coverage also belongs within a larger narrative, where Russia is the defender of the past. Russia's need to always be the victor taking the cultural spoils or the winner writing so-called kind histories is central to the Kremlin's vision of Russia and its rights to a sphere of influence – even when it entails invading and destroying other countries. Russia sees itself as culturally authentic, in stark contrast to the supposedly amoral and generic Americanised culture that has (allegedly) taken over modern Europe's moral compass and identity. This narrative is now being deftly folded into Russia's war on Ukraine.

Amid the massacres in Bucha and Mariupol, Russia's claims to the historical and moral high ground sound obscene to many foreigners but not to many Russians domestically – and for two core reasons. First, this self-aggrandising narrative is an act of propaganda and disinformation that distracts from Russian damage in Ukraine, reinforcing the notion that Russia only ever does good and casting doubt on accusations of atrocities. Second, the Kremlin's own claims to legitimacy rely heavily on tracing the right historical antecedents, as there is little to nothing it can offer its people in the present or future. As such, it needs to be able to seize control of history as much as possible to better feed it into the Kremlin's own narratorial grinder. The core ingredient of this congealed amalgamation of defrosted historical glory is the Great Patriotic War.

Soviet liberationism as imperialism

Nazism is irrelevant to understanding Ukraine's resistance to the Russian occupation but the obsessive invocation of the myth of Ukrainian fascism is useful for understanding Russia. In his 2020 article '75th anniversary of the Great Victory: shared responsibility to history and our future', Putin does not just put the blame for Nazism on the whole of Europe, but appropriates the victory over it as not even just a Soviet, but solely a Russian achievement. Unlike WWII, the Great Patriotic War starts in 1941 – avoiding the 1939 Molotov Ribbentrop Pact, in which Nazi Germany and the USSR agreed to carve up Eastern Europe between themselves. There is little space in any government-approved retelling for the disastrous retreats of summer 1941 but plenty for the heroic defence of Moscow in November 1941.[32] Stalingrad in 1943 is seen as the epic turning point and then, naturally, the liberation of Eastern Europe in 1944–1945. There is little or no mention of the West, except to say that they tried to bleed Russia dry by delaying the opening of a second front and to suggest the US and UK were going to make a secret pact with Nazi Germany to attack Russia. This plan features in several very popular parahistorical spy dramas, including Putin's personal favourites, *The Sword and the Shield* and *17 Moments of Spring*. This mythical betrayal completely overshadows the USSR's actual betrayal of Eastern Europe and cooperation with the Nazis, including providing the engine fuel for the Luftwaffe's Blitz of British cities. The war ends with Soviet liberation of Europe but not, in this retelling, with the continued occupation of these countries, the ensuing repressions of their people, or the mass rapes of German women.

As well as allowing Russians to bask more luxuriously in the 1945 victory by cutting everyone else out of the moral spoils (a strong tendency in the USA and UK too), the ubiquity of this narrative is designed to affirm Russians' right to dictate to others. In their highly selective interpretation of 1941–1945, the Russian government has often locked horns in so-called memory wars with countries that were in the former communist bloc; see, for example, the 2020 arguments over the removal of Marshall Konev's statue in Prague, or the 2019 diplomatic spat between Poland and Russia over the origins of WWII. The vitriol of such disputes reflects the extent to which all countries' legitimacy is partly based on history, with perhaps an added flourish in the post-communist part of Europe. In Russia's case, there is an extra level, as its great power status is (viewed as) dependent on the legacy of the Great Victory over Nazism in 1945.

The political uses of WWII are also the most vivid example of the government's continued discursive emphasis on the relevance of the Soviet past to Russia's current political identity and ambitions, which are still firmly rooted in a sense of Russia's right to great power status. Anyone who doesn't agree with this interpretation of history or with Russia's right to a sphere of influence similar to that which the USSR had after 1945 is deemed a Nazi, since they are 'disagreeing with' or 'wish to overturn' (both popular phrases in Kremlin coverage of historical issues) the results of 1945.

That is what 1945 means. It isn't just about remembering war, it is about justifying internal politics and also imperial expansion. These colonial ambitions mean that any attempt to shed light on the Red Army's war crimes or dismantle Soviet victory monuments (that often also demarcate Russian colonial domains) inexorably provoke diplomatic crises in relationships with Russia. But, as noted elsewhere, it is hard to take at face value criticisms of dishonouring the dead or rehabilitating Nazism from a country that follows up its soldiers with mobile crematoria, invites neo-Nazis to form battalions and forges close relations with neo-Nazi organisations, including those who openly glorify Nazi collaborationist regimes as, for example, with People's Party Our Slovakia, which glorifies the Nazi collaborationist government that ruled Slovakia from 1939 to 1945.[33]

Timothy Snyder has coined the term 'schizo-fascism' to describe actual fascists who call their enemies 'fascists', using Russia as a case study. Professor Snyder has argued that the tactic follows Hitler's recommendation to tell a lie so big and outrageous that the psychic cost of resisting it is too high for most people – in the case of Ukraine, an autocrat wages a genocidal war against a democratic nation with a Jewish president, and calls the victims Nazis. Personally, I remain unconvinced that the label of fascism adds much, if anything, to our understanding and evaluations of what has happened in Russia while locking us into the same 1930s–40s analogies and WWII-centric view of the world that contributed to Russia's own moral demise. If it was a discussion that extended beyond Nazism, the 'fascism' debate would perhaps be useful but, as it often doesn't, for me the label occludes rather than clarifies.

Moreover, it takes us further away from understanding how Russians view the war, the resonance of certain narratives, and any logical consistencies on which the other lies are scaffolded but which a term like schizo-fascism discounts. In the Russian view, their soldiers spilt blood for European lands, they liberated them from fascism. Therefore, they have a right to at least some of that land. In this way, the anti-fascism of 1945 merges into one with the generalised and imperialist sense of ownership over other countries' territory that is a central feature of Russia's invasion of Ukraine. This retelling of WWII reinforces Russia's moral right to dictate terms to others.

These presentist and politicised depictions of history are facilitated by the way Putin has sought to de-ideologise the Soviet Union: the anti-fascism element has been voided, only the imperialistic land grabs remain. 1945 bestows upon Russia the moral right to do this, as represented in the Nuremberg trials – which they have been promising to restage since 2014.[34]

With the Kremlin's proposed show trial of the Mariupol defenders, it looked as though Russia would finally stage its fake Nuremberg, using it as an opportunity to renew the argument that Russia has a right to dictate at least part of the world order, given its role, self-appointed or otherwise, as the chief national hero and chief national victim of Nazism.[35] Instead, Putin overruled his security services to swap the defenders for Russian soldiers and his long-time friend and former pro-Russian Ukrainian politician Victor Medvedchuk.

Russian elites use the selectively remembered ideology of Stepan Bandera, with its hatred of Russians, to introduce comparisons between the ways Nazis targeted Jews and Ukrainians, and the way the wider world has targeted Russians. See Dmitri Trenin's tortured word order, for example, in the following quotation: 'Banderite ideology, so it is thought, is today's Nazism, where the role of Jews is given to the Russians and where the main eternal enemy is Russia. In other words, this time of Banderism is ultranationalism directed at the eradication of everything that is Russian in the Ukraine and at confrontation with Russia.'[36] If Soviet leaders glossed over the specifically Jewish nature of the Holocaust, then Putin has acknowledged and tried to benefit from that legacy, promoting the argument that 'Russians are the new Jews.' For example, in answer to a question about Russian interference in the 2016 US presidential elections, Putin argued (about Clinton's team): 'It reminds me of antisemitism: the Jews are to blame for everything. The halfwit cannot do anything but the Jews are the ones who are to blame.'[37] The comparison appropriates the victim status of the Jews for Russians and ties into a broader effort by Russian politicians to depict their nation and people exclusively as heroes or as victims, fuelling grievance narratives and justifying violence now in the present as a means of avenging those who deny Russia's mythologised past.

8

'We will go to heaven, they will just croak'

What do Poltava, Borodino and Stalingrad have in common? The West is using the war in Ukraine to avenge these historical losses, or so says Dmitrii Kiselev, head of the Rossiya Segodnya news agency.[1] The Battle of Poltava in 1709 saw Peter the Great defeat the Swedes to secure Russian ascendancy in eastern Europe. The Battle of Borodino of 1812 ended in an indecisive victory for Napoleon's Grande Armée against Russian troops. The Battle of Stalingrad, from 1942 to 1943, was fought against invading Nazis and ended in a Soviet victory. Most Westerners are probably only fleetingly familiar with all but the last battle, so what these three events actually have in common is Russia's own obsession with viewing these long-past moments of military glory as central to its identity.

In any secular society, the many discussions over history are not about history at all, but about autobiographical narratives, or the mirror in which nations and people wish to see themselves. This often assumes a militarised bent, especially in Russia, where the Great Patriotic War is at the centre of historical and contemporary identity. The cultural memory of 1941–1945 is the only narrative that can cohere the rest of Russia's unwieldy past, functioning as a one point of agreement around which select episodes from contradictory histories can be threaded and neutralised to feed a broader historical sense of Russian greatness. Anyone who challenges this narrative is dismissed as a 'falsifier' who lives outside of a historical truth rooted firmly in the present. Such preoccupations extend into the highest reaches of Russia's political elites, as reflected in government doctrine. The Kremlin's 2021 National Security Strategy mentions 'history and memory' alone almost thirty times, highlighting the existential importance placed on Russia's need to own and control historical narratives.[2]

History as a weapon

The selective episodes of history promoted by the Kremlin form part of a vague and adaptable official narrative. It is aimed at creating a coherent Russian identity out of the past in order to derive political legitimacy from it in the present. The narrative compromises three broad arguments: that Russia needs a strong state; that Russia has a special path of development; and that Russia is a messianic great power with something unique to offer the world. It matters far less whether it is Peter the Great's state or Brezhnev's – the important factor is that the state being celebrated is authoritarian in nature.

History and past wars in particular are useful ways of devising emotive narratives as they are based on a shared past that appeals to a sense of kinship – or race – but also can be extended to allow anyone to join the nation by espousing the national view of history – and culture. Ideas of nationality are deeply embedded in Russian understanding of its past, which, at least theoretically, functions as the 'special tie' that binds the (ethnic and non-ethnic) Russian peoples.[3] Although many claim he is a nationalist, Putin's imperialism, like that of many Russians, rather guards against the overindulgence of ethno-nationalism. Instead, he might be more faithfully described as a historical nationalist, in that he is adamant and extreme about interpreting and defending history in a peculiarly pro-Russian way.

Putin's understanding of history shows the influence not only of Marxist teleology but also of the nationalist writer Aleksandr Solzhenitsyn. The famous Soviet dissident wrote an essay on how to rebuild Russia that has proven very influential on Putin's and other elites' thinking, justifying, as it does, Russia's right to possess Belarus and eastern and southern Ukraine. Framing these colonial appetites as the defence of historical Russia, Solzhenitsyn's arguments are underpinned by a sense of national exceptionalism, messianism, right to others' land and right to dictate to others. Yet, on another level, the essay is perturbed by absence; Solzhenitsyn is not focused on Belarus or Ukraine, but rather seeking ways to justify Russia's existence and to create a sense of collective identity in a diverse country where very few people trust one other.[4]

In recent years – as well as throughout history – knowledge of history has been seen not only as a means but also as an end in itself, as an attribute that sets Russia apart and makes Russia a great power – almost as if it were a civilisational advantage. As Andrei Sushentsov, a professor at MGIMO and public intellectual argues:

> the language in which the political elites of the leading countries of the world speak, is not the language of money, of institutes, or of laws but the language of history. [...] Far from every country has preserved the principle of historicism in long-term planning. Only leading countries, for whom the experience of politics from the position of being a great power has not dried up, have preserved it. [...] This is the parameter according to which leadership is defined today. We can suggest that for this reason negotiations between Russia and the USA will take place significantly earlier than with the EU since in Europe

there are no countries who could take their own large stake in
the unfolding geopolitical game.[5]

Of course, in Western parliaments the application of history
to solving present-day policy solutions is also commonplace.
History – or historical narratives – have always shaped and
been shaped by the different ways different peoples see the
world. The Russian example is peculiar only in terms of the
intensity of the obsession with controlling the past, combining
as it does the authoritarian political situation and a sense that
the democratisation of historical truth is an attack on the very
core of Russianness. This securitised obsession with the past
has replaced any hope for the future that might have been
contained in Communism, as encapsulated in the words of
Vladimir Putin when he declared the war 'a matter of life and
death, a matter of our historical future as a people'.[6] Writing
in the *New York Times*, the writer Peter Pomerantsev put it
another way: 'Humiliated people can struggle to imagine a
future as they play out old traumas over and over. We won't
let you emerge into a future, the Kremlin seems to be saying to
Ukrainians; we want you stuck in the past we can't overcome.'[7]
Mired in atavism, lacking a design for the future, Russia's leaders and people instead look back to find out where it went
wrong, where they lost the golden age, how can they improve
the past, or at best relive a bygone golden era.

This must partly account for the popularity of the *popad-
nichestvo* (roughly translatable as 'time travelling') book genre,
in which the heroes go back into the past to right a historical
injustice. Oleg Tarugin is a particularly productive author in
this field, having written best-selling works in which the protagonists must go back in time to convince Stalin to prevent
impending war (*If There Should Be War Tomorrow*) or are
accidentally transported to the 1945 Battle for Berlin but they
are kitted out with the latest military technology, meaning they
can save many Soviet lives that would otherwise be lost (*Storm*

Battalion). The plots of these books often reflect an under-standable desire to minimise the horrific number of Soviet deaths (estimated at 27 million in WWII) as much as to right any sense of historical injustice.

These very popular books seek to impose order on the ter-rifying randomness of history, just as the state seeks to coerce the past into a more acceptable and usable form. In their efforts to instrumentalise the powerful memory of the Great Patriotic War but also to render its power less unwieldy, the government, through various GONGOs, schemes and funds, encourages the banalisation of the war memory, introducing it into any and every sphere of everyday life in Russia, from street murals of General Zhukov to WWII themed metro car-riages to St George Ribbon-themed burger wrappers in the McDonalds replacement chain 'Tasty and That's It'. It has the effect of trivialising the war, making it more accessible and less mobilisational but still capable of imbuing mundane events with pathos and making you feel like a hero for eating a burger.

In schools, there has been a concerted effort to conflate WWII heroes with the heroes of the 2022 Ukraine war, although, as ever, this is not simply a top-down propaganda exercise but also teachers reproducing the rituals they know, as the ubiquity of the Great Patriotic War cult begets ever greater ubiquity.[8] Such rituals include erecting special stands with photos of soldiers fighting in Ukraine, presenting them as heroes and liberators, as well as the reintroduction of 'hero desks', where pupils line up in uniform to inaugurate a desk in honour of a soldier killed in Ukraine. Headmasters explain that these former students sacrificed their lives fighting Nazis to liberate Russian lands, such as (in their view) Donetsk or Zaporizhzhia. Shortly following the invasion, the Ministry of Education ordered history textbooks to be rapidly rewritten to include the 2022 war. Schools in Russia have been ordered to conduct 'patriotic' classes parroting the Kremlin line on the war. Teachers who refused were fired. Some students told their parents about their teachers' insufficiently patriotic views, quickly settling into a narrative of denunciations that echoed the dark days of the 1930s. History teachers across Russia have been instructed to stage trivia games designed to cultivate 'patriotic education'. The name really sets the scene; it is called 'Those who come at us with the sword . . . [Shall die by the sword].'

On the town planning level, Russian cities used to feature posters of WWII veterans but they are now being replaced by today's veterans – the young soldiers fighting in Ukraine. They are portrayed as brave men continuing the mission their forefathers began in 1941. This concept is encapsulated by the Russian slogan, *mozhem povtorit'*, literally 'we can repeat', which refers to the ability to relive the feats of the Great Patriotic War. Visible in bumper stickers (often in the guise of a hammer and sickle anally raping a swastika) and newspaper headlines (invariably in the guise of words), this catchphrase, and others like it, are popular in Russian society but also promoted by the Kremlin, which uses WWII not only to denigrate Ukrainian identity but also to reinforce Russian identity.

Through all these examples, and there are millions more, the state provides 'infrastructure' for a militarised patriotism, but it has traditionally lacked the tools or willingness to make popular conceptions and practices follow a script. At the federal and local level, officials make patriotism a quasi-mandatory label for public demonstrations but their mistrust of ordinary people and lack of clarity of mission, render them incapable of filling it with meaningful content and so they leave new symbols empty, to be filled by others' imaginations, so people can see what they want to see. If organic popular events or movements do emerge and develop in a different way, such as the Immortal Regiment processions in honour of family members who contributed to WWII, the state will take it over in fear of a genuine and uncontrollable emotional outpouring. Otherwise people take matters into their own hands, as in one town in occupied Zaporizhzhia where the chief of the collaborationist police force, and enthusiast for the Russian Empire, was beaten up and arrested by a newly arrived higher ranking officer with a penchant for the USSR.[9] Their battle over whether Suvorov or Zhukov is the real hero continues, justifying in its small way the Kremlin's refusal to leave history to the people, or to the historians.

Redemptive masculinity

The reliving of heroic history appeals to a need for redemption, a search for heroism after the humiliations of the 1990s. This tendency has led many – albeit not as many as the Kremlin would like – men to sign up to fight in Ukraine, lured in like so many soldiers before them by an element of redemptive masculinity. The best symbol of this redemptive masculinity is the enduringly popular Danila Bagrov, the protagonist of the hit movies Brother (1997) and Brother 2 (2000). Danila is a young veteran of Yeltsin's war in Chechnya. Hailing from a poor provincial town, he travels to Petersburg where he becomes an earnest vigilante who hurts the bad guys (especially men from the Caucasus) and protects the weak (poor Russian women and men).

In the sequel, Danila travels to Chicago to rescue the victims of an evil business empire run by American businessmen in cahoots with local Ukrainian mafia and 'new Russians' in Moscow. In the climactic scene, Danila avenges the death of his friend by carrying out a mass shooting at a nightclub in the city's Ukrainian district. Moral righteousness is clearly on his side: Danila declares his love for the motherland and repeats Second World War-era slogans such as 'Russians in war don't abandon their own.' Brother 2 was released in 2000, the year that Vladimir Putin ascended to the presidency.[10] It was the perfect film to usher in the new politics of resentment and Putin frequently makes reference to the film.

Danila's characterisation follows a similar pattern to the way many modern Russian soldiers are depicted, especially those who die in the line of duty. In a televised hagiography of one such soldier, Anton Fedoseev, the viewer learns of the debilitating illness that he overcame, making his way into the army to prove he was just the same as everyone else. On 19 May, Anton died in battle, and he was awarded the Order of Valour posthumously, proof of masculinity redeemed. The Kremlin and Russian media try very hard to maintain this stylised image of epic heroism and military might.

However, there is another way to understand Danila: as a young man traumatised by war (in Chechnya), unable to reacclimatise to civilian life, able to murder the 'other' with little hesitation. While people may not immediately see that side of the character right now, they may begin to recognise these traits more and more as damaged, injured Russian men once again return from another bloody war. Perhaps people already do recognise these features, as reflected in the comments on war correspondents' Telegram channels, demanding honesty about Russian losses and setbacks, rather than ridiculous claims of Russian supremacy. For example, if you tally up all the Ukrainian military kit which Russia claimed to have destroyed in the first six months of war, it exceeded the total amount of weaponry Ukraine has ever possessed.[11]

After Ukraine's successful counter-offensives in September and October, the war correspondents were open in their criticism of the army and generals, in particular. However, when this went too far, the state threatened to prosecute the pro-war correspondents who had overstepped the mark. To not have done so would have undermined public trust and also the foundations of war acquiescence among the 'loyal neutrals' group. Many Russians have served in the army and the military mindset that one shouldn't publicly criticise either the institution or the commander-in-chief is an essential element consolidating the 'loyal neutral' pro-war group. This may also be the correct lens through which to understand the unexpected transformation of Dmitri Trenin, as a former GRU officer who has taken an oath of loyalty to his country. Although I understand why people were upset with what they read of his views in certain newspapers, in my exchanges with Dr Trenin, he was excruciatingly careful not to present his analysis as personal opinion but rather as his view of what those who do support the war think. My understanding of his own position is that he will not criticise this dishonourable war out of a (in my view misplaced) sense of loyalty towards his country. I am a British academic, so hardly in a position to criticise a venerated Russian thinker and former GRU officer for his position on Russian patriotism but, speaking more generally, this conception of patriotism as blind loyalty strikes me as distinctly unpatriotic when that act is so damaging to one's country.

It could also become morally questionable if combined with a refusal to accept what your country is doing to others. In the words of mum-of-four Vera from Novosibirsk, 'we need this sense of honour or else Russians wouldn't support it. There is an honour in serving the army, that is why it would be best for (the West) not to show the atrocities, you will never get Russians to believe our army would commit atrocities. We wouldn't do that – we wouldn't kill peaceful citizens.'[12] It only takes a few minutes to find Russian language accounts from Russian soldiers willing to discuss the execution of civilians on Telegram. Moreover, the difficulty of attracting soldiers, reflected in Wagner Group's recruitment of Russian prisoners and contractors paying their own way home in order to get out of Ukraine as soon as possible, were widely known even before the call for mobilisation led thousands to flee.[13] When I contacted my interviewees to ask for their views on mobilisation and the large exodus, most were dismissive and highly critical of the 'deserters', even as they expressed fears for their own sons and family members. The large numbers of Russian men fleeing the fighting and, prior to this, refusal of soldiers to sign contracts to serve in Ukraine, clearly frustrated politicians, with Dmitrii Medvedev even ranting that 'if you wimped out and ran home, you are a nobody and nobody will ever come and ask you to go anywhere. But if you were out of the breaks first, then the chances to defending what is yours are considerable higher. That's how it is. This is exactly why it is so important that the country is respected, taken into account. This is exactly what Great Russia must be.'[14]

It is difficult to square the reality of the Russian Army's shameful and criminal behaviour in Ukraine – the looting, the murders, the spiteful destruction – with Medvedev's vision of Great Russia. But the Kremlin will have on its side a public reluctance to admit a core pillar of their identity, the military, is rotten. Faced with a choice between a comforting lie and an inconvenient truth, many people will opt for the former. You don't need a terrifying dictatorship threatening to shoot you for thought crimes, just a pervasive and persuasive media offering a half-credible alternative to the inconvenient truth. Imagine someone blaming your country (or if you're not that patriotic, your football team, or your family or friendship group, basically somewhere you feel proud to belong), accusing them of terrible atrocities and crimes. Someone you didn't trust. Would you believe them or would you believe a more palatable narrative?

Probably you would take the more palatable option, especially if you already had a difficult life, were struggling to make ends meet, trudging home from an underpaid job on an overcrowded *marshrutka* through the slush and sludge of winter to see if your son, who is serving in the military because he couldn't find a job close to home, has written. This is why support for the war does not correlate with the total militarisation of Russian society. Russia is a very diverse country, some areas are more militaristic than others, but in most of the country, people are not baying for blood so much as impervious to understanding the pain they and their co-citizens are inflicting. This is the way the Kremlin wants it, since mobilising people in an active way, to take up arms, is dangerous for those in power. The Kremlin learnt the lessons from 2014, when state propaganda created a frenzy among the public who began to demand more support for Donbas than the government was willing to give at that point. This time around, the authorities preferred to encourage people to sit at home, offering them banal ways to perform their patriotism and using financial incentives to get people to sign contracts, offering wages seven to ten times higher than regional averages.[15] Eventually, the authorities issued a call for partial mobilisation, applied haphazardly and unevenly before being cancelled, at least on paper, just a few weeks later.

Given the demobilised dynamics of Russian society and the Kremlin's spectrum of allies approach, Russian society's tolerance for, or ability to ignore, the violence and cruelty of the Russian Army is better interpreted through what the author Sergey Medvedev has called the 'ubiquity of violence', where 'violence hardly has any legal or cultural limitations in Russia [. . .] violence is normalised everywhere: in families and schools, in the army and prisons, in relationships between parents and children and between men and women, bosses and their subordinates, police and citizens'.[16] In this atmosphere – and Russia is anything but unique here – violence and war become background noise, silently increasing one's tolerance to war and suffering. Since 2014, audiences would have grown used to television displaying close ups, with barely blurred faces, of dead Ukrainian bodies, for example. In turn, viewers would have been prepared for this by the bloody, gruesome images splashed across the media during the Chechen Wars. By 2022 the horror of such images would barely register with most Russian viewers. Nor would the murals of Z-festooned soldiers standing atop dead Ukrainian soldiers. One Russian 'comic' even gave a show to which he brought the skull of an Azov fighter. The audience laughed. Other Russian soldiers have put Ukrainians' heads and hands on spikes. This is not just the horror of war but a fluency in violence born only of familiarity and of need – a need for an outlet for visualising violent fantasies of revenge on one's humiliators.

Apocalypse now (and again)

Why do we need a world if Russia isn't in it? This question has become a catchphrase from overuse by prominent people, from Putin to Dmitrii Kiselev. There is a terrifying blitheness to Russian media's violent rhetoric, especially in relation to nuclear weapons, which is summed up in this simple yet impossible-to-answer question. If previously Russia's frequent nuclear bragging could be dismissed as rhetoric, that feels less possible in the current crisis, when the old nuclear age, governed by Ronald Reagan's maxim 'a nuclear war cannot be won and should never be fought', may no longer be in force. Take one nightly discussion show aired on 5 June 2022, when the host, Vladimir Solovev argues that the world is descending into a nuclear abyss but that Russians should be happy about it. Guests, including Margarita Simonyan, agree, seemingly avid to meet the rapture. At the very start of the war, Dmitrii Kiselev asked the question that began this paragraph: do we need a world if Russia isn't in it? RT's Margarita Simonyan has on several occasions voiced this same question and self-consciously mirrored Vladimir Putin's 2018 Valdai interview (with Fedor Lukyanov) in which he jokes about how, in the event of a nuclear war, Russians will go to heaven and everyone else will just 'croak'. In the 2022 Valdai discussion, Fedor Lukyanov returned to this question, which Putin addressed with similar, chilling, levity.

By emphasising Russia's nuclear power, television hosts and presidents alike are simultaneously petrifying viewers with the prospect of apocalypse but also reassuring them, reminding them of Russia's great power status, since nuclear weaponry is one of the few areas where Russia truly is a superpower. Its military performance in Ukraine has been woeful and clearly everyone, not least the Russians themselves overestimated their military prowess. But they still have lots of nuclear weapons, nobody can take that away. On the contrary, Putin has invested a great deal of money and effort into repairing nuclear stocks so that Russia can once again boast of having the largest nuclear arsenal in the world.

In the most recent edition of the Russian military doctrine, written shortly after Russia invaded Ukraine and annexed Crimea in 2014 – the Russian military significantly reduced the threshold for using nuclear weapons.[17] There is considerable ambiguity as to whether Russia has allowed for the idea of using tactical (or limited) nuclear strikes as a means of escalating to de-escalate, believing that a limited strike against enemy targets would effectively deter conventional attacks by NATO. This horrific backdrop must be a constant in any prognostications. But what can or does this nuclear talk tell us?

Not that much in terms of intention. On the one hand, it is a useful tactic for the Russians, a way of reassuring Russian viewers while also making the other side think you are willing to use such weapons, that you are not quite rational. In return, your opponents take fewer risks, and send fewer or less powerful weapons to Ukraine. This is a good tactic, especially as ultimately nobody can discount that Putin is not bluffing – the stakes are simply too high. Indirectly, such threats also convey to enemies the degraded moral and ethical state of the Russian nation. What happy nation constantly references launching nuclear weapons at other people, calling for radioactive tsunamis to submerge Britain? I am not a fan of the 'let's psychoanalyse Russia as if it were in therapy' approach but all the same, if this is the public discourse, it doesn't suggest an especially healthy society.

There are alternative interpretations. The art historian, Natalia Sevagina, sees the talk about nuclear annihilation as a martyrological mark of Russian readiness for sacrifice: 'Russians go to war not to kill but to die.'[18] It is a struggle to locate much of this self-abnegating patriotism in Russian society. It is much easier to identify evidence to the contrary. Take the example of Ivan Kulyak, the Russian gymnast who was disqualified for a year after competing in Qatar with a Z on his chest. The Russian Gymnastics Federation then went on to ban him from domestic events as well for fear of all its other athletes being sanctioned by international bodies. And Ivan Kulyak got off rather lightly compared to some other patriots, like the volunteer soldiers whose bodies have been left to the dogs of Kharkiv region so their commanders and comrades had more space to send home looted white goods.

The turgid and depressing lack of camaraderie on the Russian side stands in stark contrast to the resilience and engagement of ordinary Ukrainians in their nation's defence. There are so many inspiring examples, but let's focus on a group of people whose work will be familiar to many in the West: the marketeers at Banda agency in Kyiv, who forfeited their salaries to help out their government and country. Before the war, Banda was a profitable agency in flashy offices in Kyiv, working with retailers to improve their communications and marketing strategies but

> when the war started, our business just stopped but we became like volunteers – we wanted to help communicate the reality to the world. For example, we created a popular advertisement about asking NATO to close the sky, it was just people in the agency doing this off their own back. It was just that sense of we need to do something. By the middle of March, we had to do something bigger – we were inspired by how people spoke of

Ukrainians as being the bravest people in the world. Everyone thought the war would be one week then Russia would win but look at us now. That takes bravery. The idea was to raise morale so Ukrainians felt proud especially as people tired after the first month, when people were losing friends and families, we needed to give them a feeling that we are united in bravery, we are together, and to thank them for their bravery. And outside, it was to bring more attention to the war – one simple message: Be Brave like Ukraine. Help us, because we can't resist without your help.

The understated patriotism of the Be Brave creators jars with the jingoistic stories coming from Russia, where the writer Saltykov-Shchedrin's apocryphal statement that 'if politicians are calling for patriotism they must have stolen a lot' is ageing like a fine wine. The Russian Army has been plagued by mouldy ration packets, lack of equipment, and the absence of hygiene products. Inevitably, this destroyed morale and is traceable to the corruption and mismanagement that blight almost every industry and area of Russian life. Russia is a country in which zany corruption stories are both a national disgrace and a coffee-table book waiting to be written, from the governor who stole a road in Komi Republic to the destroyer captain who stole the bronze propellers from his own ship. The dynamics reveal the core of Putinist patriots: not men and women trying to build a better country, but aggressive-defensive opportunists who demand constant sacrifice while they feast on the profits of resentment and tragedy.

Russian deaths, Russian killings

It is never those calling loudest for sacrifices who will have to make them. The Russian Ministry of Defence refuses even to acknowledge the numbers of young Russian lives lost in

Ukraine, telling the individual parents bombarding them with questions that they should not put their own interests over the interests of the fatherland. Perhaps there should not be much surprise in this heartless response, given that rejection of human dignity has been a hallmark of Vladimir Putin's devastating war in Ukraine and so many other pivotal moments, from the sinking of the Kursk submarine to the aerial bombardments of Syria. The little people are to be sacrificed at the altar of the ruler's need to be leader of a great state, not a good one.

This sense of being a statistic, of not being in control of your fate, is common for lower-class Russians who are unable to pay their way out of conscription or who sign an army contract due to lack of job opportunities. Their lives are not valued and they, in turn, do not always value others' lives. Across just six months of war, the Ukrainian government was investigating more than 11,000 suspected incidents of war crimes by Russian soldiers, accusing the Russian military of intentionally targeting schools, museums and other civilian infrastructure. This behaviour speaks to the dehumanisation of Russian society at large.[19] The scale of atrocities is such that it is not about one institution or one mental breakdown but about a history, not only of invasions but of disregard for human life, encapsulated somewhat paradoxically in the phrase 'we don't leave our people behind'. This phrase is not about leaving a man behind, but about not leaving 'people' behind, specifically the Russian people, as symbolised by territory rather than human beings. It is about taking 'what is Russia's', in the words of Catherine the Great, discussing the second partition of Poland. It is a way of glorifying assaults on Ukrainians and Belarusians ('Orthodox populations') and rendering it a defence.

In the name of these imagined (non) Russians, more and more Russian lives are being sacrificed. What impact will that have on people? Will it convince the parents to turn against the war? Surely once lots of young Russian men start coming back in body bags, Russians will turn against the war? But there are sufficient stories about Russians refusing to believe the truth of the war in Ukraine from their relatives, or even their own POW sons to suggest it won't be that simple. Take the story of one mother who responds to her son's death by arguing that something went wrong in the plan for invading Ukraine but this only means Russia must fight harder and further, onwards to victory. Yet, she readily admits not really understanding what the war is about.[20]

Plenty of people believe the Kremlin propaganda because it is easier and preferable to admitting or accepting that you are the bad guys. Now, imagine accepting that your son died in a pointless war and that he was part of a genocidal campaign. It is natural that anyone would try to resist believing that, especially when the entirety of the state is offering you a much more consolatory version and when you can't really do anything about the situation, so avenging your son or acknowledging your anger is pointless and even dangerous. Instead, frightened by the cognitive dissonance, you choose the only palatable option available and become even more attached to the myths and propaganda of brave Russian heroes fighting Nazis. Because you want your son to have died for something epic, not for nothing, or even worse as a villain, waging a genocidal campaign against an innocent people.

On a much less profound or emotional level, this same process will happen to many sectors and groups of people in Russia, such as those who will lose their life savings and business or lifestyle due to the war and sanctions. It is much easier to accept this loss as a sacrifice, in the name of an epic civilisational fight against fascism, that it is your part in defeating a new Hitler, than to accept everything you ever worked for disappeared because of an ill-conceived and pointless assault on an innocent neighbour. This is yet another way for the Kremlin to make ordinary Russians complicit in their war. Ordinary citizens become invested in the lies and in the continuation of this horrific war until victory is achieved at whatever price and in whatever guise – whatever it takes, as long as it justifies the loss. It would be hard to face reality even in a supportive atmosphere let alone one where the government is terrorising even mild opposition. Why resist the comfort of lies and myth?

For reality to emerge victorious against the allure of the sunken costs fallacy, certain phenomena will need to occur. Drawing on the Soviet war in Afghanistan and both wars in Chechnya, the first variable is time. It took ten years for the war in Afghanistan to have any major effect on civil society, which is much weaker in the 2020s than it was in 1989. Second, Afghanistan's impact on mass consciousness stemmed from the fact it was conscripts from ordinary families dying. For a long time, Putin resisted this by ruling out conscription. However, in September Vladimir Putin announced partial mobilisation, calling up at least 300,000 military reservists – and possibly many more – to bolster the struggling Russian forces.

Until that point, the Kremlin had done everything in its power to keep the structure of sociopolitical life in Russia such that it actively and deliberately hinders political agency, both for the Kremlin as well as against. This is why the decision to mobilise, in temporarily resolving a military issue and possibly an intra-elite dispute, raised the potential for protest and the risk therein. In recognition of this, within one month elements of mobilisation began to be cancelled.

Even these shifts may not be enough to turn the tide of public opinion, given that resistance to previous wars is often mythologised, as the sociologist Aleksei Levinson reminded me during our interview:

> Anti-war feelings during the Afghanistan and Chechen wars emerged only at that point when in war the existential questions lose impact, when it isn't a question of life or death of the nation but of life and death of specific individuals. That is when

the anti-war mood begins. But in Russia, the anti-war mood has never been great. During the first Chechen war, according to mass polls, the anti-war mood was large but there were no real mass protests, it was not convincing for the authorities. Yeltsin stopped the war because the elites put pressure on him, not just the public [..] and now for the war in Ukraine there is no strong anti-war mood, the mobilisational potential for support for the war at this beginning phase is large.

In keeping with their careful management of the spectrum of allies, prior to mobilisation the Mayor of Moscow, the city most prone to protest, tried to maintain a façade that there was no war. Even after the call for mobilisation, Sergei Sobyanin announced the campaign over after just a couple of weeks, seemingly independently of Kremlin approval. The emphasis has been on demobilising anti-war sentiment, much more than fuelling it. Speaking to me before mobilisation, Fedor Lukyanov, who lives in Moscow, described how

the situation is strange. There is a large armed conflict in which Russia is taking part, very active, the scale of the action is very large. But not just in Moscow but in any part of Russia, with the exception of border areas, you won't see any sign that this war is going on. Society lives like before. Nothing has changed. This is deliberate on the part of the leadership. Everyone says they don't have enough soldiers. To achieve their objectives in Ukraine they require more armed forces, and for that you need mobilisation, but our leadership doesn't want to do that because bringing the war into civilian life – it isn't clear what it will lead to. It could give rise to unintended consequences like protests or nationalist outpouring which can be difficult to control. The government doesn't want to do that, it prefers to rely on resources it has and can control, like contractors and Chechens. Thanks to this approach, although losses are big, quite significant, they get away with it because even though

people will bury them, that will be in the provinces and not in
Moscow because practically no one from Moscow is fighting.[21]

Given that they do not recognise their own death tolls, it is
unsurprising that the Russian military authorities are even less
forthcoming about atrocities they have committed against the
other side. In the liberated town of Bucha, investigators found
458 bodies, of which 419 bore markings that suggested they
had been shot, tortured or bludgeoned to death. This amounts
to one in ten of the town's residents having been killed, even
though mainly the elderly stayed behind. Despite overwhelming evidence of culpability, Russian authorities have denied
this, just as they have also denied they killed the inmates at the
Olenivka POW prison, contending improbably that Zelensky
had ordered the execution of Azov prisoners for telling the
truth to their Russian captors. Such flagrant lying recalls the
Soviet authorities' refusal to admit guilt for the infamous precursor of Olenivka – Katyn, the forest where the Soviet Union
shot thousands of Polish officers and then blamed it on the
Nazis for four decades. In the worst instances, the denial is no
less vociferous for being delivered with a smirk. For Bucha,
there is as much denialbragging, as there is outraged rebuttal.
Denialbragging is when you dismiss accusations but in such a
ludicrously uncredible way you are essentially farming interest
and outrage to brag about your own responsibility for the crime
and how little you care. The RT video with the two intelligence
officers responsible for poisoning the Skripals, Alexander
Petrov and Ruslan Boshirov, is the ultimate in denialbragging.

Among ordinary Russians, many dismiss any hard and fast
evidence of war crimes by blaming them on Chechens and
Buryats, a natural tendency in which members of a group
emphasise the marginalised characteristics of any other members who commit crimes, so as to show they do not really
belong or are not typical of the group. For example, when the
American public found out about the war crimes and torture

at Abu Ghraib, a lot of effort was spent on pointing out the mental difficulties of one of the men and the lesbianism of a female participant, to disavow culpability. Kirill Shamiev, an expert on relations between military and civilians in Russia, says that when he talks to Russian Army officers they just say 'the army is a reflection of society – what can we do? It isn't the army's fault',[22] and Kirill concedes they have a point. Lower levels of officers and commanders have much more responsibility in the Russian Army than corresponding ranks would have in Western armies, meaning it is harder for them to instil order but also that if one commander is immoral or uneducated it can have a notable impact on their regiment. There are also fewer institutional levers to challenge or check such tendencies. Nor is there much appetite to do so when everyone is already under considerable pressure to increase recruitment, including by persuading conscripts to sign contracts at the end of their year's service.

Once on the field of battle, the war follows its own logic. Hatred breeds hatred. Morale comes from avenging your slain brothers, not from essays about unification or historiographical debates pertaining to the Treaty of Pereyaslav. Even if a Russian soldier didn't hate Ukrainians before, he will start to hate them when they kill his best friend. This will impact even those who disagree with the war and contribute to a lack of sympathy for Ukrainians from Russians. In fact, many mothers, rather than calling for peace, are helping to spread pro-war sentiment, going to schools, organising online and offline meetings with students to 'form in their minds the correct picture of the world'.[23] They are urging kids to show support to the soldiers and officers of the Russian armed forces and separatists of the Donetsk and Luhansk People's Republics as they are 'fighting fascism and Nazism in Ukraine'.[24] The constant framing of everyone else as a foe is useful in making sure Russians never focus on who the real enemy might be.

Conclusion

How Russia lost the war

'A lot of malice had accumulated in people . . . An outlet needed to be found for that.' This is how Innokenty Platonov, the protagonist of Evgenii Vodolazkin's novel, *The Aviator*, explains the anarchic violence that accompanied the 1917 October Revolution. *The Aviator* describes Innokenty's miserable life as a Gulag inmate, before he is offered a way out – an opportunity to participate in a cryogenic experiment. He agrees, is frozen and then thawed back to life in 1999.

In his second life, Innokenty finds one of his prison-guard tormentors, a sadistic man, a killer and a torturer, living comfortably, unencumbered in his old age. In the intervening years, Innokenty's torturer has not faced punishment, he has not been ostracised or subject to justice. Nor is he sorry; in fact the former prisoner has to beg his captor for a conversation. The old hierarchy and power structures remain, then as now, real as imagined. Since 1999, these structures have only been reinforced.

The long shadows of Russia's senseless historical traumas are a powerful tool in demobilising active opposition, shunting it towards passivity and acceptance. If human beings don't cope with or manage to rationalise trauma, they will start to feel apathetic and disconnected from everyday life; it is a way of handling the pain. The Russian government knows this and exploits it. In early March 2022, Putin delivered a speech declaring those who opposed the war to be 'traitors of the nation' with a slave-like mind, the 'fifth column', 'scum' and 'gnats in the mouth' that the Russian people will 'spit out on the panel'.[1] Putin's carefully chosen comments about the need to cleanse society of national traitors were a deliberate invocation of Stalinist language to conjure the memory of the repressions and murders of that age. These were not just words; they were followed up by legislation that carried echoes of the dark 1930s.

Does understanding ordinary Russians' acquiescence to their country's war require unravelling these traumas and their political uses? In the words of the journalist Ira Shcherbakova:

> The lack of active opposition to the war is also about the collective experience Russians have had for decades, it is about our history. We are a nation that has gone through a lot of political repressions. The 1930s, 1920s, 1917 and civil war, and political repressions before that in the Russian Empire, of course political repressions in the Soviet Union and the dissidents of the 80s, the 60s. What I mean by this is that this collective experience of political repressions that spans generations is something that has affected the Russian collective mindset and its determination not to stick out, not to get yourself in trouble. My grandfather always told me not to speak up or get into trouble and I think this is related to his experience because his grandad was repressed, taken away at night and nobody knew what happened to him and he was killed – we learned this thanks to Memorial. That mentality was influenced by repressions. The fact so many are quiet now is linked to the reality that even if they don't understand themselves as descendants of victims, the shadows of repression that existed in family life have impacted their view and mentality.[2]

Ira is right: millions and millions of innocent Russians were repressed. But coming to terms with Russia's past means admitting that many of the dissidents and ordinary Russians cited by Ira as victims can also be understood as perpetrators, as in the example of Lev Kopelev. There has been no historical reckoning with Soviet perpetrators in Russia, indeed the fact that those responsible for the extrajudicial murder of millions have never faced justice and that many of them even remain heroes, with their heirs in charge of the country, at a conscious and subconscious level encourages the same cult of violence to continue.

Yet, the same is or has been true, to varying degrees, of many post-Soviet countries, including Ukraine for a long time. The problem is not the lack of atonement for the past so much as its reproduction, especially in forms that leave the heirs to the perpetrators in power and rewarded. It makes it hard for societies and individuals to establish morality, to identify who is good and who is bad. Instead, *good* denotes those in your group and *bad* denotes those in the other group, subsuming moral autonomy within allegiance to the group narrative.

In today's Russia, the past repeats itself mostly as tragedy: many have slipped back into historical roles, from committing war crimes to denouncing family members. One young woman, Elmira Khalitova, explained how her father reported her to the authorities for criticising the 'special military operation' because he 'thought it was his duty to go to the police and file a report. He'd found another enemy of the people and brought them to justice.'[3] Perhaps it is not surprising to see these patterns of behaviour return so readily, when the FSB and security services rank as Russia's third most trusted institution (after the presidency and the army). That such a terrible institution should enjoy so much support is an indictment of Russian politics and society.

The structures described above have channeled and repressed the fear passed down through generations. The terror has been internalised, denied and then misdirected onto ordinary Ukrainians. 'Who allowed you to live so well' – that is the graffiti spray painted not on Putin's mansion or Solovev's Lake Como home but on the bombed-out interior of a flat in Kyiv. These words are the physical expression of the accumulated malice that needs to go somewhere.

Many Russians working within or for the state system not only misdirect their malice, they misunderstand it, refusing to admit their culpability for any crime, pretending militaristic denial of guilt and shame is, in fact, righteous anger. These attitudes are found across society, but take an especially cynical form among pro-Kremlin intellectuals who have benefitted from Western educations. Take, for example, Vladimir Orlov, who does not see himself as responsible for the invasion; he is just the director of an influential think tank and close adviser to Russia's deputy Foreign Minister.

> When I went to Europe I gave money to Ukrainian refugees who are there who need clothes, something to feel better. They are innocent unless they are aggressive anti-Russian people who want to shoot me; other than that, they are just a lost generation. We do not need to feel aggression towards them. We should feel sympathetic. Being sympathetic is in the Russian character. Empathy is something I think should be in the global genes and I know that I am speaking to an Anglo-Saxon person [who will struggle to understand empathy] but I must say I see more and more people around the world who are just feeling empathy. But empathy is not a synonym for ignorance . . . we want peace, no loss of life, of civilian life, neither from Russia, my neighbourhood, nor from my Ukrainian brothers.[4]

I agree that empathy is not and must not be a synonym for ignorance and I hope that this book has been both enlightening and empathetic in its explanations of why Russians acquiesce in, and deny the reality of, their genocidal war on Ukraine.

This is a war that did not begin in 2022, that is not between Ukrainian and Russian 'brothers', and that cannot end while large swathes of Russian society, including Dr Orlov, lack the strength and moral autonomy to separate themselves from national narratives and reassert their humanity. This end will not happen until Russian elites and ordinary people alike lose, or preferably surrender, in their battle against reality.

In this book, I have traced the importance of that battle to how Russians came to support the war on Ukraine. Arguing, uncontroversially, that the way you tell a story will influence its reception, the first part of the book sets out the core Russian narratives about the war, how they are mediated, how they dovetail, and how they diverge. To do so, I apply large-scale and longstanding data analysis of television, print and social media, interpreting the results, and Russians' reactions to the war, as part of a shared human experience and within the peculiarities of Russian history, society and politics.

The first few chapters also examine the case for Putin's popularity and propaganda's success, even if neither are quite as they first seem. Propaganda doesn't work by convincing everybody – especially not in a country like Russia, with a population grown cynical over the Soviet years and capable of reading between the lines. It doesn't work by persuading them that this or that event is true because of this or that fact. It works by reinforcing people's emotions and prejudices; confusing them so they think there is no truth and just fall back on what they do know, or instinctively feel is true; making them think everyone has a point so they should just stick with their side; or that there is absolutely no point in saying anything as the propaganda is everywhere and you are the odd one out. Sometimes it works by encouraging just one of these reactions, and at other times it might provoke a mixture of responses – but some reactions are more desirable than others.

The Russian government is not concerned with mobilising widespread popular support but manipulating public acquiescence and encouraging ritual support in certain target audiences (e.g. mobilisation-age men). This process works in a range of ways thanks to the Kremlin's spectrum of allies approach, which is central to my understanding of pro-war narrative resonance. Pro-Kremlin media actors stress the evil, disruptive role of the West and the impossibility of ever knowing the real facts on the ground to demobilise those actively opposed to the war, rendering them apathetic. Meanwhile, these same narratives, combined with others about the ideological cruelty of Ukrainians, work to consolidate loyal neutrals around the concept of 'my country, right or wrong'. Such messaging in a time of war might work on others to encourage them to embrace a passive, or ritualised, form of support for the government. By creating an atmosphere in which the war feels far away, almost unreal, alongside careful shuffling of narratives, the Kremlin is also able to reduce the risk of active mobilisation of the wider public, affording them a political agency that would put undue pressure on the government over its lack of results. The call to mobilisation in September 2022 represented a direct threat to this approach, although after just a few weeks, the Kremlin settled back into its spectrum of allies communications approach. Further attempts at mobilisation, which are inevitable in light of Russia's military performance and needs, will undermine Kremlin propaganda unless the authorities are able to present serving in the army as ritual support (difficult when it is a matter of life and death!).

Even if people stop believing Kremlin propaganda, this will have little direct impact on whether they believe the Western narrative. More likely, they will find an alternative to the two options. Rather than pretending the cure is as simple as fact-checking – information versus disinformation – anyone wishing to engage or change Russians' views will need to address the sources of why people want to watch disinformation, what are they looking for? The watching of propaganda is as much symptom of an underlying problem, as it is cause of further problems. And rather than exoticise Russian propaganda, and Russian responses to it, the West should understand both as existing on a spectrum of disinformation and propaganda that also blight our own societies, where distrust in sources of information has encouraged people to seek out new ones.

From Chapter 5 onwards, I interrogate further why pro-war messages resonate as they do. Shifting my analysis from what Russians are watching to why they want to watch that in the first place, the second half of the book draws in more detail on interviews and first-hand analysis of Russian society. It uses this background to unpick the ressentiment, resentment and desensitisation that underpin Russia's especially aggressive form of patriotism, denigratory attitudes towards Ukrainians, inferiority complex towards the West, refusal to acknowledge historical realities, and conflation of victims with perpetrators in the past and present.

To me, both halves of the book are essential to understanding why Russians acquiesce to the war. Ultimately, I see Russia's genocidal war of conquest against Ukraine as a deranged quest to prove an imagined essentialist vision of Russianness spurred by the fear and trauma of having to overcome and address Russians' lack of national 'bondings', to borrow Putin's neologism. The war has been conceived and packaged based on an internal Russian World that often does not correlate to external reality but is shaped by Russians' interpretations of it. As such, while the war is over or about Ukraine it cannot be solved in Ukraine because its roots lie in the Russian political and societal imagination of what their own country is and what it must be. It is about Russia's right to spheres of interest, to be a great power, to avenge the humiliation of the 1990s as it has misremembered it, to be a separate civilisation, to call out Western hypocrisy. It is about security concerns that gave rise to paranoid thinking. It is about fetid obsessions that are now doing more to undermine Russian security and great power status than NATO could ever wish to achieve.

Will defeat in the war, or failure to achieve any meaningful victory, cause Russians to reassess their support for the war? Perhaps. Although the Kremlin is adept at communicating with the Russian people, at finding those topics that interest them and folding them into stories that resonate, the Russian military's humiliating performance in Ukraine, combined with the high level of losses could, over time, significantly reduce support for the vision of Russia that the Kremlin offers. Mobilisation has decreased the popularity of the war, and will continue to do so, as it requires active involvement, not acquiescence. But being against fighting in a war is not the same as opposing or regretting the war per se. In the short-to-medium term, I am sceptical of any sudden shift in Russian national self-conceptualisation, for all the reasons laid out in this book. Moreover, the chance that Russia will discover a conciliatory and positive alternative path of development has been made considerably more difficult by this invasion, with which it has cast upon itself and future generations a terrible sin, rendering Russians pariahs in much of the Western world. This will only strengthen the diseased thinking that led to Putin and that leads many Russians to accept the theft of natural resources, and suffering of its own and other peoples at the altar of an abstract sense of great power status.

More to the point, even if Putin were to lose control of the narrative, he does not need public support to prosecute this war. As the wise psephologist Aleksei Levinson points out: 'the authorities really don't directly depend on this support and don't depend on it a lot. They can manipulate it . . . the results of our surveys, the emotions and feelings they connect with television, on television there are great masters of manipulation and with their help the authorities can put public opinion where it needs to be. But I repeat, even if it couldn't and public opinion started to change in the direction of ending the war or a different direction, really that won't hinder the authorities or this hindrance will be relatively insignificant.'[5] Given this, Western leaders and publics, and probably all of my dear readers and especially the author herself, need to ask – why do we care? What then does it matter to us, or to anyone, whether Russians support the war?

Ironically, I think part of the interest stems from the lack of empathy expressed by Vladimir Orlov and, at least partly, caused by him. The dreadfulness and falsehoods spread by people like Dr Orlov are frightening to many non-Russians, revealing the darker parts of humanity and of Russian culture. This book is a journey into those dark spots, to understand why Russians accept and agree with the war. But many people, understandably, prefer not to travel there and give pro-war Russians the benefit of the doubt: they must just not know what they are supporting. This is an infantilising narrative and one that overlooks the way that large numbers of people in Western democratic societies also believe conspiracies, or express deeply unsympathetic views about human beings drowning in the English Channel or Mediterranean Sea.

The risks of being uncurious about Russian society, and our own societies, should be made clear enough by Russia's disastrous invasion of Ukraine. The biggest problem of those Russians who planned war was that they didn't understand Ukrainian society and how it is constructed. Moreover, Russia's leaders only partially understood the way their own society works – underestimating the impact of corruption and the cronyism of the power vertical, even if they correctly grasped public apathy and societal insecurity.

Increased learning, and honesty, about the realities of Russian society requires empathy but not sympathy. Western countries should not focus their efforts on shaping Putin's calculations; they cannot be confident the Kremlin would interpret any action in the intended way. Nor should they seek to target messages at the Russian public. They should expend their energies on what they can control. In other words, they should not try to defeat Putin but to make sure Ukraine wins, and the West wins. The latter means focusing on their own societies' structural issues, from ownership to disinformation, and on achieving their own objectives, as defined by values and interests. It also includes avoiding nuclear conflagration. As such, this is not a call for hawkish intervention so much as for deterrence, containment and minimising all possible interactions with the Russian authorities and those who support them. There can be no grand reset in European–Russian or US–Russian relations that does not begin with a fundamentally different Russia professing a fundamentally different view of the world.

As a Russianist, this feels slightly like shooting myself in the foot, or head, but I am compelled by honesty to advise any government to expend its budget and policy efforts not on unravelling the Russian enigma but on supporting Ukraine and renewing its own society. When it comes to helping Ukraine, the broad strokes are clear: invest in Ukraine, turn it into the West Berlin of democracy and opportunity, a living advertisement of what happens when powers that share values come together to allow a vibrant people to flourish. The West should do everything needed to ensure Ukraine is victorious and re-establishes itself on as much territory as possible. If there is any ceasefire, it should be used as an opportunity to train Ukrainians on new defensive weapons and to reinforce its defensive capabilities. Until such a point, Ukraine's allies should provide all the military support required for them to achieve their victory without starting a nuclear war. As well as training and teaching, the West should listen to Ukrainians and take lessons from them on how to renew their societies because no other European country would have been so resilient and heroic in the face of the world's second largest army invading. Put another way, in 2013, Ukrainians refused to bow to pressure from Russia to take the cheap energy deal and easy finance. The same cannot be said of any Western European country.

In light of the above, Western support for Ukraine should not be mitigated by shapeshifting claims of 'not humiliating Russia'. It is not in the West's gift or Ukraine's gift to humiliate Russia, Putin has done that on his own. If Russia stopped fighting, the war would end and if Ukraine stops fighting, Ukraine would end. And so it will continue until not only Putin but this parasitical vision of Russian identity dies, because the more the Ukrainians hold out and affirm the health of their identity, the more it undermines Russians' identity. The latter's cruel revenge then further strengthens Ukrainian identity and unleashes a cycle of destruction, insecurity and hatred among Russians. It is as if neither can live while the other survives. But only one country's current conception of identity is worthy of respect: Ukraine's.

In the meantime, Putin has made it clear he sees no prospect for a peaceful settlement and appears determined to capture as much Ukrainian territory as possible. Russia, in its current mindset, will always want Ukraine in its orbit. The only way to prevent Russia acting on this is to make it too costly by arming and supporting Ukraine. Even if Russia were to voluntarily redraw from Ukrainian territory – rather unlikely – under Putin's rule, Russian agencies would always try to hamper Ukraine's development because a democratic Ukraine, outside Russia's orbit, is not acceptable or amenable to Russia's interests. Moreover, prolonged conflicts have an important role in Russia's foreign policy, a fact to which the experiences of Transnistria, Georgia, and Ukraine in 2014 attest. So, the first step is for the West to provide commitment to long-term military training and investment programmes, as well as including Ukraine within Western structures as quickly as is practically possible.

The second step, convincing Russia that the West is not a bunch of moral degenerates interested only in its own comforts, is much more complicated. Returning to an earlier point, the trick here is not to focus on persuading Russia but rather to address the plentiful evidence of the West's lack of moral fortitude. All the West's talk about moralising is viewed as cheap, because ultimately it is cheap, or at best selectively priced. For the one billion euros it provided in aid to Ukraine in the first two months of the war, the EU spent some 35 billion on energy, paying it directly into Gazprom bank, which the regime then used to pay soldiers' salaries, since the EU had also excluded Gazprom bank from sanctions.

As if arranging for the EU to pay the very soldiers it says it is fighting was not embarrassing enough, in a mark of sheer contempt, Putin himself ended up pausing certain gas supplies into Europe, demanding the removal of sanctions. He was doing Europe a temporary favour. German exports to Russia were up 29.4 per cent from April to May, reversing losses that occurred when Germany sanctioned Russia for its invasion of Ukraine. Germany's naive maxim of *Wandel durch handel* (change through trade) certainly worked, only in the opposite way to expected, with Germany vulnerable to Russian pressure due to its dependence on NordStream gas. Taken together, such dependence, combined with the UK's warm welcome for dirty Russian money, French weapons sales, and Italian efforts to soften existing sanctions, all paved the way for Putin's February invasion by convincing him there would be no real consequences.

Putin called his own bluff by invading Ukraine – and he called the West's. If we assume that Russians have brought into their own internal reality then we need to see where the break is – the point at which reality touches the unreality. To me, the break in Russian reality is money and children, that's where it is clear they don't believe the lies about Western imminent collapse, because if they do, then why keep their money in the West? This hypocrisy can be called out through a policy of radical transparency: let the Russian people see where the patriots sending their sons to die keep their money. And this should not just be transparency for Russians but for all because liberal democracies aren't punishing Russia by cutting out the cancer of kleptocracy, but healing their own societies. The West needs to be honest with itself about the ways it has facilitated this war – not by NATO expansion but by allowing Russian elites to steal at home and spend abroad, to use London's law courts while they removed any prospect of criminal justice at home, and to keep their families in Spain or Cyprus so they don't have to invest in Russian schools, infrastructure and public amenities. The EU, UK and USA protected those who launched this horrific war from tasting their own medicine, fuelling cynicism at home and abroad. For too long the West mouthed phrases about its commitment to democracy, accountability, clamping down on corruption, building resilience, being a force for good in the world. The Ukrainian nation's unthinkably courageous defence has reminded everyone that those phrases should mean something.

The West's mistakes and behaviour are the only thing it could control about Russia's march to war and yet even now its responses are deficient. Western hypocrisy weakens its security policy at the same time as Ukrainians fight and die for the values and liberties supposedly inscribed into the European story. The West can choose to share those sacrifices and renew its societies or it can embrace the current path to polarisation, atomisation and meaningless ritualisation and phrases, in place of a true collective identity and sense of ownership over the communities and nations that make up the 'West'.

Part of this radical transparency agenda is about being honest and, in that same vein, the West should stop pinning its hopes for change within Russia on the idea of a small and unrepresentative intelligentsia, who very often see Russia through Western eyes. Most of those who are implacably imposed to the war and have not been demobilised by fear have largely fled. As Fedor Lukyanov argues 'The Bolsheviks had to use repressions and exile to get rid of the unhappy. Putin didn't have to do anything, they all just left. And now that most active protest part of society is not in Russia.'[6] Rather than pretend Russia is just a liberal waiting to be freed from tyranny – an idea with implications beyond just policy and rooted in Western self-mythologisation as liberators – the

West would do better to focus on the reasons Russians do support the war and engage with a cult of the dead and of death. That said, the West cannot change either of these situations in any meaningful way. For change to happen, Russians will need to acknowledge the cult *en masse*. For this, Russian society needs its 'Unamuno moment'.

Miguel de Unamuno was an academic, philosopher and influential intellectual – as well as one-time Socialist candidate – in early twentieth-century Spain. During the Spanish Civil War, Unamuno sided with the Francoist nationalist forces out of exasperation with the chaos and killing from the Red Terror by forces loyal to the Second Spanish Republic. Three months into the war, at a conference at the University of Salamanca, where he was rector, Unamuno appeared to recognise the horror of his choice when Franco supporters shouted the monstruous paradox: '¡Viva la Muerte!' (Long Live Death). Unable to accept this, on an intellectual as much as moral level, he immediately decried the slogan, and all it stood for, arguing publicly with a senior Francoist official. Unamuno was stripped of his rectorship and lived broken-hearted from his terrible mistake until he was seemingly murdered by a Falangist.

Such moments of realisation and rejection can only be spurred by a readiness to embrace the truth and confront cognitive dissonance, resolving it by accepting reality as opposed to telling tall tales of trauma and triumph. The West can help itself and Ukraine by developing a vision for its future, one in which Ukraine is deeply embedded. A workable vision of the future, or rebirth, is the only way to halt the force that Russia currently represents, and tries to spread around the world: an atavistic force that feeds on apathetic violence, obsesses over past and power, and cares only to ask *kto kogo (who dominates whom)*. A place where the dead aren't allowed to lay to rest but are at best abandoned in foreign lands and at worst forced to wander the television screens, drawing in more and more bodies, freshly massacred, newly misidentified, to the churn of the mass graves.

That is how we got to Mariupol, where the dead lie piled up in supermarkets or restless in shallow graves, infecting the water supply of the living, never answering desperate calls on phones that no longer ring. This need to unbury the dead, to search through their belongings and remains to find identifying marks in which Russians can make sense of often bloody and traumatising personal pasts – this is the gaping hole with which the Kremlin's monstruous narratives resonate. Maxim Trudolyubov, former Editor-at-Large of Meduza has argued that Russia lives in a closet stuffed with skeletons and this war will only add more.[7] These skeletons are the source of the resonance of the war with many Russians: to some they can be used to fuel anger and injustice, mobilising into action, for others it consolidates their sense of group belonging – we might as well stick together – for yet others the horror of the skeletons demobilises them out of fear or out of confusion.

The skeletons beget only more skeletons and Russia can never be at peace with its neighbours until it is at peace with itself and its history. Having launched a war based on unstable history, the Kremlin will continue trying to force reality to match a mythologised past, attempting to manhandle senselessly bloody history into something usable and meaningful. The Russian vision of the past must change in order for Russian society to recognise the realities of the present. Until Russians *en masse* make that choice, there will only be more death poisoning society and creating the diseased conditions for this war and for leaders like Putin. Without that, as the war and deaths continue, the situation will only become more extreme.

Until one day it all collapses.

When it does collapse, it will be quick, unexpected, and probably miserable. Most likely, it will lead to something worse than Putin; to look at Russia now, as someone who loves the country, is to despair. But then in studying, rather than forcing, historical parallels with other countries, perhaps we can find practical solutions but also hope. After all, Putin is wrong. Nations aren't essences, they are creations and the Russian people, as other nations have done prior, can choose to bond over something different: a shared belief in redemption, a rich and critical culture of dissent, a traumatic history from which they have taken and learnt lessons. Rather than silently acquiesce to it, Russians as a people could loudly reject an identity that requires amorality, apathy and abnegation of reality to avoid cognitive dissonance. Russian patriots could focus on their vulnerabilities rather than their power. They could invest in developing themselves rather than destroying others. They could define themselves by their own success rather than in relation to the West or bloody tyrants of the past. This is Russia's war, not Putin's alone. The Russian president can call off the 'special military operation' but only Russians can stop the war. If they choose to do so, then, one day, Ukraine's victory could become Russians' victory too.

Notes

Prologue: Credence and incredulity

1 RIA Novosti, 25 March 2022, video archived. See here for further details on the graves: https://apnews.com/article/russia-ukraine-mariupol-mass-grave-af9477cd69d067c34e0e336c05d765cc.

2 The term 'collaborator' is used in conjunction with the designations of the General Prosecutor's Office of Ukraine.

3 I am using the term 'West' here as an imperfect synonym for the EU, UK and North America.

1 The bad Tsar

1 Interview with Vadym Prystaiko, London, Ukrainian Embassy in the UK, 21 June 2022.

2 Aleksandr Etkind, 2013, *Warped Mourning: Stories of the Undead in the Land of the Unburied (Cultural Memory in the Present)* (Stanford University Press, 2013).

3 '1111 zhertv Sandarmokhu: rozstril pid richnitsyu bil'shovits'koï revolyutsiï', *BBC News Ukraïna*, https://www.bbc.com/ukrainian/blogs-41734955; 'Anna Yarovaya: Rewriting Sandarmokh', *The Russian Reader* (blog), 29 December 2017, https://therussianreader.com/2017/12/29/anna-yarovaya-rewriting-sandarmokh/.

4 Francis Fukuyama, *The End of History and the Last Man* (London, New York, Toronto, Dublin, Melbourne, New Delhi, Auckland Parktown North: Penguin Books Ltd, 2012).

5 'Memories of Iraq: Did We Ever Support the War?' YouGov, https://yougov.co.uk/topics/politics/articles-reports/2015/06/03/remembering-iraq.

6 https://twitter.com/abcnewslive/status/1493687915859386374, https://www.whitehouse.gov/briefing-room/speeches-remarks/2022/03/26/remarks-by-president-biden-on-the-united-efforts-of-the-free-world-to-support-the-people-of-ukraine/.

7 Joshua Yaffa, *Between Two Fires: Truth, Ambition, and Compromise in Putin's Russia*, 1st edn (London: Granta Books, 2020).

8 Jeremy Morris, 'Russians in Wartime and Defensive Consolidation', *Current History* 121, no. 837 (1 October 2022): 258–63, https://doi.org/10.1525/curh.2022.121.837.258.

9 Haifeng Huang, 'The Pathology of Hard Propaganda', *Journal of Politics* 80, no. 3 (July 2018): 1034–38, https://doi.org/10.1086/696863.

10 Interview with Slava, via Telegram, 24 May 2022, pseudonymised.

11 Ibid.

12 Thank you to Andrei Tsygankov for our discussion and his help in outlining the views here.

13 'Filosof Boris Mezhuev o tom, chto Rossiya mozhet prinesti na osvobozhdennye territorii, Ukraina.ru, – 14.08.2022 Ukraina.Ru', https://ukraina.ru/20220812/1037583183.html.

14 'How Russia Must Reinvent Itself to Defeat the West's "Hybrid War"', Dmitri Trenin, *Russia in Global Affairs* (blog), https://eng.globalaffairs.ru/articles/russia-must-reinvent-itself/.

15 Svetlana Erpyleva, 'Why Russians Support the War against Ukraine', *openDemocracy*, 16 April 2022, https://www.opendemocracy.net/en/odr/russia-ukraine-war-support-interviews-opinion/.

16 Interview with Timothy Frye via Zoom, 25 May 2022.

2 Putin's polls

1 Interview with Ira Shcherbakova via Zoom, 23 June 2022.
2 The last available polls before the submission of this book were carried out in August 2022.
3 Interview with Aleksei Levinson via Zoom, 28 June 2022.
4 Timothy Frye et al., 'Is Putin's Popularity Real?', *Post-Soviet Affairs* 33, no. 1 (2 January 2017): 1–15, https://doi.org/10.1080/1060586X.2016.1144334.
5 Interview with Aleksei Levinson via Zoom, 28 June 2022.
6 Maxim Alyukov, 'Propaganda, Authoritarianism and Russia's Invasion of Ukraine', *Nature Human Behaviour* 6, no. 6 (June 2022): 763–65, https://doi.org/10.1038/s41562-022-01375-x.
7 'The Conflict with Ukraine', https://www.levada.ru/en/2022/04/11/the-conflict-with-ukraine/.
8 'Konflikt s Ukrainoy: iyul' 2022 goda', https://www.levada.ru/2022/08/01/konflikt-s-ukrainoj-iyul-2022-goda/.
9 'The Conflict with Ukraine', Levada Center, https://www.levada.ru/en/2022/04/11/the-conflict-with-ukraine/.
10 Felix Krawatzek, 'Adrift from Politics: Youth in Russia before the War', FES, July 2022, https://library.fes.de/pdf-files/bueros/wien/19388.pdf.
11 'Dolya storonnikov priema DNR i LNR v Rossiyu dostigla pika s 2014 goda', RBK, 20 February 2017, https://www.rbc.ru/rbcfreenews/58aa9caf9a7947283b5b0740.
12 Ukraine and Donbas', Levada Center, https://www.levada.ru/en/2021/04/16/ukraine-and-donbas/.
13 'A Russian Sociologist Explains Why Putin's War Is Going Even Worse Than It Looks', Jacobin, 22/07/2022, https://jacobin.com/2022/07/russia-ukraine-war-media-public-apolitical-vladimir-putin.
14 Yudin, Greg, 'Do Russians Support Putin?' *Journal of Democracy* 33, no. 3 (July 2022): 31–7.
15 Katya Arenina, 'Nenatural'nye chisla. Chast' 2', Proekt., 7 July 2022, https://www.proekt.media/narrative/rating-putina/.
16 'OVD Info. Svodka antivoennykh repressiy', *OVD Info*, 20 July 2022, https://data.ovdinfo.org/svodka-antivoennih-sobytiy-iyl-2022#1.

17 'What Low Response Rates Mean for Telephone Surveys', *Pew Research Center Methods* (blog), 15 May 2017, https://www.pew research.org/methods/2017/05/15/what-low-response-rates-mean-for-telephone-surveys/.

18 Ibid.

19 Philipp Chapkovski and Max Schaub, 'Solid Support or Secret Dissent? A List Experiment on Preference Falsification during the Russian War against Ukraine', *Research & Politics* 9, no. 2 (1 April 2022): 20531680221108330, https://doi.org/10.1177/205316802 21108328.

20 Interview with Aleksei Levinson via Zoom, 28 June 2022.

21 A longstanding liberal radio station that had made many compromises with the Kremlin to stay on air. The shutdown of Ekho Moskvy, and its near-immediate replacement by Radio Sputnik, was interpreted as the end of any grey areas in Moscow's tolerance of dissent.

22 Interview with Aleksandr Dmitriev via Zoom, 21 June 2022.

23 Interview with Aleksandr Dmitriev via Zoom, 21 June 2022. Several Ukrainian academics I have spoken to, including Yuliya Bidenko of Karazin State University in Russian-speaking Kharkiv dispute this assertion.

24 Interview with Oleksandr Danylyuk via phone, 8 June 2022.

25 Interview with Aliona Hlivco, London, 16 September 2022.

26 'Vo Vladivostoke siloviki zaderzhali mestnuyu zhitel'nitsu, kotoruyu podozrevayut v povrezhdenii pamyatnika', OVD-News, https://ovd.news/express-news/2022/05/15/vo-vladivostoke-si loviki-zaderzhali-mestnuyu-zhitelnicu-kotoruyu.

27 Interview with Venya (pseudonym), Petersburg, over Signal, 17 March 2022.

28 'Spaset tol'ko patriotizm', 7 June 2022, Kommersant, https://www.kommersant.ru/doc/5393609.

29 Nikolai Gogol, 'Vybrannye mesta iz perepiski s druz'yami "Nuzhno proezdit'sya po Rossii" Iz pis'ma k gr'. A.P. Tolstomu.

30 Interview with Katya in London, pseudonymised, 24 March 2022.

31 Interview with Lena from Perm, via Zoom, 12 June 2022.

32 'Women in Dagestan and Other Regions Protest Mobilization "Our Children Are Not Fertilizer!"', Meduza, https://meduza.io /en/feature/2022/09/26/women-in-dagestan-and-other-regions -protest-mobilization.

33 *Address by President to the Peoples of the Caucasus, Siberia and Other Indigenous Peoples of Russia*, 2022, https://www.youtube .com/watch?v=eRjaAQAekkk.

34 'Boris Bondarev on Vladimir Putin's Craven Diplomats', *Economist*, https://www.economist.com/by-invitation/2022/07 /02/boris-bondarev-on-vladimir-putins-craven-diplomats.

35 'The Banker's Dilemma: How Elvira Nabiullina and Her Team Have Tried to Save Russia's Economy amid War and Sanctions', Meduza, https://meduza.io/en/feature/2022/07/07/the-banker -s-dilemma.

36 Michael Alexeev, 'The Nature of Russian Patriotism', *Moscow Times*, 28 September 2022, https://www.themoscowtimes.com /2022/09/28/the-nature-of-russian-patriotism-a78786.

37 Interview with Tolya, London, 15 June 2022, pseudonymised.

38 Alexeev, 'The Nature of Russian Patriotism'.

39 Interview with Dmitri Trenin conducted via email, on 7 June and 8 June 2022.

40 Interview with Vladimir Orlov via Zoom, 4 July 2022.

41 Ibid.

42 'Roskomnadzor ob"yasnil blokirovku video s pesney "Khotyat li russkie voyny" — Sekret Firmy', SecretMag, 07.04.2022, https:// secretmag.ru/news/roskomnadzor-obyasnil-blokirovku-video- s-pesnei-khotyat-li-russkie-voiny-07-04-2022.htm.

43 'A Russian Sociologist Explains Why Putin's War Is Going Even Worse Than It Looks'.

44 Basic Myths of Russian Culture: Strategies of Survival. A Lecture by Andrei Zorin, 2022, https://www.youtube.com/watch?v=Nia KuE8gjkw.

45 Morris, 'Russians in Wartime and Defensive Consolidation'.

46 Interview with Ira Shcherbakova via Zoom, 23 June 2022.

47 Pål Kolstø, 'Symbol of the War — But Which One? The St George Ribbon in Russian Nation-Building', *Slavonic and East European*

Review 94, no. 4 (2016): 660–701, https://doi.org/10.5699/slaveas teurorev2.94.4.0660.

48 Interview with Aleksei Levinson via Zoom, 28 June 2022.

49 Ibid.

3 How do you say 'war' in Russian?

1   Mediascope: internetom   v   Rossii   pol'zuyutsya   80% naseleniya starshe 12 let, Mediascope, 18 May 2022, https:// mediascope.net/news/1460058/?sphrase_id=238412.

2   'Documented Losses', *UN Human Rights Commission*, 30 June 2022,   https://pbs.twimg.com/media/FYmmTvQWIAYrrCh? format=jpg&name=900x900.

3   *Ob antirossiiskom proekte Zapada govoril sekretar' Soveta bezopasnosti Nikolay Patrushev. Novosti. Pervyy kanal*, 17 maya 2022, https://www.1tv.ru/news/2022-05-17/429034-ob_antiros siyskom_proekte_zapada_govoril_sekretar_soveta_bezopasnos ti_nikolay_patrushev.

4   Interview with Natalia Sevagina via Zoom, 30 May 2022.

5   Interview with Vadym Prystaiko, London, Ukrainian Embassy in the UK, 21 June 2022.

6   Interview with MFA official, via Signal, anonymous, 1 May 2022.

7   Ibid.

8   Interview with Modest Kolerov via Telegram, 10 June 2022.

9   Date of Nazi Germany's attack on the Soviet Union in 1941.

10 Interview with Fedor Lukyanov via Zoom, 13 June 2022.

11 A puppet show in the vein of *Spitting Image.*

12 Scott Gehlbach (2010) 'Reflections on Putin and the Media, Post-Soviet Affairs', 26:1, 77–87, doi: 10.2747/1060-586X.26.1.77.

13 Sergei Guriev and Daniel Treisman, 'A Theory of Informational Autocracy', SSRN Scholarly Paper (Rochester, NY: Social Science Research Network, 3 April 2019), https://doi.org/10.2139/ssrn .3426238.

14 For those interested in learning more about Stepan Bandera as a historical figure and about the cult of Bandera in Ukraine, I would recommend Grzegorz Rossolinski-Liebe's *Stepan Bandera: The Life and Afterlife of a Ukrainian Nationalist. Fascism, Genocide,*

and Cult, an even-handed and well-sourced account. My own position is that Stepan Bandera led a fascist movement and his followers readily collaborated with the Nazis during WWII. He bears responsibility for unspeakable and terrible crimes in an era of terrible crimes. However, I recognise that very few people in Ukraine celebrate him for that, just as few people celebrate Winston Churchill for Tonypandy, or Thomas Jefferson for slavery. His fascist ideology is seen as secondary to his zeal for Ukrainian independence and also as irrelevant, since many younger Ukrainians will not know the history but will embrace him as someone hated by Russia. To me, any celebration of Bandera is regrettable. Given the sheer amount of Ukrainian heroism now on display, it is to be hoped that he is squeezed out of the pantheon as soon as possible and his crimes dissected in the intellectually free and flourishing atmosphere of a democratic Ukraine.

15 Howard Amos, "'There Was Heroism and Cruelty on Both Sides'": The Truth behind One of Ukraine's Deadliest Days', *Guardian*, 30 April 2015, sec. World news, https://www.theguardian.com /world/2015/apr/30/there-was-heroism-and-cruelty-on-both-sides-the-truth-behind-one-of-ukraines-deadliest-days.

16 I use the Ukrainian spellings of all Ukrainian locations; however, I translate the speaker's choice since this also reflects a political, or at least sociolinguistic, reality.

17 Given the salience of this issue, it is worth adding here that the Ukrainian constitution also guarantees 'Free development, use, and protection of Russian and other languages of national minorities of Ukraine' in Article 10, https://unece.org/fileadmin /DAM/hlm/prgm/cph/experts/ukraine/ukr.constitution.e.pdf.

18 Interview with Dmitri Trenin conducted via email, on 7 June and 8 June 2022.

19 Rossiya-1 (archived), Pryamoi efir, spets vypusk, 18 May 2022.

20 Vremya pokazhet, Rossiya-1 (archived), 20 May 2022.

21 Interview with Paul Goode via Zoom, 9 June 2022.

22 Please find overviews of Paul Goode's findings here: https://twit ter.com/RuMOR_CarletonU.

23 Interview with Donbas inhabitant, anonymised, Signal, 29 March 2022.

24 Roman Horbyk, 'Little Patriotic War: Nationalist Narratives in the Russian Media Coverage of the Ukraine-Russia Crisis', *Asian Politics and Policy* 7, no. 3 (2015): 505–11, https://doi.org/10.11 11/aspp.12193.

25 Charlie Smart, 'How the Russian Media Spread False Claims About Ukrainian Nazis', *New York Times*, 2 July 2022, sec. World, https://www.nytimes.com/interactive/2022/07/02/world /europe/ukraine-nazis-russia-media.html.

26 Jade McGlynn, 'Historical Framing of the Ukraine Crisis through the Great Patriotic War: Performativity, Cultural Consciousness and Shared Remembering', *Memory Studies* 13, no. 6 (2018): 1058–80, https://doi.org/10.1177/1750698018800740.

27 Jade McGlynn, 'Beyond Analogy: Historical Framing Analysis of Russian Political Discourse', in *Researching Memory and Identity in Russia and Eastern Europe – Interdisciplinary Methodologies*, ed. Jade McGlynn and Oliver Jones, Memory Studies (Basingstoke: Palgrave Macmillan, 2022).

28 Kremlin.ru, 'Obrashchenie Prezidenta Rossiskoi Federatsii', Kremlin.ru, 18 March 2014, http://kremlin.ru/events/president /news/20603.

29 'Vse podaetsya v sravnenii', Kommersant, 11 July 2022, https:// www.kommersant.ru/doc/5457819.

30 Interview with Yuliya from Voronezh, pseudonymised.

31 Interview with Modest Kolerov via Telegram call, 10 June 2022.

32 AFP, 'Top Pro-Russian Official Shot Dead in Ukraine's Kherson', *Moscow Times*, 30 August 2022, https://www.themoscowtimes .com/2022/08/30/top-pro-russian-official-shot-dead-in-ukrai nes-kherson-a78677.

33 'Nebenzya: Plennye soldaty VSU priznalis', chto im prikazyvali strelyat' v mirnykh zhiteley', *Rossiiskaya gazeta*, 25 May 2022, https://rg.ru/2022/05/25/nebenzia-plennye-soldaty-vsu-prizna lis-chto-im-prikazyvali-streliat-v-mirnyh-zhitelej.html; 'Soldat VSU rasskazal o prikaze rukovodstva strelyat' po mirnym zhitelyam', Lenta.RU, https://lenta.ru/news/2022/04/07/order/.

34 'Nastuplenie Rossii i Novogo Mira – RIA Novosti, 26.02.2022', https://web.archive.org/web/20220226051154/https://ria.ru/20 220226/rossiya-1775162336.html.

35 The Russian Military leadership describe the retreat from Snake Island, scene of the immortal words 'Russian warship, go fuck yourself', as a goodwill gesture.

36 'Telegram: @Sladkov_plus', 29/05/2022, https://t.me/Sladkov_plus/5575.

37 'MO RF soobshchilo o podgotovke kievom provokatsii v odesse s Primeneniem KassetnykhBoepripasov – TASS', TACC, 1 July 2022, https://tass.ru/armiya-i-opk/15103473.

38 Kak ubivayut svobodu SMI faktchekery – instrument zapadnoy kontrpropagandy i tsenzury, Moscow, 2022, https://eisr .ru/upload/iblock/0a5/0a504c58c32cc4db1baf8cf3f1161625. pdf.

39 Interview with Vladimir Orlov via Zoom, 4 July 2022.

40 Jade McGlynn and Ian Garner, 23 April 2022, 'Russia's War Crime Denials Are Fuel for More Atrocities – Foreign Policy', https://foreignpolicy.com/2022/04/23/propaganda-russia-atro city-bucha/.

4 Washing brains

1 'Telegram: Contact @arinab1973', 25 May 2022, https://t.me /arinab1973/2782.

2 "Besogon" is an allusion to a fourth-century saint called Nikita Besogon (Nicetas the Goth) who drove out demons.

3 Svetlana Erpyleva, 'Why Russians Support the War against Ukraine', *openDemocracy*, 16 April 2022, https://www.opendemoc racy.net/en/odr/russia-ukraine-war-support-interviews-opin ion/.

4 Gregory Asmolov 'Why Propaganda Survives in the 21st Century: Eight Points about Russian Propaganda', *Media@LSE* (blog), 7 June 2022, https://blogs.lse.ac.uk/medialse/2022/06/07/why-pro paganda-survives-in-the-21st-century-eight-points-about-russi an-propaganda/.

5 *ZOMBOYASHCHIK | "SVYASHCHENNAYA VOENNAYA*

OPERATSIYA", 2022, https://www.youtube.com/watch?v=hw_VYBEXpTM 20.30.

6   Vera Tolz and Yuri Teper, 'Broadcasting Agitainment: A New Media Strategy of Putin's Third Presidency', *Post-Soviet Affairs* 34, no. 4 (4 July 2018): 213–27, https://doi.org/10.1080/106058 6X.2018.1459023.

7   Interview with Liza, housewife from Voronezh, pseudonymised, 12 June 2022.

8   Harley Balzer, 'Managed Pluralism: Vladimir Putin's Emerging Regime', *Post-Soviet Affairs* 19, no. 3 (2003): 189–227, https://doi.org/10.2747/1060-586X.19.3.189.

9   Interview with Hennadiy Maksak via Zoom, 6 June 2022.

10 Ibid.

11 'Truth Unclaimed: Why Russians Trust Propaganda and Distrust Independent Media', NYU Jordan Center, 18 November 2021, https://jordanrussiacenter.org/news/truth-unclaimed-why-russi ans-trust-propaganda-and-distrust-independent-media/.

12 Jeremy Morris, 'On Russian War Enthusiasm, Indifference, Militaristic Sentiment, and More', *Postsocialism* (blog), 17 August 2022, https://postsocialism.org/2022/08/17/on-russian -war-enthusiasm-indifference-militaristic-sentiment-and-more/.

13 Bruce Patton et al., *Difficult Conversations: How to Discuss What Matters Most*, re-issue edn (New York: Penguin, 2011).

14 Anthony Giddens, *Modernity and Self-Identity: Self and Society in the Late Modern Age* (Stanford University Press, 1991), 31–6.

15 Maslow, A. H. (1943). A Theory of Human Motivation, *Psychological Review*, 50(4), 370–396. https://doi.org/10.1037/h0 054346.

16 Without wishing to distract from the analysis of this book, it is of course worth noting quickly that this approach is not unique to the Russian government.

17 Interview with Hennadiy Maksak via Zoom, 6 June 2022.

18 Sam Greene, 'Beginnings and Ends', Substack newsletter, *TL;DRussia* (blog), 4 August 2022, https://tldrussia.substack .com/p/beginnings-and-ends?utm_medium=reader2. See also Samuel A. Greene and Graeme B. Robertson, *Putin v. the People:*

The Perilous Politics of a Divided Russia (New Haven: Yale University Press, 2019).

19 'Internet, sotsial'nye seti i VPN', Levada Center, 8 April 2022, https://www.levada.ru/2022/04/08/internet-sotsialnye-seti-i-vpn/.

20 Sergei Satanovskii, 'Russians Back under COVID Lockdown', DW, 28 October 2021, https://www.dw.com/en/corona virus-vaccine-why-are-so-many-russians-skeptical-of-the -covid-shot/a-59644858.

21 'Televidenie stoit na meste, sotsseti rastut', Levada Center, 29 April 2020, https://www.levada.ru/2020/04/29/televidenie-stoit-na-meste-sotsseti-rastut/.

22 'Telegram: Contact @planerka_org', 15 June 2022, https://t.me /planerka_org/14151.

23 Masha Gessen, 'Inside Putin's Propaganda Machine', *New Yorker*, 18 May 2022, https://www.newyorker.com/news/annals-of-com munications/inside-putins-propaganda-machine.

24 After the Orange Revolution of 2004.

25 Interview with Vadym Prystaiko, London, Ukrainian Embassy in the UK, 21 June 2022.

26 Volodymyr Artiukh and Taras Fedirko, 'No, the West Didn't Halt Ukraine's Peace Talks With Russia', 17 October 2022, Novara Media, https://novaramedia.com/2022/10/17/no-the-west-did nt-halt-ukraines-peace-talks-with-russia/.

27 'Telegram: Contact @readovkanews', 22.04.2022, https://t.me/ readovkanews/31656; Yuriy Mayboroda, 'V tselyakhekonomii britantsy stali myt'sya v "Makdonalds"', kp.ru, 20 May 2022, https://www.kp.ru/daily/27395.5/4589878/.

5 We are at war with the West

1 R. I. A. Novosti, 10.08.2022, 'Zapad proschitalsya, nadeyas' na vnutrennie problemy v Rossii, zayavil Kirienko', RIA Novosti, 20220810T1417, https://ria.ru/20220810/rossiya-1808577582 .html.

2 Aleksei Levinson, 'Why Continue Polling in Russia?', Riddle Russia, 21 June 2022, https://ridl.io/why-continue-polling-in-rus sia/.

3   Team of the Official Website of the President of Russia, 7 July 2022, 'Meeting with State Duma Leaders and Party Faction Heads', President of Russia, http://en.kremlin.ru/events/preside nt/news/68836.

4   William Pyle (2021) 'Russia's "Impressionable Years": Life Experience During the Exit from Communism and Putin-era Beliefs', *Post-Soviet Affairs*, 37:1, 1–25, doi: 10.1080/106 0586X.2020.1833558.

5   'Dve treti rossiyan negativno otsenili 90-e', Levada Center, 6 April 2020, https://www.levada.ru/2020/04/06/dve-treti-rossiyan-negativno-otsenili-90-e/.

6   Adrian Campbell, 'The Wild Decade: How the 1990s Laid the Foundations for Vladimir Putin's Russia', *The Conversation*, http://theconversation.com/the-wild-decade-how-the-1990s-laid-the-foundations-for-vladimir-putins-russia-141098.

7   Mark R. Beissinger, *Nationalist Mobilization and the Collapse of the Soviet State*, Cambridge Studies in Comparative Politics (Cambridge, UK; New York: Cambridge University Press, 2002).

8   Gulnaz Sharafutdinova, *The Red Mirror: Putin's Leadership and Russia's Insecure Identity* (New York: Oxford University Press, 2020).

9   Interview with Fedor Lukyanov via Zoom, 13 June 2022.

10 Ibid.

11 Ivan Golunov, 'Medinskiy i partnery Kak byvshie kollegi po biznesu pomogayut ministru kul'tury Rossii v ego rabote. Rassledovanie Ivana Golunova', 27/12/2016, Ivan Golunov, Meduza, https://meduza.io/feature/2016/12/27/medinskiy-i-partnery.

12 McGlynn, 'Beyond Analogy: Historical Framing Analysis of Russian Political Discourse'.

13 'Rossiisko-amerikanskie otnosheniya', Levada Center, https://www.levada.ru/2022/05/25/rossijsko-amerikanskie-otnosheniya/.

14 'Levada-Center: Sanctions', Levada Center, https://www.levada.ru/en/2022/06/10/sanctions-6/.

15 Margarita Lyutova, 'The Banker's Dilemma: How Elvira Nabiullina and Her Team Have Tried to Save Russia's Economy amid War and Sanctions', Meduza, https://meduza.io/en/feature/2022/07/07/the-banker-s-dilemma.

16 Interview with Dmitri Trenin conducted via email, on 7 June and 8 June 2022.

17 Dmitrii Nekrasov, '"Naselenie za vse zaplatit". Pochemu, nesmotrya na sanktsii, u Putina ne konchatsya den'gi na voynu', Russkaya sluzhba Moscow Times, 30 May 2022, https://www.moscowtimes.ru/2022/05/30/naselenie-za-vsyo-zaplatit-pochemu-nesmotrya-na-sanktsii-u-putina-ne-konchatsya-dengi-na-voinu-a20792.

18 'V Rossii stalo na 69% bol'she bednykh', Sever.Realii, 14.06.2022, https://www.severreal.org/a/v-rossii-stalo-na-41-bolshe-bednyh/31897550.html.

19 Interview with Natalia Sevagina via Zoom, 30 May 2022.

20 This is presumably a reference to Edwin Starr's song but the random insertion of 'Frankie Goes to Hollywood' made me smile and hopefully will give the reader a microsecond of mirth in what is otherwise a pretty depressing book.

21 This song from 1981 is an anti-Vietnam song. The original was made by Bolland (two Dutch brothers who also produced 'Rock me Amadeus' by Falco). It was later covered by Status Quo (and they made it a hit).

22 Interview with Vladimir Orlov via Zoom, 4 July 2022.

23 Ibid.

24 R.I.A. Novosti, 'Lavrov rasskazal o grubom otvete NATO na vopros o rasshirenii al'yansa', RIA Novosti, 04.06.2022, https://ria.ru/20220604/lavrov-1793205477.html.

25 'Foreign Minister Sergey Lavrov's Interview with RT Television, Sputnik Agency and Rossiya Segodnya International Information Agency, Moscow, 20 July 2022 | Botschaft Der Russischen Föderation', https://russische-botschaft.ru/de/2022/07/21/foreign-minister-sergey-lavrovs-interview-with-rt-television-sputnik-agency-and-rossiya-segodnya-international-information-agency-moscow-july-20-2022/.

26 Interview with professor of history in Moscow, anonymous, via Telegram, 17 May 2022.
27 Interview with professor at regional university, anonymous, via Telegram, 24 April 2022.
28 Pryamoi efir, 20 April 2022 [video archived and available].
29 Email correspondence with Patrick Porter, 18 July 2022.
30 *Russia's Soft Power | Marlene Laruelle and Vuk Vuksanovic*, 2022, https://www.youtube.com/watch?v=c5FR_4Ltimk.
31 https://web.archive.org/web/20220226051154/https://ria.ru/20 220226/rossiya-1775162336.html as in this article for example.
32 Interview with Fedor Lukyanov via Zoom, 13 June 2022.
33 Andrei P. Tsygankov, 'The Final Triumph of the Pax Americana? Western Intervention in Yugoslavia and Russia's Debate on the Post-Cold War Order', *Communist and Post-Communist Studies* 34, no. 2 (2001): 133–56, https://doi.org/10.1016/S0967-067X(0 1)00008-3.
34 Regina Heller, 'Russia's Quest for Respect in the International Conflict Management in Kosovo', *Communist and Post-Communist Studies* 47, no. 3–4 (2014): 333–43, https://doi.org /10.1016/j.postcomstud.2014.09.001.
35 For reference, the term "Yugoslav wars" denotes the events spanning from the ten-day war with Slovenia, in June 1991, to the Kumanovo agreement that ended hostilities in Kosovo in June 1999.
36 Data taken from author's own unpublished conference paper.
37 Vladimir Putin, 'Zasedanie Mezhdunarodnogo diskussionnogo kluba "Valdai"', Prezident Rossii, 27 October 2016, http://krem lin.ru/events/president/news/53151.
38 Vladimir Putin, 'Zasedanie mezhdunarodnogo diskussionnogo kluba "Valdai"', Prezident Rossii, 27 October 2016, http://krem lin.ru/events/president/news/53151.
39 Vladimir Putin, 'Vladimir Putin otvetil na voprosy zhurnalistov', Prezident Rossii, 18 October 2016, http://kremlin.ru/events /president/news/53103.
40 Team of the Official Website of the President of Russia, 'Address by the President of the Russian Federation', 21 February 2022,

President of Russia, http://en.kremlin.ru/events/president/news
/67828.

41 'Zasedanie Soveta Bezopasnosti' Prezident Rossii, 21 February
2022, http://kremlin.ru/events/president/news/67825.

42 'Telegram: Contact @rian_ru', 26 April 2022, https://t.me/rian
_ru/160556.

43 Sergey Radchenko, 'What Drives Vladimir Putin?', *Engelsberg
Ideas* (blog), 9 August 2022, https://engelsbergideas.com/essays
/what-drives-vladimir-putin/.

44 Interview with Fedor Lukyanov via Zoom, 13 June 2022.

45 'Moskal'kova o rusofobii za rubezhom: ya mogu sravnit' eto
tol'ko s kholokostom', rossiiskaya gazeta, 30 June 2022, https://
rg.ru/2022/06/30/moskalkova-o-rusofobii-za-rubezhom-ia-mo
gu-sravnit-eto-tolko-s-holokostom.html.

46 'O narusheniyakh prav rossiiskikh grazhdan i sootechestvennikov
v zarubezhnykh stranakh', Ministerstvo inostrannykh del
Rossiiskoi Federatsii, https://www.mid.ru/ru/foreign_policy/hu
manitarian_cooperation/1815559/#_Toc104561466.

47 'Maria Zakharova', Telegram, 31 August 2022, https://t.me/Maria
VladimirovnaZakharova/3582; 'Telegram: Contact @medvedev_
telegram', 30 August 2022, https://t.me/medvedev_telegram/170.

48 'Patriarshaya propoved' posle liturgii v khrame ravnopostol'nykh
Kirilla i Mefodiya v Kaliningrade, Patriarkhiya.ru, http://www
.patriarchia.ru/db/text/5941811.html.

49 Timofey Bordachev, 'Ostrov zlodeev i geniev', *Profil'* (blog), 8
June 2022, https://profile.ru/columnist/ostrov-zlodeev-i-geniev
-1097600/.

50 Interview with MFA official, anonymous, phone call over Signal,
15 July 2022.

51 Interview with Fedor Gaida via Zoom, 8 June 2022.

52 Interview with Fedor Lukyanov via Zoom, 13 June 2022.

53 Ilya Yablokov, *Fortress Russia: Conspiracy Theories in Post-Soviet
Russia* (Cambridge: Polity, 2018).

54 'Top Russian Official Blasts Anglo-Saxon Doctrine of "Select Few
Entitled to Prosperity"', TASS, 24 May 2022, https://tass.com/po
litics/1455011.

55 Interview with Fedor Gaida via Zoom, 8 June 2022.

56 Aleksandr Dugin, *Osnovy geopolitiki: geopoliticheskoe budushchee Rossii* (Moskva: Arktogeĩa, 1997).

57 *Baunov – Chto proiskhodit s Rossiey / What's Happening to Russia*, 2022, https://www.youtube.com/watch?v=rY_XyEVHK5M.

58 The 'shopping centre issue' is a reference to the Russian armed forces launching two Kh-22 anti-ship missiles into central Kremenchuk, hitting a shopping centre and the region's largest toy shop, killing at least twenty people.

59 Interview with Vladimir Orlov via Zoom, 4 July 2022.

60 Liah Greenfeld (1990), 'The Formation of the Russian National Identity: The Role of Status Insecurity and Ressentiment', *Comparative Studies in Society and History*.

61 Interview with Dmitri Trenin conducted via email, on 7 June and 8 June 2022.

62 Jade McGlynn, *Memory Makers: The Politics of the Past in Putin's Russia* (London: Bloomsbury, 2023).

63 Interview with Fedor Gaida via Zoom, 8 June 2022.

64 Michael Kimmage, *The Abandonment of the West: The History of an Idea in American Foreign Policy* (New York: Basic Books, 2020), 18.

65 Interview with Natalia Sevagina via Zoom, 30 May 2022.

66 Bol'shaya Igra, 15 April 2022, Pervyi kanal, video archived.

67 Jade McGlynn, 'Defender of the Faiths: How the Russian Government Uses Religious Diplomacy' (Henry Jackson Society, September 2021), https://henryjacksonsociety.org/publications/defender-of-the-faiths-religious-diplomacy/.

68 'Putin sdelal vazhnye zayavleniya na vstreche s rukovoditelyami SMI', Rossiiskaya gazeta, https://rg.ru/2021/02/14/putin-sdelal-vazhnye-zaiavleniia-na-vstreche-s-glavnymi-redaktorami-glavnoe.html.

69 'Amerikantsy Otmechayut Odin Iz Poslednikh Dney Nezavisimosti – RIA Novosti, 4 July 2022', https://ria.ru/20220704/ssha-1799945182.html.

70 'Afganskaya dilemma Zapada na Ukraine', Timofei Bordachev, VZGLYAD.RU, https://vz.ru/opinions/2022/6/9/1162310.html.

71 60 minute, 16 August 2021, pervyi kanal. Screenshots archived. Thank you to Thomas Brenberg for sharing with me his unpublished research into Russian coverage of the US withdrawal from Afghanistan.

6 The Ukrainophobes

1 Uilleam Blacker, 'What Ukrainian Literature Has Always Understood About Russia', *The Atlantic*, 10 March 2022, https://www.theatlantic.com/books/archive/2022/03/ukrainian-books-resistance-russia-imperialism/626977/.

2 Interview with Modest Kolerov via Telegram call, 10 June 2022.

3 Interview with Fedor Gaida via Zoom, 8 June 2022.

4 This is a reference to shutting down Victor Medvedchuk's television stations, which were major sources of disinformation and were to be used to prepare the country for the Russian takeover and enforce the occupation. Russian occupiers envisaged Medvedchuk as the second-in-command.

5 Interview with junior academic from Belgorod, anonymous, via Signal, 12 July 2022.

6 Interview with lady from Voronezh, anonymous, via Signal, 18 April 2022.

7 This is a reference to the pejorative term 'Washington Province Party Committee', used in Russian to imply that many crucial decisions by political elites of Russia and some other post-Soviet states have been and are agreed with and/or taken in the United States.

8 Interview with Vadym Prystaiko, London, Ukrainian Embassy in the UK, 21 June 2022.

9 Interview with young woman from Petersburg, anonymous, 4 August 2022.

10 'Obrashchenie Prezidenta Rossiiskoy Federatsii', Prezident Rossii, 21 February 2022, http://kremlin.ru/events/president/news/67828.

11 Vladimir Putin, "On the Historical Unity of Russians and Ukrainians", President of Russia, 12 July 2021, http://en.kremlin.ru/events/president/news/66181.

12 https://www.rbc.ru/politics/15/07/2021/60f0475d9a7947b61f09 f4be.

13 Putin, "On the Historical Unity of Russians and Ukrainians".

14 Interview with Fedor Lukyanov via Zoom, 13 June 2022.

15 MID Rossii RU [@MID_RF], 'S.V. Lavrov: Ukraina pytalas' vystraivat' svoy suverenitet na otmene svoey istorii. U nee net svoey istorii bez russkogo naroda. Zapad, potiraya rukami i podtalkivaya ikhpo etoy "skol'zkoy" doroge, pooshchryal takoy podkhod i kontseptual'noe videnie ukrainskogo gosudarstva. https://t.co/sXjUAVwtW5', Tweet, *Twitter*, 23 June 2022, https://twitter.com/MID_RF/status/154008033130653286.

16 Elizaveta Nesterova, '"Pered nami zadacha – sdelat' tak, budto Ukrainy prosto net". Iz uchebnikov izdatel'stva "Prosveshchenye" ubirayut upominaniya Kieva i Ukrainy', 23 April 2022, Mediazona, https://zona.media/article/2022/04/23/enlightenment.

17 Voskresnyi vecher s Solovyovym, 22 May 2022, Pervyi kanal (video archived).

18 Benedict R. O'G. Anderson, *Imagined Communities: Reflections on the Origin and Spread of Nationalism*, revd edn (London: Verso, 2016).

19 Interview with think tanker from Moscow, anonymous, via Signal, 15 July 2022.

20 Based on discussions with think tankers close to the Kremlin.

21 Interview with Ministry of Culture employee, name supplied but I anonymised him, via Signal, 20 December 2021.

22 A small minibus frequently used as a form of popular transport in the former USSR.

23 Interview with Hennadiy Maksak via Zoom, 6 June 2022.

24 Jake Epstein, 'Captured Ukrainian Troops from Mariupol Were Barely Fed and Woken up to the Russian National Anthem Each Morning', Business Insider, https://www.businessinsider .com/captured-ukrainians-mariupol-azovstal-barely-fed-russian -national-anthem-report-2022-7.

25 In the Soviet Union, citizens had internal passports for travel around the USSR and external passports for travel abroad. The former had a category for nationality. For more detail on the

fascinating history of the Soviet passport, please see *The Soviet Passport: The History, Nature and Uses of the Internal Passport in the USSR* by Albert Baiburin, Polity, 2021.

26 Interview with Vadym Prystaiko, London, Ukrainian Embassy in the UK, 21 June 2022.

27 A detailed discussion of the language issue and the merits or otherwise of Ukrainian language laws deserves the type of close attention that lies beyond the scope of this book, but I would recommend those interested turn to the following article, which examines the post-2014 laws and the criticism of them from various quarters: 'Language, Status, and State Loyalty in Ukraine', *Harvard Ukrainian Studies*, Dominique Arel, published in Volume 35 (Number 1–4), 2017–2018 (pages 233–64), https://www.husj.harvard.edu/articles/language-status-and-sta te-loyalty-in-ukraine.

28 Interview with a Ministry of Foreign Affairs official via Signal, anonymous, 23 May 2022.

29 Vremya pokazhet, 19 May 2022, Pervyi kanal video archived.

30 Most military experts estimate that the actual number was between 160,000 and 190,000.

31 Interview with Dmitri Trenin conducted via email, on 7 June and 8 June 2022.

32 Ibid.

33 Vremya pokazhet, 30 June 2022, Pervyi kanal, video archived.

34 60 minute, 23 May 2022, Rossiya-1, video archived.

35 60 minute, Rossiya – 1, 6 June 2022, video archived.

36 'Gosudarstvennyi Doklad o Sostoyanii Kul'tury v Rossiiskoi Federatsii v 2017 Godu', Ministerstvo kul'tury Rossiiskoi federatsii, 2017, https://www.mkrf.ru/activities/reports/report2017/.

37 'Propagandist ot boga', iStories, 1 August 2022, https:// storage.googleapis.com/istories/investigations/2022/08 /01/propagandist-ot-boga/index.html.

38 Interview with Modest Kolerov via Telegram call, 10 June 2022.

39 Interview with Natalia Sevagina via Zoom, 30 May 2022.

40 'Dying to Kill The Russian Neo-Nazis Fighting Vladimir Putin's

War to "Denazify" Ukraine', 15 July 2022, Meduza, https://medu
za.io/en/feature/2022/07/15/dying-to-kill.

41 Interview with Fedor Lukyanov via Zoom, 13 June 2022.

7 Restoration, redemption, revenge

1 'Extracts from Putin's Speech on Ukraine', *Reuters*, 21
February 2022, https://www.reuters.com/world/europe/extra
cts-putins-speech-ukraine-2022-02-21/.

2 Ilya Kalinin, 'Nostalgic Modernization: The Soviet Past as
"Historical Horizon"', *Slavonica* 17, no. 2 (1 November 2011):
156–66.

3 Timothy Snyder, 'Vladimir Putin's Politics of Eternity', *Guardian*,
16 March 2018, sec. World news, https://www.theguardian.com
/news/2018/mar/16/vladimir-putin-russia-politics-of-eternity
-timothy-snyder.

4 Jeremy Smith, *Red Nations: The Nationalities Experience in
and after the USSR* (Cambridge, United Kingdom; New York:
Cambridge University Press, 2013), http://www.loc.gov/catdir
/enhancements/fy1307/2013006196-t.html.

5 Emil' Pain, 'Russia Between Empire and Nation', *Russian Politics
and Law* 47, no. 2 (2009): 60–86, https://doi.org/10.2753/RUP
1061-1940470203; Emil' Pain, *The Imperial Syndrome and Its
Influence on Russian Nationalism* (Edinburgh University Press,
2016), https://doi.org/10.3366/edinburgh/9781474410427.003
.0003.

6 'Foreign Minister Sergei Lavrov's interview with RT France,
Paris Match and Le Figaro', MID, 18 October 2018, https://www
.mid.ru/en/web/guest/maps/fr/-/asset_publisher/g8RuzDvY7q
yV/content/id/3377331.

7 'Interview between Sergei Lavrov, the Russian Foreign Minister,
and Rossiiskaya gazeta, Moscow, 19 November 2013', MID,
https://www.mid.ru/en/web/guest/foreign_policy/news/-/asset
_publisher/cKNonkJE02Bw/content/id/87526.

8 Vladimir Putin, '*Vladimir Putin: Rossiya: Natsional'nyi Vopros*',
Nezavisimaya gazeta, 2012, http://www.ng.ru/politics/2012-01
-23/1_national.html?insidedoc.

9 George Breslauer and Catherine Dale, 'Boris Yeltsin and the Invention of a Russian Nation-State', *Post-Soviet Affairs* 13, no. 4 (2013): 303–32; Alfred B. Evans, 'Yel'Tsin and Russian Nationalism', *Soviet and Post-Soviet Review* 21, no. 1 (1994): 29–43, https://doi.org/10.1163/187633294X00089; Oxana Shevel, 'Russian Nation-Building from Yel'tsin to Medvedev: Ethnic, Civic or Purposefully Ambiguous?', *Europe–Asia Studies* 63, no. 2 (2011): 179–202, https://doi.org/10.1080/09668136.2011.547693.

10 Prezident Rossii, 'Pryamaya liniya s Vladimirom Putinym 2014', Kremlin.ru, 17 April 2014, http://kremlin.ru/events/president/news/20796.

11 Claudia Walner, 'If Russia Is Serious about De-Nazification, It Should Start at Home', RUSI, 21/04/2022, https://www.rusi.or ghttps://www.rusi.org.

12 Mark R. Beissinger, 'Nationalism and the Collapse of Soviet Communism', *Contemporary European History* 18, no. 3 (2009): 331–47, https://doi.org/10.1017/S0960777309005074. page 333.

13 Yeltsin spoke at the Russian Congress of People's Deputies in June 1990.

14 Geoffrey A. Hosking, *Rulers and Victims: The Russians in the Soviet Union* (Cambridge, MA; London: Belknap Press of Harvard University Press, 2006).

15 Yuri Slezkine, 'The USSR as a Communal Apartment, or How a Socialist State Promoted Ethnic Particularism', *Slavic Review* 53, no. 2 (1994): 414–52, https://doi.org/10.2307/2501300.

16 David Chioni Moore, 'Is the Post- in Postcolonial the Post- in Post-Soviet? Toward a Global Postcolonial Critique', *PMLA* 116, no. 1 (2001): 111–28, page 114.

17 'No Middle Way between Being Independent Country and Colony, Putin Says', TASS, 9 June 2022, https://tass.com/politics/1462989.

18 'Eks-razvedchik Bezrukov poyasnil prichinu spetsoperatsii: "Osvoboditel'naya voyna"', 17 June 2022, https://tsargrad.tv/ne ws/jeks-razvedchik-bezrukov-pojasnil-prichinu-specoperacii-os voboditelnaja-vojna_568027.

19 As identified by the Prosecutor General of Ukraine.

20 *V tsentre Khersone taino rabotaet pasnaya laboratoriya Pentagona*, 2015, https://www.youtube.com/watch?v=1vIYRvA qbPA.

21 Interview with Anzhelika (surname held back by author), over Signal, 12 June 2022.

22 'Izvestnaya v Khersone storonnitsa separatizma', Kherson Onlain, 20 October 2016, https://khersonline.net/novosti/ politika/69620-izvestnaya-v-hersone-storonnica-separatizma-tatyana-tomilina-stanet-doktorom-nauk-v-nacakademii-gosuda rstvennogo-upravleniya.html.

23 This is a reference to Brodsky's derisive poem 'On Ukrainian Independence' when he writes such gifted lyricisms as: 'Away with you, Khokhly, and may your journey be calm! . . . It's over now. So hurry back to your huts . . . Good riddance, Khokhly, it's over for better or worse, I'll go spit in the Dnieper, perhaps it'll flow in reverse.' Khokhly is a racist term denoting Ukrainians.

24 A Russian-language monthly literary journal.

25 Interview with Aleksandr Dmitriev via Zoom, 21 June 2022.

26 Andrei Kolesnikov, 'When Culture Reaches for a Gun', *Moscow Times*, 28 June 2022, https://www.themoscowtimes.com/2022 /06/28/when-culture-reaches-for-a-gun-a78129.

27 Interview with Dmitri Trenin conducted via email, on 7 June and 8 June 2022.

28 Interview with Alyosha, academic, over Signal, 4 June 2022.

29 Daria Mattingly, 'Idle, Drunk and Good-for-Nothing: The Rank-and-File Perpetrators of 1932–1933 Famine in Ukraine and Their Representation in Cultural Memory', DPhil Thesis, University of Cambridge, 2018.

30 Daria Mattingly, 'Recollections May Vary', in Jade McGlynn and Oliver T. Jones (eds) *Researching Memory and Identity* (Palgrave Macmillan, 2022).

31 Putin, 'On the Historical Unity of Russians and Ukrainians'.

32 Jade McGlynn, 'Covering up Tragedy and the Myth of the Great Patriotic War', *New Eastern Europe*, 30 September 2021, https:// neweasterneurope.eu/2021/09/30/covering-up-tragedy-and-the -myth-of-the-great-patriotic-war/.

33 Miroslava German Sirotnikova, 'Far-Right Extremism in Slovakia: Hate, Guns and Friends from Russia', *Balkan Insight* (blog), 20 January 2021, https://balkaninsight.com/2021/01/20/far-right-extremism-in-slovakia/.

34 Kseniya Akhmetzhanova, '"Boets 'Berkuta': Radikalov na maidane uchili, kak nas nado ubivat'", Komsomolskaya pravda, 26 February 2014, http://www.kp.ru/daily/26206/3091625/.

35 Andrew Roth, 'Kremlin Mulls Nuremberg-Style Trials Based on Second World War Tribunals', *Guardian*, 28 May 2022, https://www.theguardian.com/world/2022/may/28/kremlin-mulls-nuremberg-style-trials-based-on-second-world-war-tribunals.

36 Interview with Dmitri Trenin conducted via email, on 7 June and 8 June 2022.

37 'St Petersburg International Economic Forum plenary meeting', President Rossii, 2 June 2017, http://en.kremlin.ru/events/president/news/54667.

8 'We will go to heaven, they will just croak'

1 Vesti nedeli s Dmitriem Kiselyovym, Rossiya-1, 14 August 2022, video archived.

2 'Strategiya Natsional'noi Bezopasnosti Rossiiskoi Federatsii', Konsul'tant.ru, http://www.consultant.ru/document/cons_doc_LAW_191669/61a97f7ab0f2f3757fe034d11011c763bc2e593f/.

3 Mark Bassin and Catriona Kelly, *Soviet and Post-Soviet Identities* (Cambridge; New York: Cambridge University Press, 2012), 17–20, http://www.loc.gov/catdir/enhancements/fy1117/20110 40511-t.html.

4 'Edelman Trust Barometer 2021', Edelman, IPSOS, January 2021, https://www.edelman.com/sites/g/files/aatuss191/files/2021-01/2021%20Edelman%20Trust%20Barometer_Final.pdf https://www.ipsos.com/sites/default/files/ct/news/documents/2022-03/Global%20Advisor%20-%20Interpersonal%20Trust%202022%20-%20Graphic%20Report_0.pdf https://www.worldvaluessur vey.org/wvs.jsp.

5 Andrey Sushentsov, 'Lichnyy opyt ili istoricheskoe znanie? Chto pomozhet sovremennoy diplomatii', Klub "Valdai", https://ru.val

daiclub.com/a/highlights/lichnyy-opyt-ili-istoricheskoe-znanie
-chto-pomozhe/.

6 'Obrashchenie Prezidenta Rossiiskoi Federatsii', 24 February 2022.

7 Peter Pomerantsev, 'Ukraine Is the Next Act in Putin's Empire of Humiliation', *New York Times*, 26 July 2022, sec. Opinion, https://www.nytimes.com/2022/07/26/opinion/russia-ukraine-putin.html.

8 Anton Troianovski, 'Putin Aims to Shape a New Generation of Supporters, Through Schools', *New York Times*, 16 July 2022, sec. World, https://www.nytimes.com/2022/07/16/world/euro pe/russia-putin-schools-propaganda-indoctrination.html.

9 'Telegram: Contact @holmogortalks', 18 July 2022, https://t.me /holmogortalks/22780.

10 Mark Lipovetsky, 'Brother 2 as a Political Melodrama. Twenty Years Later, Balabanov's Film Serves to Justify War with Ukraine', 2, Russia Post, https://russiapost.info/society/brother_2.

11 Ekaterina Reznikova, 'Podmena mest slagaemykh', Proekt, 30 June 2022, https://www.proekt.media/research/ofitsialnaya-sta tistika-minoborony/.

12 Interview with Vera from Novosibirsk, 22 April 2022, over email.

13 '"Komandovaniyu prosto-naprosto nasrat' na vsekh voenno sluzhashchikh"', iStories, 19 August 2022, https://istories.media/ reportages/2022/08/19/komandovaniyu-prosto-naprosto-nasrat-na-vsekh-voennosluzhashchikh/.

14 Medvedev nazval uzhe reshennuyu zadachu spetsoperatsiyu, 9 June 2022, Lenta, https://lenta.ru/news/2022/07/09/medvedev/.

15 Whether these payments are paid is another matter entirely, of course.

16 Maksim Martem'yanov, 'Anatomy of a Genocide', *Holod Magazine*, 8 August 2022, https://holod.media/en/2022/08/08 /anatomy-of-a-genocide/.

17 'Voennaya Doktrina Rossiiskoi Federatsii 2014', Konsul'tant.ru, http://www.consultant.ru/document/cons_doc_LAW_172989/.

18 Interview with Natalia Sevagina.

19 Sergei Medvedev, 'Putin's Dehumanized Russia', Wilson Center',

https://www.wilsoncenter.org/blog-post/putins-dehumanized-russia.

20 Oksana Ivanovna, 'Mat' soldata iz RF', 29 October 2022, https://www.dw.com/ru/mat-soldata-iz-rf-pogibshego-v-ukraine-tam-prosto-mesivo/a-61263854.

21 Interview with Fedor Lukyanov via Zoom, 13 June 2022.

22 Interview with Kirill Shamiev over Zoom 28 June 2022.

23 Chronicles of war: How families of Russian soldiers are engaging in social media, Sec Dev Analytics, 15 May 2022, https://www.secdev.com/Whitepapers/Chronicles+of+the+war+in+Ukraine_+How+families+of+Russian+soldiers+are+engaging+in+social+media.pdf.

24 Ibid.

Conclusion: How Russia lost the war

1 'Soveshchanie o merakh sotsial'no-ekonomicheskoy podderzhki regionov', Prezident Rossii, http://kremlin.ru/events/president/news/67996.

2 Interview with Ira Shcherbakova via Zoom, 23 June 2022.

3 *Russians Are Snitching On Friends and Relatives Who Oppose the War*, 2022, https://www.youtube.com/watch?v=z3Z174zEnC8.

4 Interview with Vladimir Orlov via Zoom, 4 July 2022 notes.

5 Interview with Aleksei Levinson via Zoom, 28 June 2022.

6 Interview with Fedor Lukyanov via Zoom, 13 June 2022.

7 '"We Live in a Closet Stuffed with Skeletons" Maxim Trudolyubov on How Russians' Inability to Condemn the Crimes of the Past Has Led Them to War', Meduza, https://meduza.io/en/feature/2022/04/05/we-live-in-a-closet-stuffed-with-skeletons.

Index